EVERYTHING®

PARENT'S GUIDE TO

OVERCOMING CHILDHOOD ANXIETY

Dear Reader,

I am a specialist in alternative practices for anxiety, but I am also a mom and a former anxious child. Looking back, I can see how anxiety made its way through the generations of my family, contributing to the life events I endured. However, by applying the practices in this book, I have not only overcome anxiety but have learned to thrive from it. I no longer see anxiety as an obstacle, but rather as an opportunity for growth. I have experienced this firsthand, and now see my children, students, and clients benefiting from the teachings and practices you are about to learn.

My background and years of vocation allow me to see anxiety from many angles. I have a tremendous respect for traditional and nontraditional approaches when they are applied with integrity, ethics, and respect for the entire family. I am confident in the information in this book, and passionately continue my work to support and serve children, families, and educators. To gain more information about my services, workshops, and updates on additional resources, please visit my website: *http://sheriannaboyle.com*.

I hope this book offers you strength, clarity, and reassurance that the path you and your child are on is well worth exploring.

Sherianna Boyle

HILLSBORO PUBLIC LIBRARIES
Hillsboro, OR
Member of Washington County
COOPERATIVE LIBRARY SERVICES

WELCOME TO THE

EVERYTHING®

PARENT'S GUIDES

Everything® Parent's Guides are a part of the bestselling Everything® series and cover common parenting issues like childhood illnesses and tantrums, as well as medical conditions like asthma and juvenile diabetes. These family-friendly books are designed to be a one-stop guide for parents. If you want authoritative information on specific topics not fully covered in other books, Everything® Parent's Guides are your perfect solution.

 Alerts

Urgent warnings

 Facts

Important snippets of information

 Essentials

Quick handy tips

 Questions

Answers to common questions

When you're done reading, you can finally say you know **EVERYTHING**®!

PUBLISHER Karen Cooper

MANAGING EDITOR, EVERYTHING® SERIES Lisa Laing

COPY CHIEF Casey Ebert

ASSISTANT PRODUCTION EDITOR Alex Guarco

ACQUISITIONS EDITOR Brett Palana-Shanahan

DEVELOPMENT EDITOR Brett Palana-Shanahan

EVERYTHING® SERIES COVER DESIGNER Erin Alexander

Visit the entire Everything® series at *www.everything.com*

THE
EVERYTHING®
PARENT'S GUIDE TO
OVERCOMING CHILDHOOD ANXIETY

Professional advice to help your child
feel confident, resilient, and secure

Sherianna Boyle, MEd, CAGS

HILLSBORO PUBLIC LIBRARIES
Hillsboro, OR
Member of Washington County
COOPERATIVE LIBRARY SERVICES

Copyright © 2014 by F+W Media, Inc.
All rights reserved.
This book, or parts thereof, may not be reproduced in any form without permission
from the publisher; exceptions are made for brief excerpts used in published reviews.

An Everything® Series Book.
Everything® and everything.com® are registered trademarks of F+W Media, Inc.

Published by
Adams Media, a division of F+W Media, Inc.
57 Littlefield Street, Avon, MA 02322. U.S.A.
www.adamsmedia.com

ISBN 10: 1-4405-7706-4   *5440 6730*   *07/14*
ISBN 13: 978-1-4405-7706-2
eISBN 10: 1-4405-7707-2
eISBN 13: 978-1-4405-7707-9

Printed in the United States of America.

10   9   8   7   6   5   4   3   2   1

Library of Congress Cataloging-in-Publication Data

Boyle, Sherianna.
  The everything parent's guide to overcoming childhood anxiety / Sherianna Boyle.
    pages cm
  Includes index.
   ISBN 978-1-4405-7706-2 (pb) -- ISBN 1-4405-7706-4 (pb) -- ISBN 978-1-4405-7707-9 (ebook)
-- ISBN 1-4405-7707-2 (ebook)
  1. Anxiety in children. 2. Parenting. I. Title.
   BF723.A5B69 2014
   155.4'1246--dc23

                        2014002372

Many of the designations used by manufacturers and sellers to distinguish their product
are claimed as trademarks. Where those designations appear in this book and F+W Media,
Inc. was aware of a trademark claim, the designations have been printed with initial capi-
tal letters.

This book is intended as general information only, and should not be used to diagnose
or treat any health condition. In light of the complex, individual, and specific nature of
health problems, this book is not intended to replace professional medical advice. The
ideas, procedures, and suggestions in this book are intended to supplement, not replace,
the advice of a trained medical professional. Consult your physician before adopting any
of the suggestions in this book, as well as about any condition that may require diagnosis
or medical attention. The author and publisher disclaim any liability arising directly or
indirectly from the use of this book.

This book is available at quantity discounts for bulk purchases.
For information, please call 1-800-289-0963.

Acknowledgments

I dedicate this book to God. I would also like to extend deep gratitude for all the blessings in my life: my mother, Judy Zradi, and father, Larry Zradi. My husband of sixteen years, Kiernan Boyle, and our three daughters Megan, Mikayla, and Makenzie; I am so proud and grateful to be your mother. Thank you to my team members and mentors who supply me with the guidance and support to blossom: Ana Zick, Jason Peterson, Mary Blair, Julie Garfinkle and yes, you too Sue Tilton. To the amazing team of professionals at Adams Media: Brett Palana-Shanahan, my editor; Lisa Laing; and Karen Cooper; it has been a pleasure. To my wonderful students who have trusted me as their teacher and who always seem to show up with such grace. Finally, thank you to the authors of the first edition, Ilyne Sandas, Christine Siegel, and Deborah White for providing me with a solid framework.

Anxiety (ăng-zī-ĭ-tē) *n.* **1.** A treatable, uncomfortable state of mind, often described as an overwhelming feeling of apprehension, worry, and/or fear, marked by physical symptoms such as heart palpitation, nausea, tension, physical pain, trembling, sweating, and psychological symptoms that include self-doubt and inability to cope.

Contents

Introduction

What we have learned about the brain has dramatically changed over the past five years. New scientific research has substantiated how vast, viable, and intricately connected our brains are. Yes, anxiety disorders are on the rise, but so are the reliable and sound strategies proven to alleviate it. In fact, research shows consciously choosing to work through anxiety offers much more than relief; it also activates strength, resiliency, and personal fulfillment.

The Everything® Parent's Guide to Overcoming Childhood Anxiety recognizes the uniqueness of each child and family by providing you with an array of tools, strategies, and resources. Each one has been backed up by valid research and evidence. Whether you are concerned about your child's anxiety or feeling anxious yourself, you can benefit from the advice in this book.

The lessons in this book cover treatment for a child who may fit the standard criteria for an anxiety disorder, as well as strategies for children and parents who may not. Many of the strategies are free of cost, easily implemented by parents and taught to children. Others require connecting with credentialed professionals who may deliver a service or prescribe treatment. Discipline and simple steps for updating your parenting skills to incorporate current scientific viewpoints are sprinkled throughout the book. Old forms of thinking can be replaced by fresh mindsets that support the integration of the subconscious and conscious mind.

In the end, anxiety will no longer be something you or your child needs to beat, but rather an opportunity to strengthen who you are. Consider this book to be a doorway to revealing the true nature of you and your child. Enjoy.

CHAPTER 1

What, Me Worry?

Kids today have to keep pace with a faster lifestyle than any other past generation. They are faced with greater academic expectations and responsibility, have additional pressures due to changing family structures, and look forward to an uncertain worldview economically and politically. In short, growing up is probably very different from how you remember it, and, for some, a lot more worrisome. New science however, confirms a promising viewpoint illustrating how thoughts, beliefs, feelings, and pressures are a reflection of neurological pathways and habits. Similar to optimizing a computer, you can change the brain's programming and patterns and how it chooses to register present experiences like anxiety. The process begins with a simple shift from wanting to know what is happening *to* your child to becoming curious about how this may be happening *for* him.

What's Happening *for* My Child?

Anxiety has a unique way of serving both you and your child. Your child will have an opportunity to learn about the magnificence of his brain, body, and feelings. He will learn how thoughts manifest into words, self-talk, and in some cases belief systems. He will also learn the difference between suffering and feeling.

It is through feeling that he will connect to the deeper parts of himself and because you are along for the ride, you get to join him in discovering your inner values, how you interpret the world, what triggers uncomfortable feelings for you, and your unconscious and conscious fears and desires. With your guidance, rather than becoming overwhelmed by his symptoms, your child will learn how to appreciate them, and, with practice use them to make healthier choices. The process of overcoming anxiety takes your child along a journey of creating healthy boundaries, developing resiliency, self-discipline, creativity, autonomy, and most of all self-love. As her parent, you are an important guide and supporter.

 Fact

Ninety percent of children and adults successfully decrease their anxiety through lifestyle changes that foster empowerment, confidence, and independence. This can be achieved through a combination of mindfulness training, complementary therapies, psychotherapy, alternative medicine, and, when necessary, medication.

How to Recognize Anxiety

Adults experiencing anxiety feel nervous, jittery, uneasy, moody, and worried. You may not sleep well, and others might see you as agitated, irritable, or distractible. Children and teens can experience anxiety in much the same way. Younger children often do not have the words to let you know what is going on for them, and teens get confused about how to balance what they know logically in their heads with the emotions they are feeling. As a result, the anxiety creeps into their behavior, and shows itself in both overt and covert ways. *Covert anxiety* may show itself while your child is studying for a test, if he keeps biting his nails until they bleed. You see the damage, but do not know why it has occurred. Or your child complains that she has a stomachache, which (unbeknown to you) disappears after a school test is over. *Overt anxiety* is more pronounced; for example, before going to dance class your child has a meltdown when you ask him to put his dance gear in his bag. During the yelling, you hear things like "I can't go to class tomorrow, I won't have enough time to study tonight," or, "Stop getting on me about everything, I'm only one person, how much can I take?"

 Alert

> Studies show children typically worry about school and personal safety. A child's developmental age also seems to influence worries. For example, adolescents with more abstract thinking abilities tend to worry more about worldly events. Younger children (preschool and elementary) may be more concerned about friendships.

While every child occasionally feels stressed, worried, or fearful, an anxiety disorder is diagnosed when your child feels excessively, unreasonably, persistently, and often uncontrollably worried. This worry will take over the child's thoughts, sometimes lasting for an extended period, and the hardest part for her is that she will feel like she can't make it stop. You can sit down and discuss your child's fears with her, showing her they are not warranted, but she still cannot seem to make the worry and apprehension go away. If the distress your child feels extends to all areas of life including home, school, and with friends, then it is no longer "normal or expected" anxiety. Specific areas of concern occur when anxiety affects school attendance, academic motivation, learning, concentration, memory, friendships, activity level, or sleep patterns.

The Two Components

Your child's anxiety typically will have two parts: physical sensations and emotional experiences. The most common physical sensations include stomachaches, headaches, back or neck aches, nausea, and sweating. The emotional component will consist of nervousness, worry, negativity, and fear. Because there are physical symptoms, it is important to see your family doctor to rule out an illness first. Doctors have found that anxiety can be caused by thyroid disorders, encephalitis, hypoglycemia, irritable bowel syndrome, Group A strep, or even pneumonia.

Is Fear the Same as Anxiety?

Although fear and anxiety are related, there is an important distinction between them. Fear is the appropriate reaction to a real danger or threat. One example is when a siren sounds to warn you of a tornado in your neighborhood, and your child gets scared of what the sound implies. In that scenario, the brain is just responding to protect your child. Anxiety is the reaction to a *perceived* danger or threat, such as a thunderstorm in a neighboring county that your child has heard about on the news. Although there is no danger in your own neighborhood and you tell him that, his brain, which has been evolutionarily primed by our ancestors to overreact as a means of survival, jumps into action anyway. Symptoms of anxiety are also reinforced through our environment. Perpetual rushing is one way this happens. Rushing promotes panicked, high pitched or a yelling tone of voice occupied by statements such as: *we are going to be late, hurry up,* or yelling the child's name over and over.

What Triggers Anxiety?

Anxiety can be triggered by a myriad of things. Thoughts trigger anxiety, particularly ones that focus on flaws or unworthiness. Emotions such as shame and guilt are anxiety magnifiers, along with worry, learning difficulties, pressure, uncertainty, feeling emotionally unsafe, and fear of criticism and/or failure. Unrealistic expectations, striving for perfection, and an imagined sense of doom also contribute to this state. Long-term anxiety leads to a habit of racing thoughts and a persistent desire for things to be a certain way, or different from the way they are at that moment. Finally, anxiety may be triggered by the memory of past events, both those that are within the child's current awareness as well as some that may be buried in her subconscious mind.

 Essential

Teach your children not to believe everything they hear and think. Words are a physical manifestation of your child's thoughts. Not all thoughts represent your child's truth. For example, your child might say, "I hate school" one day and later you may find out that your child did poorly on a math test. Children experiencing anxiety tend to generalize their thoughts to all-or-none thinking.

Anxiety can also be triggered by development. Children go through several stages of anxiety as they grow, and their brain develops and readjusts to newly acquired knowledge. For example, an infant of a certain age can experience anxiety when a parent or caregiver leaves a room. The infant believes the parent has ceased to exist, when in reality the parent may just be in the next room. This is a type of separation anxiety, which can occur from around eight months old through the preschool years, and it is normal for a child of this age to show intense feelings if separated from his parents. At two years old, your child may be scared of the dark, loud noises, animals, changes in the house, or strangers. At age five you can add "bad people" and fear of bodily harm to the list. By age six, it is common for children to still be afraid of the dark and have separation issues again, as well as fear of thunder and lightning, supernatural beings, staying alone, or getting hurt. Within the age range of seven to eight, it is common for children to unconsciously bite their pencils or twirl their hair as a temporary way to relieve tension. Kids aged seven through twelve often have fears that are more reality-based, like getting hurt or of some kind of disaster happening, because they are now more aware of the world around them.

All these fears are developmentally normal phases, but if your child seems stuck in a phase or fixated on a certain fear it may be a sign of something more. Many children can be described as intensely oversensitive, or "high maintenance," which may just be a normal expression of your child's developing personality. The deciding factors of whether to seek help lie in the frequency and intensity of the fears, and how much the fear and worry interferes with life.

Worry Makes Anxiety Grow

Everyone worries. On the positive side, worry can motivate you to do well at a task, accomplish a goal, or take care of a problem. With mental discipline and patience, your child will be able to reflect back on his experiences as opportunities rather than obstacles. He will eventually realize there are no monsters hiding in the closet; that if he makes a mistake, he will live through it; and sometimes he has to keep trying to get what he wants. However, for some children, anxiety is so overwhelming that it becomes paralyzing and prevents any movement whatsoever. Worries become a full-time job. As a parent, it will be important for you to notice when you exchange a worry for a worry. Similar to a ping pong game, parents may get in the habit of hearing a worry, and sending (silently or verbally) one of their own worries back to their child. Instead of sending back a worry pause, close your eyes and rest your attention on your own feelings. This allows you to send your child frequencies of higher emotions such as trust, love, and acceptance, rather than worry.

When the "What Ifs" Kick In

Worry involves both thoughts and feelings, and is defined as a lasting preoccupation with past or future events. This type of thinking causes your child to feel as if she were reliving an event repeatedly, or constantly readying herself for the worst outcome in a future event. When you see your child "becoming her anxiety," you might think to yourself, "I don't get it, where did this come from?" The worry will often seem out of proportion to you and sometimes seem as if it came out of nowhere. You see your child get stuck in a vicious cycle that in turn increases her dread, and nothing you say or do seems to help. When your child is trapped by worry, you will often hear the phrases "if only . . ." and "what if . . ." over and over.

The "What Ifs"

"What if" refers to thoughts about the future. In the case of worry, these thoughts are about any number of emotionally charged things that could possibly happen. *What if I am not liked by the other kids, do not do well on the test, cannot hit the ball in gym,* or *do not get chosen for the team? What if my face turns red during my speech,* or *my teacher gets upset that I forgot my homework again?* When the worry starts and your child cannot stop it, it grows in intensity like a runaway train, and your child ultimately ends up with the thought of *What if no matter what I do, it is not enough?* It is an endless cycle that can never be satisfied and often results in negative self-talk, low self-esteem, and ultimately, being unsure of who they are. It also shows itself behaviorally. When *what if* takes hold over your child's life, he may seem paralyzed, unable to participate in activities or unable to perform to his capability. You then will hear phrases like, "What if I don't catch the ball when it comes my way, I can't be on the team," or "I can't try out for the play, what if I forget my lines? Everyone will make fun of me—I'll just die."

Redirecting What Ifs

There are two ways to handle *what if.* The first is to focus on the moment by redirecting your awareness to your body. Parents can model this by saying, "Gee, I notice when I think about *what if,* my jaw tightens and my shoulders tense up. My eyes grow wide, and

I stop noticing what is around me." Dr. Lawrence J. Cohen, author of *The Opposite of Worry*, suggests you teach children to change their thoughts from *What if,* to *What is.* This can be encouraged by directing your child to his own body as a resource for restoring balance. Initially, children may be fearful of noticing what is happening physically; however, when practiced in a gentle, nonjudgmental way, noticing transforms into expanding awareness and observation of the situation. Go ahead and try it on yourself. Notice if one of your shoulders feels tight, and watch how your body naturally begins to relax itself simply as a result of that noticing.

The second way is to reframe "what if" to "I look forward to." For example, your child may say, "What if my face turns red while I give my speech?" Teach her to reframe this and say, "I look forward to getting through this speech." *Reframing* teaches children how to shift present thinking from the negative to the positive. This shift functions on a neurological level; because negative thinking increases stress hormones, giving your child's body the impression that what he is thinking is actually happening, reframing it in a positive way reduces those stress hormones, allowing the body to relax. Reframing is a technique you will learn about in greater detail in Chapter 6.

 Fact

Your body does not know the difference between a real or imagined threat. If you imagine yourself having a conflict with someone, your body will respond as if it is in danger. Most likely your breathing will become shallow and rapid, you may feel tense, irritated, or even angry. Your body does not know you are imagining this through your thoughts and images; it reacts as if the threat is genuine.

The "If Onlys"

"If only" refers to thoughts about an unhappy event that your child wishes had not happened. Maybe your child said something to a friend she now wishes she had not, or did something she regrets. The event has ultimately left her with an unresolved emotional feeling, and worry is how her mind tries to resolve it, by trying to figure out what went wrong and how to fix it. *If only* statements sound like this: *If only I had kept my mouth shut when Sara asked me what I thought of her new haircut, now she will never talk to me again,* or *If only I had listened in class, I would have gotten a better grade on this test.*

 Question

Are you constantly trying to soothe and reassure your child by reviewing the past?
If so, teach your child reviewing the past is like hitting the replay button on a song. If you do it enough times, your body begins to learn the words and music by heart. The next time you are in a similar situation your body will automatically hit replay because that is what you have taught it to do. Focus on the here and now instead.

In many cases, the event has already happened and your child cannot control the past, nothing can be done to alter it, and worry cycles on without resolution like a gerbil on an exercise wheel. Your child can become consumed with guilt, hypersensitive to criticism, and hesitant to take action for fear of "yet another failure." However, you can use your knowledge of your child's worry cycle to teach her how her brain works, how she has the ability to influence the activity of her brain cells and in what way her neurotransmitters fire and wire. In order to do so your child will need to follow these three basic steps:

1. Notice her thoughts
2. Observe her thoughts with nonjudgment (more on this under self-reflection)
3. Experience her thoughts through breathing and bodily sensation

Thoughts can be either conscious or unconscious. In the purest form they are units of energy. Each thought therefore gives off an electromagnetic frequency. These frequencies are the building blocks of her emotions. High frequency emotions are ones that lift you up such as joy, love, and appreciation. Low frequency emotions such as guilt and shame weigh you down often coloring your perception with negativity and doubt. As your child becomes more skilled in self-observation she will learn you can feel your feelings without labeling or creating a story around them. Habitual thoughts tend to get memorized and therefore familiar. This means the same neurochemicals get wired in the same routine way. As your child begins to change, her neurochemicals will fire in a new way. Like most things your child attempts for the first time this approach may initially feel a bit uncomfortable or uncertain. See this discomfort as a sign of growth. Thoughts spark feelings, therefore as your child learns the relationship between thoughts and feelings she will soon recognize her own ability to influence it.

According to Joe Dispenza, author of *Evolve Your Brain: The Science of Changing Your Mind* and *Breaking the Habit of Being Yourself*, "Thoughts are the language of the brain and feelings are the language of the body." The body is always in the present moment (where anxiety cannot live). For example, imagine you are studying with your child and he says, "I don't know the answer." Rather than tell your child the answer you might suggest they pause, and sit (relax) with it a minute before stating "I don't know." Very often a child has the answer but they have developed a rote response as a way to push through uncomfortable feelings. Once they sit and let the question rest in their body rather than push it through with their thoughts, often they discover they knew more than they initially thought.

Your Child's Identity

Identity is who you are, and who you are not. Creating and maintaining a healthy identity is another key part of your child's development. Identity is self-awareness, for example how much your child knows about her likes and dislikes, her beliefs about who she is, and what she thinks her capabilities are. As your child's sense of self develops, so does her ability to blossom in school and in social relationships. Just as self-esteem is how she *feels* about herself, identity is how she *thinks* about herself. A child with a strong sense of identity might state, "I am a short person, I like pizza, and I am funny."

Anxiety is so overpowering that it interferes with your child's ability to make the distinction between how she *feels* about herself and what she *thinks* about herself, and prevents her from seeing herself clearly. Filled with a sense of "I can't" or "I do not," the child experiencing anxiety cannot even begin to see her way clear to a strong sense of self. This creates a foundation that feels unsteady and magnifies negative self-statements that interfere with the development of confidence. Learn more about the development of identity and the influences of social media in Chapter 5.

 Question

My child is so hard on herself when she doesn't do well on a task. How can I help her feel better?
The best way to help your child is to truly listen, without simultaneously reviewing in your head how you could respond. Simply listen, and if you feel compelled to speak, consider sharing a developmentally appropriate story about how you got through a frustrating task. Your story will be far more meaningful than a lecture or pity.

Autonomy

An important skill for your child to learn in order to develop a healthy identity and be less affected by stress and anxiety is to grow in autonomy. *Autonomy* is defined as the ability to act independently as a product of self-awareness, a sense of identity, and self-control. If you have ever heard a three-year-old say, "I can do it

myself!" you have experienced a child experimenting with autonomy. Your child's sense of knowing he can make it on his own, and
knowing what type of person he is and is not, become building
blocks for future success and happiness.

Internal Strength

For children in a difficult environment, such as a family with
alcoholism, overprotective parents, fighting, divorce, or mental illness, a strong identity means a better ability to distance oneself
from the family chaos and have a positive view of the future. These
children will be able to identify how to differentiate "what is about
me" from "this is about *them*," and to make independent judgments
about life events. This internal strength creates a buffer against
stress by allowing a child not to internalize or take on the problems
of others. A strong sense of identity, as you can see, is one of the
keys to combat stress and anxiety, and cope well through adversity.

Your Child's Self-Esteem

Self-esteem is the collection of beliefs and feelings that your child
has about himself, combined with a general sense of whether or
not he sees himself as basically good, worthy, and competent. It
is a collection of ideas about who he believes he is, what he is
capable of, and what makes him special and unique from others.
Self-esteem encompasses how your child defines himself, his attitudes and behaviors, and how he sees his ability to affect the world
around him. The three key ingredients for a child's strong self-
esteem are that he feels he is lovable, capable, and accepted for
who he is (rather than who others expect him to be). Acceptance
is fostered when parents take responsibility for learning about and
working with their own anxiety, if that is a contributing factor to the
child's anxiety issues. Parents who are willing to integrate some
of the strategies in this book into their own life will find it not only
supports their own fears and concerns, but also their child's. All it

takes is one person to make a change in how they respond to the symptoms of anxiety and the entire family will eventually reap the benefits.

The Content Child

The patterns of self-esteem begin developing soon after birth and are a lifelong process. For example, when a baby or toddler reaches a developmental milestone, he experiences a sense of accomplishment that bolsters self-esteem. In a healthy family, frustration and confusion are seen as vehicles for growth. It is this learning process of attempts and eventual success and mastery that teaches your child a "can-do" sense of self.

A healthy concept of the self builds resiliency for life challenges. Kids who feel good about themselves will most likely view their experience of moving through conflicts as a source of strength, wisdom, and knowledge. They tend to be hopeful, energetic, and have positive thoughts about the future. They are more likely to be able to solve problems on their own, and to ask for help or support when they need it.

The Self-Critical Child

In contrast, if your child has low self-esteem, challenges can become a source of major anxiety and frustration. When your child is plagued by worry and anxiety, irrational beliefs surface, such as, "I'm no good," "I can't do anything right," and "What's the point?" Ultimately, he might become passive, withdrawn, and depressed. Children with a deflated sense of self view small setbacks as permanent, intolerable conditions. The immediate response to challenges becomes "I can't." Making matters worse, they see challenge as something they need to avoid. They can feel defeated before they even begin by a need for unattainable perfection or complete control over the situation or process, enormously demanding goals that are themselves overwhelming in their magnitude, quite apart from the challenge itself.

Perfection

Perfection in a child's world might look like an inability to appreciate what she does well or intolerance for her limitations. Your child may see her mistakes as huge, creating a negative outlook full of personal criticism. The negativity may translate to seeing herself as incompetent, inadequate, imperfect, and can also lead to a rigid, inflexible view of people and life. The types of statements you might hear are, *How could I have missed that, I'm so stupid,* or *I didn't get invited . . . nobody likes me.* Often, if what your child did accomplish is not 100 percent a success, she considers herself a failure. This thinking becomes a crippling and painful way to live, and restricts your child's opportunities to be human and learn from her mistakes. Worry, stress, and anxiety take their toll. Anxiety leads to perfectionism, which is unattainable and thus inevitably leads back to anxiety via self-blame, and possibly self-hatred. In the end, mistakes become severe criticism, shortcomings become complete failure, and relationships with both the self and others can become impaired.

 Essential

Most of us grew up with the mindset that practice makes perfect. Author Jim Kwik from Kwik Learning (*www.jimkwik.com*) teaches kids *practice makes permanent.* This means what you choose to do over and over again is what you will remember. If self-criticism is something you do on a regular basis, those negative critical statements become imprinted into the subconscious mind. The good news is that you can reprogram your brain simply by mindfully changing your negative thoughts and self-statements to positive ones.

The Stress and Anxiety Connection

Stress can come from any situation or thought that causes your child to feel frustrated, angry, nervous, or tense. What is stressful to one child will not necessarily be stressful to another. Stress is subjective, and often parents do not experience stress the same way their children do. Parents also do not feel stress about the same *things* as their children do. Understanding what is stressful for your child and responding, even if the issue seems trivial, will help your child build his overall sense of security. For example, if your child tells you he is afraid of the dark and wants to sleep with a light on, it will not be helpful to say, "Oh, that's silly, there is nothing out there, I already checked." The child who tends to feel stress or anxiety will believe that you do not know what you are talking about, he might feel confused about whether to trust you or himself, and his symptoms may grow. Stress is one of the biggest contributors to children who feel anxiety, and it can lead to depression, eating disorders, or a host of other difficulties. The impact is usually cumulative, adding up over time before becoming considered as an anxiety disorder. Consider each time your child experiences stress and anxiety as an opportunity to interrupt the cycle and redirect your child's sense of security, self, and competence. Becoming aware of what seems stressful in your child's life gives you the power to intervene and re-route the cycle. The goal is to teach your child how to divert his stress-triggered anxiety before it leads to something more intense such as an illness, conflict in relationships, or a negative impact on schoolwork.

The following are some typical emotional or behavioral signs of a stressed child:

- Worry
- Inability to relax
- Irritability
- Chronic fatigue
- Over- or undereating
- Critical of self and others
- Overly sensitive

- New or recurring fears (fear of the dark, being alone, of strangers)
- Clinging or unwilling to let go of mom or dad
- Unexplained anger
- Unwarranted crying
- Aggressive or refusal behavior
- Regression to a behavior that is typical of an earlier developmental stage (like bedwetting or thumb sucking)
- Unwillingness to participate in family or school activities
- Shyness that limits activities

Is Anxiety Contagious?

Have you ever walked into a room with someone who was anxious in it? You can sense the tension and/or irritability. Before you know it, you may find your own mood becoming impatient or your heart rate elevating in response to uncertainty or frustration. Anxiety may be passed along or absorbed through observing body language, feeling it on your skin like a tightness, a shifting of the eyes, or a tone of voice. If you are around someone who is complaining, critical, or negative, you may easily get swept up into their state of mind if you are not aware enough to consciously choose to reject it. However, by remaining in the moment and aware of your own body, you create an inner resiliency, making you less susceptible to the anxiety of others, and you are more likely to make choices that support your personal self-confidence and mental and emotional health.

Self-Reflection

It is common for your child to be stressed if he sees that you are stressed. For the sake of your child, you may need to learn to reduce your stress by reflecting on it without judgment. Reflection without judgment occurs when the mind and body are in harmony with one another, thereby reducing anxiety. To achieve this balance, follow these steps:

1. First, open the doorway to nonjudgment by choosing to connect to your heart. To do this, allow yourself a moment to sit quietly, close your eyes and allow yourself to feel the present moment. If you are unsure how to do this imagine the sun is shining on your face, heart, and body. Next, take a deep breath (one inhale and one exhale). Notice how this opens you up to receiving rather than resisting what is happening in and around you.

2. After two or three receiving breaths, ask yourself: *Am I overbooked or overwhelmed, worried, or not sleeping?* or, *Am I eating well, setting boundaries in order to take time for myself?* or, *Do I allow myself to hear my child's concerns, or do I put my hand in the air and say things like, "I have had enough"* or, *"I can't handle this"?*

Once you are able to understand your emotions and what stresses you, you will feel calmer and better able to help your child. You can be a powerful model and example of healthy stress management and self-care for your children, and it behooves you to be the best person you can be for their sake, as well as yours. Research has suggested parents who are not emotionally available for their children, or who have limited positive coping mechanisms themselves, often have children who are stressed.

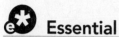 **Essential**

Play is necessary for children to learn. Studies show that it helps them learn self-control, how to interact with others, improves intellectual skills, and fosters decision-making, memory, thinking, and speed of mental processing. It is also one of the most natural ways children release anxiety.

Possible Reasons for Stress

It is normal for your child to feel stress when she is starting school or a new school year, or changing from one school phase to the next, such as between elementary and middle or junior high school. Moving, changes in peer groups, or families with high expectations in academics or other activities have also been found to be highly stressful. If your child has been abused, neglected, deprived, or has had a major loss that threatened her security, she is also at risk for stress or anxiety. Additionally, when there has been a demand for a child to carry responsibility that would normally belong to a parent, like dealing with a family member's chemical abuse or chronic illness, children often feel stressed and anxious. This is because they have to overfunction by taking on chores and emotional responsibility greater than appropriate to their age. This may lead to patterns of perfectionism and as a result your child may attempt to utilize control as a means for keeping his life in control.

Some other physical signs of a child experiencing stress are:

- Headaches
- Upset stomach
- Sleep disturbances
- New or recurrent bedwetting
- Stuttering
- Changes in eating habits

Fight, Flight, or Freeze Response

When your child is faced with a real or perceived threat, his body produces certain hormones to deal with that threat. Some of the hormones that are released are adrenaline, noradrenalin, and corticosteroids. This chemical process sets off the flight-or-fight response, compelling either escape or self-defense. Your child's heart rate may increase to pump more blood to his muscles and brain, and his lungs will take in air faster to supply his body with the added oxygen it thinks it needs. The process is automatic, happening in seconds.

Liberate Stress and Anxiety

Mindful breathing is an essential skill for reducing anxiety that all children and family members can benefit from learning. Benefits of deep breathing include increased oxygen flow to the brain and other organs, decreased muscle tension, increased energy and focus, and a general sense of well-being. Here is how it works: When your child takes a deep breath and exhales slowly, the body begins to balance oxygen (what you take in) with carbon dioxide levels (what you breathe out). Without realizing it, most people regularly engage in a shallow chest breathing pattern that limits the amounts of oxygen and carbon dioxide that move in and out. Also, the nerve endings that promote calm are located within the lower lobes of the lungs. In order to access them, one must breathe from the belly. The belly inflates like a balloon upon inhalation, and deflates (navel toward spine) upon exhalation. Teaching and practicing how to breathe optimally is an essential ability, and Chapter 11 further explains this skill in greater detail.

 Fact

Anxiety levels can actually increase through oxygen deprivation as a result of shallow chest-focused breathing. The upper chest is considered to be the area from your sternum (just under your breast bone) to the base of your throat. Training yourself to instead breath deeply into the lower abdomen, allowing maximum lung expansion, is one of the quickest ways to alleviate anxiety.

Sleep and balanced nutrition are also excellent ways to loosen the effects of stress. Replenishing your child's body in all ways goes hand in hand with a happy and healthy child. Sleep requirements vary according to age. For the most part, doctors give the following recommendations: children from birth to age six need ten to thirteen hours of sleep a night; six- to nine-year-olds need ten hours; ten- to twelve-year-olds need nine hours; and adolescents need approximately eight to nine hours of sleep a night. Depending on the child's schedule, more sleep may be required.

Remember, this list is only a recommendation, not an absolute. Your doctor's suggestions are important information to keep in mind as you work toward maximizing your child's potential.

CHAPTER 2

Causes of Anxiety

Anxiety occurs for a variety of emotional, biological, and environmental reasons. It is built on factors that are interrelated. Science is also getting closer to confirming that you can be predisposed to anxiety. Although this chapter breaks down the causes of anxiety into categories, they can, and often do, overlap.

How Common Is Anxiety?

With over 40 million adults diagnosed worldwide, anxiety has become the most widely recognized mental health problem in the general population. According to the Anxiety and Depression Association of America (ADAA), anxiety disorders affect one in eight children. If left untreated or avoided, children with anxiety disorders are at a higher risk to perform poorly in school, miss out on important social experiences, and engage in substance abuse.

Fear-based messages embedded into culture and magnified through media using visual imaging, sounds, and words stimulate stress while creating and feeding a global anxiety. Marketers often use this to their advantage, pushing quick fix strategies via a tone of needing more, being unsafe, or being inadequate. In many ways this has led to a desensitization of immoral acts, and to the suppression of the two inherent qualities that give human beings the ability to alleviate anxiety: empathy and compassion. Fortunately, the tools and strategies in this book support the growth and development of those powerful emotions.

Comparing Boys and Girls

Although there is no clear-cut reason, researchers do recognize some differences between boys and girls. Medical professionals suggest that girls are perhaps more likely to have a hormonal imbalance, an increased level of emotional, mental, and physical changes, and a higher sensitivity to others' struggles. A study led by Tara M. Chaplin of the Department of Psychiatry at Yale University School of Medicine found that boys and girls have very different emotional tendencies. Her study of over 21,000 participants found that in infancy, the boys and girls exhibited similar emotional displays. As the children aged and were introduced to social setting, the children felt the need to conform to social norms, which may have led to a sense that they could not freely express their true emotions. Adolescent girls demonstrated higher levels of shame and guilt, while boys were more likely to exhibit anger and aggression. Researcher Carol Gilligan, when comparing girls and boys, discovered that girls perceive danger in their isolation, with abandonment being a main fear, whereas boys described danger as more entrapment or smothering.

In my book *Powered by Me for Educators Pre-K–12,* I state "repeating statements such as boys are more active and girls are more emotional may at times seem harmless but in the long run have proven to negatively influence behavior and learning." It is important for parents to watch how stereotypes are reinforced in their speech used at home; phrases such as "boys will be boys" or "girls are so dramatic" can teach children to disguise their feelings and to behave in ways that they perceive as predetermined or expected by society.

Scientists also believe sex hormones may play a role in anxiety for both boys and girls. During times of intense hormonal shifts, symptoms of anxiety may occur. In some cases, it could also be the anxiety that exasperates the intensity of the hormonal shift. In general, girls are more likely than boys to seek help. This may reflect the fact that it is more socially acceptable for girls to both express and address their emotional states.

 Fact

Girls who have suffered from sexual abuse have been found to have long-term changes in the brain's structure and chemistry. Researchers found that they had abnormal blood flow in the hippocampus, which triggers memories and emotions. These girls were found to be more moody and depressed, and were more likely to suffer from anxiety attacks.

Psychological Aspects

It is helpful to keep in mind that your child learns primarily by imitation. Studies have found that 95 percent of children's learning occurs unconsciously, while children are simply living life. This makes it hard on you as a parent, because it means you are being watched and your decisions and responses are being used to make judgments about what life looks and feels like to your child. If you do not have open communication with your kids, or are not aware of their perceptions as they go through their learning process, the decisions they make about life are happening largely without your knowledge.

 Fact

Ninety percent of what children learn and remember is from what they *experience*, as opposed to 20 percent if they only *hear* it. This means that to be truly effective, it is best to provide experiences with tools and strategies rather than simply telling your child about the associated information.

Feelings in the Family

Growing up in a family where fear, worry, and anxiety are consistently modeled by parents or family members may teach a child to be anxious. In addition, if a child grows up in a home where a parent or sibling is terminally ill, in an abusive or alcoholic home where she is walking on eggshells around a parent, or constantly in an over-alert state, she may learn to expect the worst, or actually *look* for the worst. The child ends up living in a state of constant worry.

The psychological state of fear and trauma can also be present when a child is bullied at school, in the neighborhood, or on the school bus. The continuous state of anxiety that results creates children who might freeze up or withdraw in order to protect themselves. They have a tendency to lose their sense of belonging and separate themselves out from friends. A typical example is the child who is standing off on his own during lunch or recess. It is also common for a child feeling anxiety to fall into a world of his own where he might feel he has to create plans for how to safeguard himself, "just in case." When this happens, the body and mind's resources are sidetracked, and your child's growth may become interrupted.

Internal Versus External Stressors

The term *internal* refers to the vulnerability that comes from genetics and temperament. It also means how your child feels inside about what happens externally or around her. Internal triggers are more likely to affect a child who has strong emotions or who has a tendency to be a sensitive child. Examples of internal cues that can lead to anxiety are guilt, anger, shame, perfectionism, negative thinking, and frequent thoughts that are centered on *should*, *must*, and *never*.

External influences are events that happen outside of the child and have a separate point of origin. Examples of some external triggers are divorce, violence at home, school, games or TV, injury, illness or death of a family member, abuse, or a disaster. These examples will be addressed in detail later in this chapter.

Understanding the differences between the external and internal environment can be confusing. This is an area where communicating with your child, in an effort to help him understand where his fear accurately lies, would be helpful.

 Essential

> A hard, but significant, job as a parent is to understand that your child is constantly adding to her fears by how she thinks. Irrational thinking and an inability to stop that thinking are common. Once this process of worry, fear, or anxiety over an issue has begun, your child may continue to frighten herself with her own thoughts.

The amount of anxiety your child feels from these triggers will be based on how she processes it. Therefore, it will be important for you to take the time to help your child separate out what is a real threat external to her from what she is creating internally, through her own thoughts.

Biological Aspects

Fear and panic are normal reactions to danger. When fear or panic is felt, this reflects a chain of events in your child's autonomic nervous system. By learning to understand how your child's body works, biologically speaking, you can then explain it to your child. Children who understand how their body is working *for* them rather than *against* them tend to be less overwhelmed by the emotional shifts they feel inside. Explain to your child how every thought secretes a chemical, which creates a feeling. If you think fearful thoughts, your body cooperates by delivering fearful emotions. On the contrary, if you think loving thoughts, like how much you love your pet, your body delivers those emotions.

Neurotransmitters

A person's brain is a network of billions of nerve cells called neurons that communicate with each other to create thoughts, emotions, and behaviors. This process is called cell-to-cell communication, in which a transfer of information from one part of the brain to another is made possible by chemicals called neurotransmitters. The two primary neurotransmitters that affect your child's feelings are serotonin and dopamine. Other brain chemicals often referred to when speaking about anxiety are norepinephrine, acetylcholine, gamma-aminobutyric acid (GABA), corticotrophin-releasing hormone (CRH), and cholecystokinin, all of which play a role in the regulation of arousal and anxiety. This information is complex, but remember one of the best ways to free yourself from feeling anxious about raising an anxious child is to become aware.

 Essential

Children are more likely to remember things that have an emotional charge. Parents can help instill positive emotions by keeping their joyful memories alive through pictures, videos, and storytelling.

The Autonomic Nervous System

Your child is likely to learn about their autonomic nervous system in health or science class at some point in their educational journey. This system controls your child's breathing, digestion, and temperature regulation. It is composed of two parts: the sympathetic nervous system and the parasympathetic nervous system. The job of the SNS is to rev your child up, and the job of the PNS is to calm your child down, each balancing the other out. As mentioned before, when your child gets frightened the SNS releases adrenaline, his heart pumps faster, sometimes racing, his blood pressure goes up, he might get tingling in his hands and feet because blood flows away from them to his brain, and his lungs will work harder to get more air. This release allows him to focus more intently on the real or perceived danger and sets off the fight-or-flight reaction discussed in Chapter 1.

The Amygdala and Hippocampus

When the fight-or-flight response is triggered it occurs in the parts of the brain called the amygdala and hippocampus. The amygdala is the part of the brain where feelings and emotions lie. So if your child is feeling fearful and anxious, the amygdala will send this information throughout your child's body in an alert. The hippocampus holds memory, time, and place, especially for situations that are highly emotional. Once the amygdala jumps into action, your child can become overly sensitive to certain stimuli, responding to fear and anxiety in an instant, even in a safe situation.

An example might look something like this: You moved last month and your child was very upset about it. He now cannot find his teddy bear that he sleeps with every night. He becomes frantic, even though you told him you know where it is and will go get it. His heart starts to beat faster and he is becoming nervous, sweaty, and tingly all over anyway. Although you persist in reassuring him, he continues to panic.

Genetic Causes

Investigations into the causes of anxiety are clear that anxiety, panic, and depression can be hereditary, and that usually, anxiety is a concern for several members of the same family. If a parent or sibling has a history of an anxiety disorder, a child's risk increases four- to six-fold for developing symptoms herself. This is because the structure of the brain and its processes are inherited. However, science is coming out with solid science that not only can you change your brain but also your DNA (genetic makeup). Studies on consciousness and awareness now prove human beings can actually influence what gets passed on to future generations.

Families with patterns of anxiety can now take faith that the cycle of unnecessary worry can truly be broken. People who have no family history of the disorder can develop anxiety as well. Knowing your family history helps you and any professionals supporting you make clear, conscious decisions about what steps to take.

The Role of Temperament

Temperament is your child's nature present at birth. Many parents can tell almost immediately whether their child will be peaceful, irritable, sociable, or more introverted. At the forefront of temperament research is Dr. Jerome Kagan of Harvard University, now retired. The research has connected the dots between four personality traits (timid, upbeat, melancholic, and bold) to patterns in brain activity. What he discovered in timid children is that the amygdala is more easily aroused in those prone to fearfulness, creating children who are more anxious and uneasy. Compared to children in the other groups, their hearts beat faster when confronted with stressful situations, they were more finicky about eating, were introverted around strangers, and were reluctant to try anything new. Kagan found that from birth, these children had a hyperexcitable right temporal lobe in their brains, and if fear was triggered in the child, those pathways became stronger. More research is needed, but other studies have shown that the hippocampus is smaller in people who have had a significant trauma.

 Fact

Dr. Kagan and his team found only 10 to 15 percent of children who were shy, fearful, irritable, and introverted as babies had social anxiety throughout their adolescence. That means the majority of the kids they studied did not. Having an introverted child is not a sure bet for later issues.

The brain is constantly changing. It will reshape based on information it receives, changing itself in order to learn and respond. It is a work in progress and becomes stronger through repetition and time. Parents who are more successful in reducing their child's fearfulness and anxiety will allow the child to face fears so the pathways can become stronger. It is best to challenge your child in small increments, no matter how uncomfortable, while being encouraging and loving. Reshaping as soon as you notice your child is having difficulty, even in infancy when children tend to be more flexible in their thinking and have less to unlearn, works best.

Changing your child's temperament is much less difficult when the brain is still developing. The greatest influence will occur between birth and five years old when neural pathways can still be easily sculpted.

Environmental Factors

Many of the environmental factors that contribute to anxiety are discussed in detail later in the book, but here is a general explanation. The environment is composed of all events, people, circumstances, desires, needs, and situations that have a point of origin outside of your child. Any situation that disrupts your child's sense of structure and order in their world creates a change internally.

Life Events

It is common when children start school or day care, or transition to a new grade, for them to become emotional, scared, or clingy for a brief period. Usually, parents will find a few weeks are normal for the transition, and are able to hang in there. It is when the reaction becomes protracted and your child cannot move past her feelings about the incident that intervention will be necessary. Some common examples of stressful life events (which are external stressors) are:

- A trauma
- Seeing violence at home, school, or on TV
- School issues
- Divorce
- Moving
- Loss
- Anxious, overprotective, or critical parenting style
- Difficulty with friendships
- Death of a family member, friend, or family pet

Uncertainty of outcome, along with transitions and ambiguous situations, often create the most stress. In addition, if a child grows up in an environment that is actually scary or dangerous, such as when there is violence in the family or the community, the child may learn to be fearful or expect the worst.

 Alert

According to a National Television Violence Study, a child will have viewed 8,000 murders and 100,000 other acts of television violence by the time he is eleven years old. It is important to use parental controls and limit what is available for viewing to minimize the impact of trauma on your child and decrease sources of anxiety.

Uncertainty

When a situation lacks a clear outcome, your child might feel a lack of control and significant stress. Uncertain as to what type of coping response will be needed to deal with a particular situation, your child might be convinced he does not have what it takes to get through it, especially when he remembers difficulties he had in the past. A study of adolescents anxious about the future, a stressor marked by uncertainty, found they expressed their anxiety by trying to alter their mood. Often they resorted to drug-taking and impulsive or dangerous behavior to help them cope.

Children can learn how to manage environmental stressors through watching parents, siblings, friends, teachers, and peers at school. If they observe people who respond to stressful situations with uncertainty, worry, nervousness, extreme caution, and over-emphasis on danger, this can influence how they themselves will react, and create a pessimistic worldview.

Parental Influence

First, it is important to note that most parents do not *cause* their children to be anxious; rather, they unwittingly help to perpetuate it. I say *most* parents because this statement does not hold true if there is intentional violence or abuse in the home. Sometimes in your efforts to do the best you can with what you have been taught or know, you are unaware that your efforts might be hindering your children. For example, if your seven-year-old child is afraid to make new friends, you might "help" him by making the phone call to set up a playdate instead of assuring him he can get through it on his own. Parents can also affect how a child chooses to cope through their anxiety by watching the choices they make. For example, if you come home from work stressed, does your child see you reach for a glass of wine or a beer to relax? Do you yell at others and then say, "Sorry, I had a stressful day"?

Research shows that inconsistency, harsh and rigid attitudes, ambiguity, and family conflict appear to be among the primary predictors of the development of anxiety. Also identified as associated with a child's anxiety are little to no clear family rules, strong parental concern for a family's reputation, a poor relationship with the father, and an inability for the child to bond in infancy.

Trauma

Early traumatic experience can block the normal growth and development of coping skills, and affect your child's emotional and social growth. At the time of the event, intense feelings of fear and helplessness can overcome your child, causing him to feel he cannot think clearly or function well. If your child has experienced a life event that is outside the realm of normal human experience and the associated anxiety continues over time, even with your care, concern, and discussions with him, you may want to consult with your medical provider. Please note that some symptoms of anxiety may not occur at the time of the event. In some cases, there is a delayed reaction. Also, if your child has ever experienced a panic attack and continues to avoid the place it was experienced, he is more likely to grow and learn from the experience if you seek professional help from a licensed provider. When help is delayed this can complicate and/or prolong treatment.

Your child's reaction to a trauma is affected by her age, what life has felt like so far, temperament and personality, and when the trauma happened. This can result in feelings of loss of control and stability, worry about personal safety, and grief reactions. When the trauma has been long lasting or a sense of hopelessness develops, as in the case of abuse or bullying, you might see school refusal (resisting attendance), or even suicidal thinking. Trauma comes in many forms, and even if the bullying occurred one time it is important to notify the child's teacher, principal, and school nurse.

Food

When foods are full of sugar or caffeine, contain food additives, or if your child is lacking vitamins and minerals, anxiety, feelings of panic, an inability to sleep, night frights, and/or depression can develop. These foods can influence your child's thought process by altering her ability to concentrate or learn new material; they can also lower her level of awareness, weaken the growth process of her brain, increase how sick she becomes when ill, and even increase the duration and intensity of a cold. Chapter 12 covers the importance of nutrition.

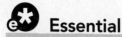 **Essential**

A number of conditions can occur when your child's body is low in potassium, including diarrhea, vomiting, and sweating, which are also symptoms of anxiety. To keep potassium levels balanced, be sure to give your child bananas, meats, fruits, fish, beans, and vegetables.

Because anxiety affects blood sugar levels, it can cause sensitivities and stomach problems such as pain, a bloated or distended stomach, discomfort, indigestion, and symptoms of hyperglycemia and hypoglycemia. When your child overeats, especially sweets and desserts, it can affect her nervous system. This can trigger moodiness, anxiousness, sleepiness, or depression. It is important to note that some people free their anxiety almost completely through a reduction of sugary or caffeinated foods and drinks.

Sleep

Sleep is a basic human need important at any age, as fundamental to feeling healthy as good nutrition and exercising regularly are. A good night's sleep, as you probably know, can make a world of difference in your child's ability to handle himself. It can refuel his body's energy, give his active brain the rest it needs, and all around put him mentally in a better mood. On the flip side, a lack of sleep is known to disrupt the body's ability to replenish hormones that affect both physical and mental health. For children experiencing anxiety, poor sleep is linked to learning problems, slower emotional and physical growth, bedwetting, and high blood pressure. Details on sleep routine and insomnia will be presented in Chapter 12.

CHAPTER 3

Signs and Symptoms of Anxiety

Children experiencing anxiety show telltale signs of the turmoil hidden below the surface. These indicators fall into several categories, but the underlying theme is that your child feels that he simply cannot meet the demands of life because they are too difficult or frightening. This chapter describes typical signs that might indicate that your child needs help with their symptoms. Pay attention to the frequency, intensity, and duration of the behaviors in your child. In addition, the more signs your child displays, the more likely the underlying cause is anxiety. It is also helpful to keep in mind the ways that your child may seem different from his peers.

Behavioral Expressions

Because children are less likely to be able to identify and verbalize feelings of worry and anxiety, they are more likely to show anxiety through their behaviors. Keep in mind that the older your child, the more likely he will be able to talk about his internal states. Children act out feelings as a normal expression of their development, which can sometimes be frustrating. As a result, parents often mistake a child's behavioral challenges for stubbornness, laziness, or willfulness. In fact, the overall message a child experiencing anxiety communicates through behavior is a state of hopelessness.

Meltdowns

A meltdown can be best described as a "total emotional break-down." Your child may sob, wail, refuse to move or respond, or talk nonstop about an event he found upsetting. He may seem inconsolable, or unable to "rally" for the next demand, like homework, an outing, or dinnertime. Adolescents may "freak out," lamenting about issues that may seem trivial or even insensible from the adult point of view.

 Essential

When supporting your child, refer to their symptoms rather than the label (anxiety). Labels give the impression that your child *is* the anxiety rather than an individual experiencing nervousness, worry, or concern for future events. Be mindful of how you speak of your child in front of others (e.g. "He's anxious" as opposed to "she is thinking fearful thoughts about the exam" or "he's always worried about his appearance").

Tearfulness

Tears in response to disappointments, loss, or injury to the physical or emotional self are normal and expected in children (and adults, too!). Tears are one of the ways the body releases stress hormones, which is why many people feel better after a good cry. If your child is tearful for no apparent reason, cannot seem to stop crying in response to an upset, or seems to "cry at the drop of a hat," anxiety could be the underlining cause.

Transitional Stress

Many children feeling anxious have difficulty switching gears between activities. This may occur at school between subjects, at particular times during the day, such as between playtime and dinner, or when a new set of skills or attention is required. A child may dawdle or show one of the behaviors discussed earlier. Parents can help their children appreciate the transitions in their life through modeling their own positive behavior. Many people regard transitions as the time in between or preparation for the next task. This may be true, but to ease pressure, consider your transition to *be* the experience. You might say to your child, "I notice that when I slow down and feel the weight of the book in my hands, the texture of my bag, or the texture and smell of my clothes as I put them on, it has a way of calming my mind and body." This is an aspect of mindfulness, focusing on physical details of the present moment rather than worrying about what might come next. Redirecting your child to the present moment (e.g. feeling their feet connected to the floor) with their senses is a way of providing them with tools to manage anxiety.

Requests

Your child may refuse to meet requests, obligations, or deadlines. Requests such as doing her chores, getting ready for bed, or participating in family activities may be pushed away. Children who are afraid they cannot do something well, or if they feel unsure if they can meet your standards, may instead avoid the request altogether. See this as a signal that they may need some encouragement or recognition for the things they have done.

Avoidance

Avoidance is one of the hallmarks of anxiety in both adults and children. Because your child wants to shy away from what is uncomfortable, she may resist doing things that take her out of her comfort zone. Children feeling nervous or uncomfortable may avoid social situations or occasions in which they fear they will be called upon to use skills they are certain they do not possess, such as a class presentation. To avoid feeling inadequate, your child may procrastinate or even shut down entirely. Parents may respond by either pushing or coddling, or by avoiding the issue themselves. Research shows that parents of children with anxiety tend to do tasks for children or respond in a way that does not increase and encourage autonomy in the child. This increases avoidance of independence in the future because the child is blocked from experiencing an internal sense of competence or mastery.

 Fact

> Procrastination is a specific form of avoidance, with an "I'll do it later" attitude. In the moment, the child experiences a temporary relief from anxiety; however, in the long run, it will return and the child will be faced once again with either having to learn skills for managing stress or repeating patterns that generate stress.

Feeling Isolated

One of the most debilitating aspects of anxiety is its power to cause people to feel different, isolated, and cut off from the world. This feeling of alienation can come in many forms and tends to feed on itself. Often, feelings of being different and separate from others can lead to increased symptoms of anxiety and withdrawal. Left unaddressed, these are overpowering feelings that can lead to depression in a child with anxiety. Overlap between anxiety and depression is discussed later in Chapter 14.

Alone in the Family

Children who are anxious may shy away from contact with family as well. Although it is common for teens or children who are more solitary or introverted to spend time alone in their rooms, children feeling anxious may avoid family contact more often than not. Your child may try to opt out of family outings, especially when extended family is included. He may appear to be indifferent, "hang back," or be slow to warm when extended family or company is present. They may opt for solitary activity, even when the opportunity for more interesting group interaction is available. It is important to note that some children are naturally more introverted than others.

Alone at School

Children faced with anxiety may be highly sensitive, and at times overreact to challenges, disappointments, or feel isolated in their school environment. Making and keeping friends can be challenging. This is very difficult for parents to witness. Some children may come home from school teary and overwhelmed by social demands they feel they cannot meet. Your child may make statements such as "no one likes me" or "everybody's mean to me." She may be afraid to try new things, like the monkey bars or the newest dance step, and may end up ostracized by her peer group, magnifying her sense of aloneness. Because peer relationships are so important, they will be addressed more fully later in this chapter in the section entitled "Friendship Fuss."

 Essential

Comparing yourself to others can reinforce the belief that you are not good enough or missing something. Parents can set the tone by being careful about comparing siblings or always measuring their child against his peers. Instead, direct your attention to your own child's milestones and hurdles with loving encouragement and praise.

I'm Different

Children who feel anxious may view themselves as not like other children. The cycle of negative thinking that so often occurs magnifies fears and shortcomings. Because his experiences are perceived as more intense or overwhelming than those of his peers, he is left with a sense of "otherness" that may prevent him from identifying with and learning from his peers. Behavioral issues such as tearfulness or frequent meltdowns can alienate the child experiencing anxiety further from his peers. Unfortunately, it is not uncommon for children to avoid or reject kids who seem immature or have low self-esteem.

They Can Do It, Why Can't I?

Anxiety has a way of exaggerating what children don't like about themselves. When this occurs, achievements of others may be viewed as more important than is due, and the child may downplay his own accomplishments. Fear of failure may cause anxious children to give up before they have mastered a new skill. In their mind they think "why bother?", believing that they are unable to measure up to the expectations of their peer group. He may give up entirely on learning a new skill, like the child who becomes afraid of trying to ride a bike and who will not ride at all because his friends have already mastered the skill. A child experiencing anxiety may believe that others accomplish things effortlessly and give up on his task, believing he is a failure because the task isn't easy. If you believe this is true for your child, try modeling persistence and/or share a story of your own frustration with mastering a skill.

Skipping School

One of the most troubling patterns that can develop in children feeling anxious is refusing to attend or stay at school. Separation anxiety, generalized anxiety, social fears, and peer issues all contribute to school avoidance. A pattern of school refusal, once established, can be extremely difficult to break and requires a team approach. Most often the team would need to include the child's teacher, parents, school nurse, and mental health professional such as a school counselor or school psychologist.

What Are the Signs?

Most children who attempt to avoid school will do so by complaining of physical symptoms. Headaches, stomachaches, and vague complaints of not feeling good are common in children with anxiety and will be detailed later in this chapter. Complaining, pleading, dawdling, "disappearing," and repeated attempts to avoid or be absent from school (for example, by regularly missing the bus) are common. In these cases it is important to gather as much information as possible. Notice any patterns such as the child not wanting to attend school on specific days or possibly to avoid certain situations. For example, make note if any tests, projects, public speaking, or competitive activities are occurring.

What Are the Consequences?

The most obvious consequence of missing school is that your child may get behind in her schoolwork. For the child who is already anxious, missing homework can become overwhelming, spiraling into more physical complaints and additional attempts to avoid school. Another consequence, particularly for a child who is socially anxious, involves missed opportunities to build competence in peer interactions. The longer a child is away from school, the more daunting it becomes to go back into the fray of social demands. In this case, the proverbial "getting back on the horse after a fall" applies directly. Typically, the longer your child is away from school, the less confident and motivated she may be.

 Fact

Meditation alters brain wave patterns, even among new practitioners. This means you can teach your child to focus on the moment and become aware of what is happening both inside and outside of her body so that she can change her brain from an alert, vigilant, stressed condition to a more relaxed, soothing state of mind. Read more about this in Chapter 11.

What Can You Do?

If you feel your child attempts to stay home from school more than she should, you can use several approaches, depending on your child's particular pattern. Sometimes, friends or siblings attending the same school can be excellent supports for your child. You may wish to spend some extra time at your child's school, for example, by volunteering, if this encourages her to stay in school. However, be prepared to wean your involvement at some point so that your child can learn to tolerate being at school on her own. School nurses, psychologists, or social workers may also be called upon to help encourage a child experiencing anxiety to stay through the day.

You may also consider taking your child to a mental health provider trained in meditation, biofeedback, or guided visualization. A shift in perception first requires a shift in brain waves from the beta frequency, a more alert state, to the alpha frequency, where she can imagine herself going back to school in a more relaxed state. (More on this and other techniques in Chapters 11 and 13.)

 Alert

Avoidance works in the short term but perpetuates stress and anxiety in the long term. It gives your child a false impression of how to relieve anxiety. In other words, you are better off seeking help rather than waiting to see if it works itself out.

Homework Hassles

Homework can be a trigger for children experiencing anxiety. They may already be feeling overwhelmed and pressured, and now they have to use their "free" time doing something that creates more stress and anxiety. At the same time, their fear of failure puts them on the wheel of frustration and cycle of perfectionism.

Some children get emotionally overwrought trying to call up the attention and focus needed to complete the work. Supervision and reassurance is often required from a parent who is busy preparing a meal, or is tired from the day's demands. Parents need to remember that they know their child best. Be an advocate for your child's learning and set realistic expectations and boundaries with teachers. Stress and anxiety impinge learning, decreasing the ability to process and recall information. In the case of anxiety, as well as learning disabilities, it is better to give less homework so the child is able to feel capable and strong rather than incapable and weak.

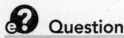 **Question**

My daughter needs help at school, but got very angry at me for suggesting I could call the teacher. What do I do now?
The importance of respecting your child and not increasing anxiety makes this a tough call. It is best to explain how parent-teacher communication is part of your role. Parents who make a habit of checking in with the teacher regardless if there is a problem set the tone for open communication early on. Developing a respectful relationship with the teacher is critical. On occasion, you may feel you are unable to communicate or work with the present teacher. If so, you may need to speak to the principal or social worker.

What Does It Look Like?

Typical patterns of homework refusal may include procrastination or dawdling, forgetting assignments or materials needed to complete the work, defiance, excessive need for reassurance, and inability to work independently. Some children become great at the disappearing act by running off to a friend's house or holing up in their rooms. As surprising as it seems, some children may even offer to do chores or help with food preparation in an effort to avoid doing their homework.

What Can You Do to Help?

First, be aware of your child's assignments and obligations for school. Make checking your child's backpack or folder a daily part of your routine, such as when she first comes home from school or when you come home from work. Communicate your belief that your child can do the work on her own, but that you will be happy to assist her if she gets stuck. If your child routinely does homework in an area with multiple distractions, consider the following tips (also read Chapter 4 where it is suggested you reframe "homework" to "home study"):

- Turn the TV or radio off. If your child feels listening to music helps, it is best if the music is low and/or does not have words.
- Give your child time to play or exercise before homework.
- Consider limiting after-school obligations, particularly if homework is forcing your child to stay up late.
- Choose an area that is well lighted, the least noisy, and clear of clutter.
- Have an organizational calendar (that is only for your child) in the work area to assist in long-term planning. That way your child can visually see and plan out how much time she has to complete an assignment.
- Have your child do homework routinely in that area, at about the same time each day.
- Encourage your child to hydrate and eat a healthy snack while tackling homework. Put out carrot sticks, or hummus and crackers for your child to graze on.
- Consider reading a book or magazine nearby so that you are available for support. You are also modeling good study habits.
- Encourage younger siblings to draw or do projects in the same area, but only if they do not overly distract your child.
- Be positive and reinforce your child's efforts.

- If homework is taking too long—meaning it is interfering with sleep, eating, and exercise—make an appointment to speak with your child's teachers.

Encourage your child to get up, stretch, and move around in between tasks. If they experience tension while sitting, suggest a seated spinal twist (putting hand on back of chair and gently twisting the spine in both directions). Also, neck and shoulder rolls and stretching arms overhead can renew attention.

When and How to Talk to the Teacher

If your child is experiencing anxiety-related concerns at school, be prepared to increase your level of contact with his teacher. Keep in mind that some teachers are more receptive than others are to emotional concerns, and it may be necessary to enlist the school social worker or other helpers to advocate for your child. Generally, it is a good idea to let your child know that you plan to talk with his teacher. But some children will be embarrassed by this, as it can increase their anxiety if they feel the teacher is watching them closely. As such, you may wish to involve your child directly in problem solving.

Friendship Fuss

Social difficulties can be a source of stress and therefore trigger symptoms of anxiety in your child. Children may experience an inward conflict of wanting to fit in, yet the amount of stress it takes to fit in is overwhelming. This may in turn exasperate or introduce a fear of failure. Feelings of alienation may or may not be an accurate assessment of the reality of the situation. Your empathy and understanding of your child's frustrations, along with your persistent and gentle encouragement, can go a long way to improving your child's social experiences. Try not to minimize the enormous power social frustration and discomfort play in a child's developing sense of independence and self-esteem.

Late elementary and early middle school (grades six through eight) years can be particularly difficult as it is normal for social cliques to develop. Cliques serve a purpose of helping children to experiment with social power and a sense of belonging; however, for those outside of the circle it can be hurtful. Consider encouraging your child to participate in activities that are less competitive. Also, both boys and girls benefit greatly from role models who illustrate how to feel and talk about their feelings comfortably, meaning without fear of being ridiculed. Children flourish in environments where their feelings are honored and accepted for what they are.

No One Wants to Play with Me

Shyness and being quiet are common traits in children sensitive to anxiety. Initiating social interaction or including themselves in a situation where other children are already involved in an activity may at times be challenging. Your child may end up feeling that she is unwanted. Conversely, as you have already learned, peers can reject children with anxiety when their behavior is seen as immature, disruptive, or odd. Consider role-playing with your child ways to handle herself in social situations (parent, you be your child and have your child be the other kids). Model rather than tell your child what to do and say.

 Essential

Notice if your child repeats statements such as: *they won't play with me* or *they are mean to me*. Encourage your child to close her eyes and visualize those thoughts being washed away in the water. Perhaps they can do this in the shower or bathtub. It can help if she gives her thoughts a color. Often these are hidden belief systems that can be cleared away through using their imagination.

Older children may compare themselves negatively to others, and may feel they have little or nothing of value to offer as a friend. Younger children may simply feel restless or uneasy around peers for reasons they are not yet able to identify. Your child may fear doing things other more gregarious children do, such as sports, video games, or sleepovers. To help your child overcome this roadblock, encourage and reward baby steps. You can also play a game or sport with your child to help increase confidence and ability and lessen fears.

They Make Fun of Me

Younger children may lack social tact, and refer to your anxious child as a "crybaby" or "fraidy-cat." Unfortunately, the aftermath of repeated teasing can be serious, especially if the teasing is brutal, sadistic, or widespread. Be as supportive as possible if your child complains of teasing, and try to "check out the facts" whenever possible. With younger children, you may be able to intervene by increasing supervision, talking with the other parents involved, or limiting contact with specific friends. With older children, it may be necessary to speak to school personnel or neighborhood parents about your concerns, or assist your child in working out an assertive solution. Keep in mind that if this intervention is not handled delicately, it may backfire and lead to increased ostracism. In extreme cases, when a pattern of teasing or alienation cannot be broken, it may be necessary to move your child to another school.

Body Talk

Homeostasis is the body's way of putting itself back into balance. For example, if your body is low on iron you may experience symptoms such as weakness and fatigue. Once you take iron supplements or eat more iron rich foods you may feel more alert, strong, and happy. Anxiety works in the same way. It is your body's way of communicating how your child may require more play, outdoor time, sleep, healthy foods, vitamin D, and habits that allow her to receive the moment (e.g. breathing, stretching, etc.).

It is not uncommon for children sensitive to anxiety to experience and complain of physical pain and discomfort. Following are some of the symptoms most commonly experienced. Keep in mind that for stress and anxiety to be the culprit of these symptoms, they must be unrelated to sports or other injuries.

Aches and Pains

Aches and pains cover a relatively diffuse variety of physical sensations. They most typically include:

- Muscle aches
- Joint pain
- Tightness or tingling, most commonly in chest or extremities
- Back and/or neck pain

If your child experiences more than one or two of the pains on this list more than once or twice a week, start with your family physician to rule out any underlying physical conditions that could be causing the discomfort. If a trusted physician rules out physical causes, it may be time to seek psychological help.

 Alert

Studies show somatic complaints are strongly associated with physical disorders in girls and with disruptive behavior disorders in boys. A pain reduction study found that four twenty-minute sessions of mindfulness meditation reduced pain unpleasantness by 57 percent and pain intensity by 40 percent. (*Journal of Neuroscience*, April 2011.)

Fat Talk

Fat talk is negative statements or put-downs your child may say directly or indirectly about her body. According to Common Sense

Media, "the pursuit of a perfect body is no longer a 'girl' thing. [. . .] Girls want to get skinny and boys want to bulk up and lose body fat." Parents can reduce body anxiety by avoiding diet language (e.g. calorie talk, weight), limiting exposure to media, and avoiding purchasing magazines that emphasize outside appearance. Pay attention to what your child watches on TV or on the Internet. Try to steer your children toward activities and websites that are developmentally appropriate, value kids for who they are, and are community driven. Equally important is to know that fat talk may be code language for "I feel unworthy" or "I am under a lot of pressure." If your child talks about how fat she is, rather than say "no, you are not," ask her about what she was just doing or thinking about. Fat talk doesn't usually just appear out of nowhere; often there is something behind it. Most of all, watch how you refer to your own body. For example, notice what you say when you are looking in the mirror or trying on new clothing. Avoid habits such as weighing yourself, calling yourself fat, or reporting how much you weigh. Focus on how amazing the human body is and the importance of living a balanced lifestyle. Comments such as, "I felt so strong on my walk today," or "when I drink water I feel a difference in my energy levels" are far more effective.

Tummy Troubles

In 1996, science writer Sandra Blakeslee of the *New York Times* reported what science now knows to be true: "The brain can upset the gut and the gut can upset the brain." It is important to be aware of the true source behind these symptoms in order to take appropriate action for treatment. Remember some of the following symptoms may also be due to gluten, dairy, or wheat allergies. If there is a food intolerance, this can exacerbate anxiety. Gastrointestinal complaints related to anxiety may include:

- Nausea
- Stomachaches
- Indigestion or heartburn
- Vomiting
- Diarrhea
- Constipation

 Fact

Teaching your child how to breathe can be an effective tool for helping your child redirect the communication between his gut, heart, and brain. One of the best times to teach this is while your child is lying in bed. Sit with him and model breathing in through the nose, inflating your belly as you inhale and deflating it as you exhale. You can find more breathing techniques and tips in Chapter 11.

Nervous Habits

Have you ever watched someone chew her fingernails, bounce her leg incessantly, twirl her hair, or snap chewing gum? These are all examples of nervous habits. Other nervous habits include knuckle-cracking, tapping fingers or objects, biting the lips, picking at the skin, or straightening clothing or other objects. Although most people have one or two nervous habits, in children these habits can go from distracting to debilitating if they are incessant. Interestingly, nervous habits develop unconsciously as a way to tame tension. If you see your child engaging in nervous habits like these, this may be a sign that they need some exercise, fresh air, support, or a break from their present task. Refrain from judging or assuming all habits are bad. Instead, see it as feedback for you and your child about her bodily needs. If you have a nervous habit, observe yourself next time you in engage in it and see how it may interfere with your ability to breathe deeply and calm your body.

CHAPTER 4

School Days

School is one of the biggest triggers for anxiety in children. Children who may not have been sensitive to anxiety before may illustrate signs of it once they experience the social, emotional, and academic pressures of the school environment. Children may find it stressful as they attempt to conform to the academic standards and expectations. School experiences require many adjustments, some of which are expected and others which are not. Some of these include adjusting to teachers, schedules, academic expectations, friendships, homework, transitions, developmental shifts, and more. However, along the way parents will have to listen and pay attention in order to guide their child, and in some cases advocate for situations that position the child for optimal growth.

Anxiety about School

A certain amount of anxiety about school is normal and expected. Making new friends, completing homework, taking tests, completing projects, athletic or performance schedules, and the demands of "fitting it all in" can tax even the most confident child. If your support and encouragement do not seem to help your child gain a sense of mastery, and if she loses sleep, avoids school, or worries more than you think she should, you will want to pay special attention to this chapter.

She Doth Protest Too Much

As you saw in Chapter 3, the most common tactic children use to avoid school is to complain about physical symptoms such as headaches, stomachaches, or general malaise. Children with anxiety may make frantic and repeated calls to be picked up from school early, or may be mysteriously ill after a long weekend or extended break. The child with anxiety may complain of over-whelming social pressures and push you to let her have a "mental health day," or she may repeatedly miss the bus. Other signs that point to anxiety may be difficulty getting up in the morning, pro-longed dawdling, or a pattern of missing school on days when tests or class presentations are scheduled.

 Question

Does your child often try to avoid going to school by complaining of illness?
After a medical checkup to rule out any true physical problems, follow the school's guidelines for illness and attendance so you do not become a part of the problem. If your child ultimately does stay home, avoid making the day an opportunity for playtime. That is, limit television, video games, and the like. If a child is truly ill, the best medicine is a restful day in bed, with a little TLC thrown in, of course.

Values Reduce Anxiety

According to author Mark Waldman "reflecting on personal values can keep neuroendocrine and psychological responses to stress at low levels." By clearly communicating your values (e.g. respect) as opposed to repeating your rules and expectations, you can encourage your child without stressing him out. Most children truly want to do the right thing and please their parents. However, when parents constantly restate the rules this can send a message that you don't trust or believe in the abilities of your child. Consider having a brief yet meaningful conversation about your values rather than quick, impulsive reminders about your rules. This can be done at a family meeting time (not dinner) when you and your family can briefly sit together without distractions.

Home Study

The word "homework" may itself be an anxiety trigger for your child, as it implies more work. Parents may want to adopt their own language when asking about homework, instead referring to it as "home study." Also be mindful of your own statements and attitude toward homework. If you speak of the dreaded homework your child will pick up on this and begin to sing the same tune. Often these statements are a sign that a parent needs to communicate to the teacher about the amount or intensity of the workload. Speaking to teachers does not mean you are attempting to change them or get them to agree with your viewpoint. It is an opportunity to provide constructive feedback about your child and in many cases parents walk away with a renewed perspective or reassurance from the teacher.

Anticipatory Anxiety

Anticipatory anxiety occurs when your child imagines a future event that he believes is outside his safe zone, and fears he will not be able to handle the situation without panic. Sometimes referred to as the "fear of fear," the overall goal is really to avoid distressing feelings. The anxiety your child feels when thinking about the feared event increases his tendency to avoid it, and magnifies feelings of distress if the situation actually does occur. Anticipatory anxiety is indiscriminate; that is, it can involve negative thoughts about performance, panic, peers, perfection, or just about anything else, and can be lifelong. Parents can help by asking questions such as who their child sits next to during the day or how the bus ride is going. It is when children believe they do not have a choice (e.g. they have to sit next to someone) that anxiety is increased.

Very often symptoms can be reduced with simple changes in seat placement, schedules, or homework load. Test anxiety is another example of anticipatory anxiety, and the suggested solutions in the next section can be used as a basis for dealing with general anticipatory anxiety as well.

Test Anxiety

It has been said that almost all children will experience test anxiety at some time in their school careers. Small to moderate levels of anxiety actually increase performance, while more severe amounts cause performance to drop off. Test anxiety occurs when strong or unpleasant emotions interfere with your child's ability to absorb, retain, and recall information. Anxiety creates a kind of "mental static" in the brain, which interferes with learning, memory, and the ability to reason and think clearly. Feelings such as worry, fear, and frustration actually derail the central nervous system, causing the SNS and PNS to get out of rhythm, thereby disrupting mental processes. Conversely, positive feelings like hope and appreciation lead to increased balance and harmony in the nervous system. This enhances performance and creates positive emotional pathways to build on success.

Be Prepared

One of the most basic approaches to managing test anxiety is to help your child maximize her sense of competence by ensuring preparation for an exam. You may wish to help by using practice questions or by encouraging her to review with friends. The younger your child is, the easier it may be to make a game out of this. How your child prepares for the review is also important. Productive study skill habits such as effective note taking, organization, and time management sets your child up for success. You and your child may ask the teacher for a study guide. Encourage your child to talk out loud when he studies similar to how an actor remembers his lines (using flexion in his voice). Some children do better when they are permitted to move their bodies or listen to background music. Be sure your child gets a good sleep and nutrition during exam time.

Counter Negative Rehearsal

Negative rehearsal or mental repetition of negative thoughts and fears is actually what drives anticipatory anxiety. The repeated negative thoughts about the feared event groove in anxiety responses, creating an endless loop and making the situation seem unbearable. As a parent it will be important that you watch for counter-productive language. For example, if your child says, *"I hate tests,"* help him to see tests are an opportunity to review, strengthen, and show what you know about a subject. If your child is not agreeable to seeing tests as opportunities ask him to imagine the word "hate" drifting down a river and away from him. What your child does not realize is these types of words and statements actually prevent him from showing his knowledge. As your child learns how to relax and breathe (see Chapter 11) these statements will naturally lessen. You can also encourage your child to imagine himself getting up, going to school, entering the classroom where the test will occur, taking, and finishing the test with ease. Through relaxation and visualization your child can begin to view himself moving through rather than being paralyzed by difficult situations. Older children may purchase an app for relaxation where he visualizes to soothing sounds. Your child can also state a mantra for himself (see Chapter 11). For example, he can repeat out loud to himself, *"Taking tests comes naturally and easy for me"* (ten consecutive times per day). For teens who may feel this is silly, you can let them know techniques such as these are used in sports psychology by professional athletes to prepare them for their mental game. Like children, even the best athletes get performance anxiety.

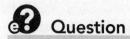 **Question**

Will talking about the test with my child only make it worse?
Generally, less is more with most children and teens. Stories and encouragement are great, however, lectures tend to turn most kids off. Try not to prolong any discussions that do take place; create boundaries—meaning allow some time for discussion, but then move on. Talking about the test right before the exam or before your child hops on the bus may actually raise anxiety.

Tapping

Tapping is a technique based on the principals of acupressure. Certain points on the body are tapped lightly over and over using the tips of the finger while making statements such as, "Even though I feel anxious about my test I completely and totally accept myself." This technique is proven to move any emotional charges. (Emotional charges are strong reactions when your child keeps revisiting the same thoughts over and over again.) Tapping helps break up the density of the emotion allowing the energy to move freely rather than becoming static in the body. When done for several minutes your child will eventually receive relief from the tension brought upon by the charge. One of the points is called the karate chop and is located on the outside of the hand halfway between the bottom of the pinky and the bottom of the hand (above the wrist). Before teaching tapping to children it is recommended that parents first try tapping on themselves. Next time you feel an emotional charge close your eyes and tap the point repeating the statement, "Even though I feel _____, I completely and totally accept myself." The tapping session can take anywhere from three to five minutes. The technique is discussed more fully in Chapter 11.

Touchstones

Have you ever found yourself toying with change or keys in your pocket, or twisting a ring on your finger? If so, you are using a touchstone to calm yourself. A touchstone is an object that your child carries with her that she can touch or hold, which becomes grounding and comforting for her. It should be small enough to be worn or carried, and be an object that has a symbolic or emotional meaning for your child. Examples include smooth stones, coins, crystals, amulets or figurines, jewelry, or key rings. Help your child to find an object she can carry with her to use like this when anxious or upset. Often items children find in nature, such as a smooth rock, will work well. Encourage your child to use her touchstone while she practices other skills such as breathing or imagery to reduce both testing and general anxiety.

 Essential

Crystals give off an electromagnetic frequency. Many children experiencing anxiety feel weak in their ability to cope with stress and negativity. By carrying a rock, mineral, or crystal in their pocket they can increase their vibration. When vibration is low you may feel drained. However, when vibration is high resiliency increases. Teach your child to go for natural resources rather than synthetic stimulants such as soda to rebalance her body.

Handling Anxiety at School

Many children choose to push through their day at school, collapsing or melting at the end of the day never really knowing they are experiencing symptoms of anxiety. Transitions are a great time for your child to utilize techniques such as breathing, stretching, yawning (a built-in stress reliever), drinking water, playing, reading, drawing, and reconnecting mind and body by engaging their larger muscles (legs and thighs). Children can even do energy techniques or tapping (see Chapter 11). Techniques such as these don't magically make the symptoms disappear. However, they can tone down the intensity of symptoms such as worrying, enough so your child can recognize and observe her thoughts without feeling overwhelmed or threatened by them. The calmer your child feels (which is the purpose of techniques such as breathing) the more likely she is able to observe her thoughts without following them, meaning she is able to think a fearful thought without personalizing or making it her current reality. She can see that she has a choice to keep thinking the same thoughts or to interrupt the cycle by yawning or laughing. Even a fake sneeze can redirect her attention to more uplifting or kind ways of thinking. After all thoughts are just thoughts and most of the time they stem from the past or future. It is when your child chooses to focus on the ones that give her information about the here and now that you can feel confident she is learning and growing from her experiences with anxiety.

Parents can help their children by discussing how they might de-stress during the day. Talk about how you had a stressful moment at work or the grocery store and what you did to restore calm and balance in your body. Open the dialogue between you and your child by asking, "How do you help yourself through the stress in your day?" Parents and children can learn a lot from each other.

Lunchtime Moans
The social melting pot of your child's lunchroom can be overwhelming if he is especially sensitive, introverted, or self-conscious. If your child is unable to eat around others, you will want to address this early. Enlist school personnel and a therapist who can help with a plan of gradual exposure so that your child can learn how to thrive from managing fears rather than be overcome by them. This requires building confidence bit by bit. For example, the school can help your child by finding familiar lunch partners or a regular

table. It is helpful when adults and teachers take a moment to check in with students. Schools may even prepare a list of conversation topics, and alternative lunch space may be an option where some children meet in a smaller group setting to practice basic conversational skills. Your child may prefer a lunch brought from home as opposed to waiting in line to purchase a prepared meal, which can be anxiety-provoking as children may worry there will be no place for them to sit.

 Essential

Family meals are one of the ways to practice social skill development. To do this well, turn off televisions and other electronic devices. Remember that a family meal does not always mean dinner. If gathering the family at breakfast is better for your schedule, that works just as well.

Staying in Class

If your child has trouble staying in class and has frequent urges to leave this may be a sign that she is choosing to run from her symptoms of anxiety. This is a temporary fix and will only increase her feelings of panic and hopelessness. Teach your child not to be afraid of her tension. The impulse to leave is often a response to bodily tension, which in some cases is simply memory of irritation or fear that may be stored in the body. The body is highly intelligent and holds memory just like your brain does. Explain tension to your child as an intersection. Imagine seeing someone wanting to cross the street. Imagine waving to the person to go ahead and cross before you drive through the intersection. It is the same thing with tension. When your child feels it in his body he can simply say to the tension in his mind "Okay, you go first, then me." This teaches children to pause and allow tension to move through and past them, rather than react to it. It will also be important to look at your child's diet to determine the amount of sweets and stimulants.

Nutritional supplements that promote calm and relaxation may also be necessary (see Chapter 12).

Transitions

Some transitions are anticipated while others are not. Your child will benefit from you giving her a heads up for transitions that are expected as well as the unexpected. For example, your child might experience a pop quiz, fire drill, substitute teacher, or something that he thought was going to happen may be canceled. Once your child is provided with strategies such as mudras (see Chapter 11), touchstones, and mindfulness he can then apply them to these unexpected moments.

Peers and Peer Pressure

The demands of social interaction can be especially traumatic for children who are experiencing high anxiety, who worry more, and are exceedingly shy or self-conscious. In fact, it is not uncommon for children with anxiety to have difficulty making, keeping, and interacting with friends.

 Fact

Your child's first best friend is truly a friend forever, because the experience of having a person outside of your family who mirrors your fears, fancies, and foibles creates a base or template for all of your child's future relationships. The developmental push to find and keep a best friend is greatest between the ages of about eight to eleven. Developmental psychologists see this as a crucial step, because the best friend or "chum" helps your child to begin fine-tuning his identity and strengthening attachment.

A child experiencing anxiety (even if it is situational, one example being a child's parents deciding to divorce) may evidence his anxiety socially rather than at home with you. The child may have previously appeared to be socially comfortable but is now experiencing some fear of rejection. Regardless of where and when the anxiety shows up, the tools, strategies, and resources remain the same. Keep in mind one of the greatest ways to support children is through active listening. Listen with full attention, without the distractions of phones, household tasks, and computers.

Peer Pressure

You have no doubt had firsthand experience with peer pressure, especially during your adolescent years. Peer pressure can add to insecurity and undermine self-confidence. As your child grows older, family influences take a back seat to those of his peer group. His circle of friends influences what he wears, watches, listens to, eats, believes in, and aspires to. Because children are trying to fit in at the same time they are learning to express themselves, the pressure to conform can become an easy solution to identity confusion. For socially anxious children, peer pressure may be especially powerful, with its promise of "safety in numbers." You can support your child by helping him talk about peer pressure, and especially any influences he finds confusing or distasteful. It may help to ask, "How would you feel about a person who does/ thinks _____? Would you want that person as a friend?"

The Importance of Anchoring

Your child's symptoms are a reminder of how important it is that she be connected and supported. Social anchors through activities such as: sports, dance, Scouts, martial arts, drama, choir or band, and church youth groups can all provide your child with a base sense of security in the social world. They are ready-made opportunities for finding friends who share similar interests and schedules. Hopefully, other children in these specialized peer groups will be a positive influence on her attitudes and behavior, encouraging her to stretch socially. You might try carpooling or hosting a small gathering for her group to encourage your child to use new skills.

Take pride and show interest in her choices by attending events or performances, or by volunteering to help if you can.

Bullies and Gossip

Estimates are that as many as 20 to 30 percent of children either bully or are bullied at some time, and that bullying is most common in the middle-school years. The effects of bullying and gossip can even be harmful to those merely observing it. It was previously believed that bullies lacked self-esteem and put others down to gain self-confidence. However, recent findings show that bullies are more confident than previously thought, but that they tend to lack empathy, are poor communicators, and may be raised in homes where aggression is an acceptable response to conflict.

 Alert

If your child is passive, especially introverted, or socially awkward, he may be an especially susceptible target for bullies. It is easy to dismiss complaints about bullying as a child being too sensitive or dramatic, so please take the time to listen to what your child is saying. Your support can provide the impetus your child needs to address the problem (more on this in Chapter 5).

Gossip is verbal bullying to which girls often resort. It can include name-calling, rumors, and lies, and can have devastating effects, particularly for a child who is already anxious socially. A child who struggles with anxiety may feel she has no recourse, and the powerlessness may lead to avoidance, isolation, and depression. If you suspect your child is the victim of bullying or gossip, listen supportively and try the following:

- Encourage your child to practice "safety in numbers."
- Help your child to widen her social circle.

- Role-play ways to ignore and walk away from teasing or pestering.
- Role-play saying no and being assertive.
- Involve the school if violence, racial slurs, or serious threats of harm occur.

Middle-School Meltdowns

Middle-school (grades six through eight or nine) can be one of the most socially tumultuous times for children. Brains are rewiring and hormones are surging, and children at this age compete for social status, which can sometimes change rapidly. If your child is already having difficulty with worry and panic, this developmental transition can be extremely painful, and making sure therapy is available is important.

A hallmark of this age is the clique, a social group that is highly exclusive and demands strict conformity. The clique usually has a "ringleader" or "queen bee," and members see themselves as superior to others outside the group. Those who do not belong can feel inferior, and even threatened, as the clique can have great social power.

 Essential

When children feel snubbed by members of a clique, they may struggle with self-doubt, anxiety, anger, and even depression. Check for meltdowns or moodiness after school, help your child to talk about social struggles, and celebrate her unique strengths. Use the ideas presented on anchoring to help your child shift focus and find alternative social outlets.

Social Support

Many elementary and middle schools offer "friendship groups" for children who are awkward or have social anxiety, or who are new to the school. Usually, a school social worker leads the groups, in addition to providing individual support to children in the school district. Groups usually meet weekly or bimonthly, and most children look forward to breaks from class and an opportunity to build friendship skills. Other social connections at school may be available through mentoring, student government, peer support, or tutoring. Check with your child's school if you think he might benefit from some of these opportunities.

Staying Connected and Getting Involved

Throughout the book, you have been encouraged to form a support team to help you become strong and confident in your own parenting abilities. If your child has school-based anxiety, it will be especially important to make and keep regular contact with various professionals at her school, and to support her by becoming more active in her educational experience.

 Essential

If you feel that your child's teacher is not receptive to your child's needs or your requests, respectfully involve other support people, such as the nurse, social worker, psychologist, or principal. You know your child best; trust what you feel and advocate when needed.

Where Do You Start?

If your child is experiencing anxiety-related concerns at school, the once- or twice-yearly conference will likely be inadequate to address his emotional needs. Your concerns for your child are important, and no doubt feel urgent. However, it is important to remember that the teacher has many students to attend to, and to respect the teacher's needs with regard to communication. Some teachers prefer to use e-mail; others may have reserved times to speak with parents about concerns over the phone. Many are happy to schedule meetings before or after school.

Classroom Volunteering

Many schools depend on volunteers to increase cooperation between families and schools, and to help things run smoothly. Volunteer opportunities vary from heading the Parent Teacher Organization to coordinating fund drives or correcting weekly spelling tests. If you become involved and interested in your child's school experience, her investment and motivation in school may improve as well. However, if you are concerned that your child might be clingy or tearful if you are there, or if your own anxiety causes you to hover or be overprotective, your child might do better without your presence. If you are unsure, talk over the options with your child's teacher or therapist to see what they might recommend.

Field Trips

Chaperoning one of your child's field trips can be a great way to learn more about your child's social world and about his daily struggles with anxiety. You may want to volunteer for field trips if your child has trouble managing them without you. However, you will also need to have a plan to decrease your participation so that your child can eventually experience independence. If volunteerism is especially popular in your child's school, you may have to speak up early. If joining a field trip is important for your child, you may have to travel separately, or arrange to share parts of the field trip with other parents.

Special Events

Most schools have dances, all-school parties, fairs, or other events for fundraising and community building. These can be great opportunities to watch your child in action, support her, and connect with other parents and children to strengthen your support network. In-school stores, book fairs, and assemblies may provide similar opportunities. Scouting (often affiliated with the school district) and after-school, homework, athletic, and drama programs usually depend on volunteers for support. But remember to be kind to yourself: if volunteering can work for your life and your schedule, that is great; if not, there are plenty of other options in this book for you to try. When supporting your child through her anxiety it is important that you feel healthy, strong, capable, and supported. You are an example for your child of what it looks like to deal with intense emotions and move through them with integrity and love for self.

CHAPTER 5

Outside Pressures and Influences

Outside pressures are influences that may intensify symptoms of anxiety in your child. Some of these include: cyberbullying, media, technology, fearful messaging/marketing, security warnings, and exposure to violence. Needless to say, there may be other pressures apart from what is listed here. Rest assured that the tips and strategies offered in this section may be applied to any situation.

Coping with Outside Pressures

Outside pressures are anything that influences your child outside of what he is exposed to within the family. Media, technology, and peer pressure are a few examples. About 50 percent of the behavior you see particularly in early childhood is developmental in nature meaning it is normal and will pass. The remaining 50 percent is due to outside influences.

Most children will experience some levels of anxiety during certain developmental periods of their life. For example, anything that is referred to as a "first," first dance, first game, or first time being left alone all evoke some level of stress necessary for motivation and growth. Outside pressures have a different feel. There is no first, and then you grow and move on. Often these pressures are ingrained into the culture, and therefore it is critical that children and families instill mindsets, boundaries, and tools that can support them through a lifetime.

 Fact

> According to psychiatrist Gary Small and Gigi Vorgan in their book *iBrain*, "Studies show that our environment molds the shape and function of our brains. We now know that normal human brain development requires a balance of environmental stimulation and human contact. Although exposure to new technology may appear to have a much more subtle impact, its structural and functional effects are profound, particularly on a young, extremely plastic brain."

Benefits and Risks of Technology

When used correctly, technology can have many benefits, including quick and easy access to learning tools, research, equal opportunity for individuals with special needs, quick and easy communication, facts, ease of access to information, supportive causes, connection to individuals/organizations that promote tolerance, empathy, and cross-culture involvement. It also increases environmental awareness by supporting the recycle movement, saving trees, and other natural resources.

However, when overused, or used as a pastime or habit, technology and media can increase aggression, decrease empathy and social skill development, weaken face-to-face communication (an essential skill for healthy relationships), decrease physical activity, increase obesity, discourage personal development, instill fears, disrupt sleep, promote isolation, increase at-risk behavior such as violence, addictive behavior, and most of all increase anxiety.

Media

The term *media* refers to communication through television, radio, news, movies, newspapers, Internet (includes blogs, videos, audio files), photos (images), and commercials. Often messages of values are embedded into the stories, advertisements, and entertainment. Before the Internet, stories were targeted specifically to individuals in a certain area, meaning a newspaper and radio program could only reach so far. Now the power of the Internet has the capacity to reach billions of people with stories and content that may or may not pertain to the person who receives it.

 Alert

Research shows television and cartoon viewing before bedtime (after 7 P.M.) can hinder sleep in preschoolers. Bedtime routines that include wind-down activities, such as bath and stories, continue to promote healthy brain development and sleep.

Commercials

Marketers are masterminds at subliminally influencing the likes, dislikes, values, opinions, tastes, and preferences of the consumer. Many times the commercials are more captivating than the show itself. Even the well-intentioned parent who carefully chooses the current program being viewed needs to stay alert to messages and violent images that occur before, during, and after the program. If your child is watching a DVD, it is best to fast-forward through advertisements and commercials. Otherwise, turn the volume down or switch the channel, and let your child know why you are taking action. This is an opportunity to restate your values. For example, "That commercial portrays women as objects, making it seem that being sexy is more important than intelligence, values, and self-worth, so I am going to change the channel for a moment." You might also say, "That word he used and his tone of voice were not okay." On the other hand, when you view a commercial that is appropriate and supports what you believe, make a positive comment. The rule of thumb is that what you pay attention to grows and is reinforced. In other words, give the positive more verbal attention than the negative.

Blogs

A blog is a journal or diary that is on the Internet. A blogger is the person who keeps and writes the blog. This person can be a professional or a nonprofessional of any age who shares her news, passions, and information. The positive side to blogging is that it allows self-expression, can contribute to good causes, and spreads information that readers may not otherwise receive through the general media. The negative side is that the information may not always be true, is often subjective, and in some cases may have alternative agendas such as selling products or swaying people to support a viewpoint. If your child is reading blogs or blogging himself, it will be important for you to monitor his activity. In order to do this, it is essential that you develop clear, consistent rules and guidelines early on. More on this later in this chapter.

 Fact

The American Psychological Association (APA) states children and adolescents who view more than two hours of screen time (e.g. computers, television, video games) per day are more likely to be less sensitive, and more susceptible to fear and aggressive behavior.

Video Games

Nowadays, children can play video games on the computer, phones, iPods, or via consoles such as the Wii, Playstation, and Xbox. Some of the most popular video games are extremely violent and disturbing. A 2010 review by psychologist Craig A. Anderson and others concluded that "the evidence strongly suggests that exposure to violent video games is a causal risk factor for increased aggressive behavior, aggressive cognition, and aggressive affect and for decreased empathy and prosocial behavior." Parents need to view and research games themselves before allowing a child to play them, and not assume that a PG rating means there is no violent material. For advice and guidance on video games, movies, and other forms of media go to *www.commonsensemedia.org*.

 Essential

The American Psychological Association and the American Academy of Pediatrics are equally concerned about the 24/7 availability and influence of media exposure on today's youth, and are working together to create guidelines based on solid research and evidence. Their intention is to guide parents and children toward healthier ways to interact and utilize technology and media for their benefit. Policy statements reporting the potential risks as well as the positive contributions of the Internet are supporting the recommendations of mental and medical health professionals.

Guidelines for Technology and Media

Children may revert to technology as a way to escape their feelings. This places them at a disadvantage as they learn to disregard, suppress, and in some cases shove away a part of themselves that stimulates inner growth. By doing so, they are likely to miss opportunities to acquire new skills that will ultimately deepen their sense of self. The following guidelines allow your children to safely experiment with technology and be exposed to media, without sacrificing values, brain development, social and emotional skills, health, and overall growth.

- Unless your child needs a cell phone for safety or communication with parents, consider putting off the purchase until a child is more mature, or at the very least in middle school.

- Set rules and guidelines before items are purchased. Consider writing a contract with specific guidelines and consequences. Keep the contract short but to the point; this will increase the chance that you will follow through. Write the contract using positive phrasing, focusing on the behavior you would like to see rather than the one you are trying to prevent. For example, rather than stating "No phones during dinner," state "Phones off during meals."

- Create tech-free times that also cover accepting phone calls and texts. Create times that are negotiable, and ones that are non-negotiable. For example, phones and texting during mealtimes would be a non-negotiable. Using the phone first thing out of bed in the morning would be negotiable.

- Teach children that tech time includes all time spent in front of a screen. This includes TV, computer, movies, video games, and phone. Teach children how to monitor their own time. Often the hardest part for children is motivating themselves to turn it off. When they are young, provide a five- or ten- minute warning before you will turn it off. You can also use a kitchen timer as a way to remind younger children when to turn it off. As they get older, have them watch the clock or use the timer themselves. Thank them for the times they turn it off on their own. If they are unable to turn it off on their own, then the logical consequence will be that you get to be in charge of turning it off. (Note that children will test you on this; it will be important not to assume they have mastered the skill once they do it a few times.)

- Create tech-free zones. Establish early on in which areas of the home computers and cell phones may be used. Tech-free bedrooms are an excellent way to keep your child safe and to ensure that they are not using technology as a means for coping with stress.

- If children are not asking for it, refrain from suggesting it. Parents have habits as well. Notice if when your child starts whining or complaining your first response is to quickly soothe them by handing them a phone or video game. Model the behavior you wish your child to display.
- Teach cell phone and computer etiquette. No matter what your child chooses to do as a career, they will stand out if they can show self-restraint and etiquette when using technology. For example, teach children never to answer a phone or text at a dinner table. Keep cell phones off at the table. Excuse yourself politely to a private location if you need to make or receive a call. Avoid answering your phone when you are being waited on or served. It is just plain rude. Keep your voice down in public so other people don't have to hear your business. Teaching etiquette also reduces the likelihood your child will utilize technology as a means for coping with his symptoms of anxiety.
- Be an example. Parents who wish to raise children to make safe choices need to model these choices. For example, pull over the car before texting something, watch your own habits such as checking e-mails, or surfing online as a pastime. Illustrate the importance of face-to-face contact by small acts such as putting away your phone when you greet your child or take them somewhere such as a playground, or on errands. Your smile has the potential to reduce anxiety in yourself and others.
- Watch television with your child so you can explain what is real and what is imagined, particularly for younger children (under age nine). Point out healthy behaviors when it comes to stress reduction from unhealthy. Many celebrities who have learned to manage their own stress and anxiety have developed personal boundaries and keep their life private. Others have found a way to lift their mood by giving back to the community.

- Watch your family habits. Do you or your children check your e-mails, texts, or play video games out of boredom? Some of these habits may actually be perpetuating the cycle of anxiety as they keep you from ever really experiencing the present moment. The next time you have this urge, choose to close your eyes and imagine feeling a warm breeze on your face. Practices such as these will teach you how to *be,* rather than *be busy* in the moment.
- Expose children to scams (when sucked in they create a lot of anxiety). If you receive an e-mail that looks fishy, show your child what they look like. Teach them to never open e-mails from strangers or provide private information over the Internet.
- Value the development of your child's inner voice. The goal is to guide your child toward self-regulation, balancing time on and off technology. For example, if your child is looking out the window while playing on the computer this could be his inner voice saying, "Hey go out and play."
- Notice if your parental stress is due to technology itself or rather a response to your own fear. Some parents avoid asking their children to stop because they fear conflict. What you avoid persists and many times escalates. Choose to respect yourself by sticking to your guidelines.

Social Media

Social media is a virtual community and network where individuals share and exchange information. Psychologists have growing concerns about the limited face-to-face contact involved, and how this may be impacting children and adolescents' identity and self-esteem. According to Howard Gardner, a Harvard psychologist who studied under Erik Erikson states, "Kids feel pushed into developing a public identity early, and since it has been widely posted and effectively branded, it is actually difficult to explore other forms of identity."

 Alert

> A study by Kent State University found that "college students who spent hours each day online, texting, or talking on cell phones are more anxious, less happy, and get lower grades."

Parents can help their child navigate the social media world by waiting until the child is at least thirteen years of age (a Facebook requirement). If your child is experiencing social anxiety, social media may keep them from developing the skills they need to overcome it. Teach your child to refrain from going on social media sites when they are angry, sad, or upset about something. These emotional states increase the chance that they might say something they could regret. Since children experiencing anxiety may feel they are alone or they may have a fear of what others think of them it will be important for you to monitor their behavior online. Behaviors such as passing photos may temporarily make your child feel good but in the long run they may put themselves at risk as what gets sent into the virtual world never really goes away. Posting hurtful comments, gossip, inappropriate content such as swearing and sexual behavior all contribute to the shaping of your child's identity, and could come at a cost later in life. On the other hand, when used appropriately, it can be a great way to market your ideas, strengths, connect with others, and send positive messages out into the world.

Boundaries

Media and technology enable people to be contacted and connected at any time of day (even if it is two o'clock in the morning). Establishing boundaries early on will not only keep your child safe, but allow time for the self-care and attention required for relieving stress and anxiety. When possible, encourage your child to avoid group texts. A group text is received by everyone in the group, even if the current conversation is not actively involving your individual child. This can be distracting, and has the potential to pull your child away from other activities. Boundaries include teaching web safety. For example, if your child does go into a chat group he should never use his real name. Nor should he ever give personal information out such as name, address, and phone number.

Be sure you and your child carve out time each day to do something for yourselves. Exercise, rest, make a healthy meal, get outside, visit face-to-face with neighbors and friends, draw, paint, and attend community events. It is experiences such as these that teach your child how to enjoy people and help him stay in touch with what is happening in real time, this exact moment, the place where anxiety does not exist.

The Power of "No"

Initially, your child may feel compelled to answer every text or message that comes her way. Without guidance, children and adolescents can get into the habit of putting the needs of others first. Allowing your child to say "no," both in and outside the tech world decrease the likelihood that they will serve as prey (see next section), or feed the insecurities of others. The ability to say "No thanks," "I will connect with your later," or "I am unable to do that" is a sign of strength.

Online Predators

Online predators are individuals with ulterior motives who prey on children and adolescents with insecurities, who are isolated, depressed, unsupervised, and/or emotionally needy. Parents of children with anxiety may hesitate to discuss the dark side of the Internet; however, children who are unaware are more likely to fall victim. Give your child the facts without going into details. Explain there are individuals who use the Internet as a way to entrap children, meaning they will pretend to be your friend, have similar likes, dislikes, and be willing to listen and be there for you when you need it. They may even offer you money or to buy you things. You may want to include a clause in your Internet contract stating that your child will never give their personal information (such as full name, address, age, passcodes, bank information, credit card, telephone number) to anyone they do not know. If someone or a website requests their personal information they should check with you, but most likely will still never provide it.

Cyberbullying

No longer does bullying only happen on the playground, or during unstructured times such commuting to and from school. Bullying can also happen right in a child's bedroom, online, with more than one bully at a time. If your child is being made fun of, harassed, tormented, teased, or gossiped about via social media, these would be examples of cyberbullying and could very well be the cause of their anxiety. All it takes is one instance to be enough to provoke a significant amount of fear and anxiety in a child. If this occurs, be sure to respond calmly, tell your child not to respond to the attack, then print and save the evidence. If you know the individual and feel safe doing so, you may address the problem face-to-face. In some cases, you may need to file a police report. On the other hand, if your child is a witness to cyberbullying, it can be equally disturbing and may show up in a child's behavior such as irritability, nervousness, and isolation. Trust your gut as a parent. If your child seems off, do not hesitate to check what is happening with social media.

Other Influences

Children today are growing up in a world of warnings. Media is constantly warning people about certain foods and how they may cause cancer, or how they might be bad for you. There are security warnings with images shown at airports, and constant exposure to reports of the violence happening all over the world. There are also warnings about germs, potentially contracting diseases, the dangers of bugs, mosquitoes, and environmental toxins, and so forth. It is no wonder that anxiety is on the rise among both adults and children. To some degree, it is important for your child to be knowledgeable about the influences of the world. However, the way your child responds will depend a great deal on how it is delivered.

 Question

I try to have a conversation with my teenager and he will barely talk back. What do I do?
Keep the lines of communication open. Instead of asking about his day, what homework he has, or if he is feeling stressed, consider talking about what he likes. Perhaps ask about his music, sport, hobby, or book he is reading. Most importantly, listen without judgment or an agenda. Teenagers can smell an agenda a mile away. A car ride is an opportunity to engage your child with minimum distractions. It is neutral territory and sometimes being away from daily tasks and chores (outside the home) can stimulate conversation. Be genuine and consistent, and know that to sit silently with someone without distractions (for example, avoiding multitasking) is a gift.

Children often hear your tone and feel your anxiety more so than the actual words you are speaking. To pass on information in a calm way, parents will want to learn how to take information in, let it settle, allow one inhalation and one exhalation (a full breath cycle) before repeating it verbally, if immediately sharing the information is necessary. This may take approximately twenty seconds. Picture yourself throwing a stone into a pond. Watch the rings on the water appear and circle outward. As the rings get bigger know that they represent you truly experiencing your feelings rather than reacting to them. After about twenty seconds notice how your thoughts and sense of urgency may have changed. Sensitive information is best delivered in a calm, brief (factual) and clear way. If it is brought on too strong your child will focus on your reaction more than the actual information you are attempting to convey. The intent is to help your child feel guided and informed rather than overpowered by the knowledge.

Building Face-to-Face Social Skills

One of the best ways to build resiliency in your child is to help her develop face-to-face social skills. Communication is much more than abbreviated words or sentences. When you communicate face-to-face, you learn the skill of reading body language, tone of voice, and expression. Face-to-face communication tends to be more empathic, conscious, and heartfelt. Adolescents who predominately communicate through texting and social media never really learn vital communication skills, such as: expressing your feelings, eye contact, listening, taking turns, conflict resolution, problem solving, and how to be vulnerable with another human being. Instead, they may develop a false persona based on a need to fit in, be liked, accepted, and popular. Anxiety lives off false and negative perceptions. By becoming comfortable with herself and knowledge about what the symptoms of anxiety are attempting to communicate she will naturally gravitate toward relationships that strengthen rather than weaken her sense of self.

Here are some ways to build healthy social skills:

- Family meals are the best way to practice skills such as eye contact, taking turns, vulnerability (through stories of making mistakes), news, and interests.
- Be a model. When speaking with your child model eye contact, refrain from multitasking, ask questions, and most of all listen without interrupting.

- Provide opportunities for unstructured play. Have your child invite a friend over. Set the rule ahead of time that technology will not be a part of the playdate.
- Play family board games. Board games reinforce taking turns, waiting, following the rules, and problem solving. Family games encourage laughter: a sign your child is feeling comfortable being herself.
- Refrain from doing things for your child because you know she is feeling nervous or anxious. For example, avoid ordering your child's food for her at a restaurant, or calling your child's friend to cancel a playdate. Instead, be confident in your child's abilities.
- Make mistakes safe. Children who feel stressed or anxious may find themselves stating things they don't mean, being overly self-conscious, or socially awkward. Share your stories of mishaps and awkwardness. Know that social skill development is a lifelong journey.
- Role-play. Your child can ease anxiety by practicing ahead of time. Role-playing can be done with another person or alone in front of a mirror. For example, a child may role-play how they might handle situations that trigger anxiety. For example: how to say no, speak in front of others, ask someone to come over and play, or join a group. Children love to do skits. Many groups such as Scouts and church groups will make skits part of their curriculum. These are all opportunities to practice overcoming, and be empowered by experiencing, anxiety.

CHAPTER 6

Building a Supportive Home Environment

Your home is the foundation of your child's physical, emotional, and spiritual well-being. The attitudes and influences you provide as parents are the basis for your child's identity, self-esteem, coping, and worldview. These influences begin in your child's early years and are combined with experiences outside of your home. Together, they form the values and expectations that will guide your child throughout her lifetime. This chapter will provide suggestions that will help you build a supportive home environment to help decrease anxiety and increase inner calm.

Open Communication

Communication is the basis of all relationships. It involves not only what you verbalize to others but also the ability to listen and observe yourself. As you and your child learn about anxiety you will see how thoughts impact how you feel and communicate with others. A large part of your child working through his symptoms will be to recognize his thoughts, which ones enhance communication and which ones disrupt it. Often symptoms of anxiety bring on thoughts that are defensive or reactive in nature. For example a child may inwardly fear failure and show this through defensive remarks. Children and adolescents who communicate with intensity and/or fear (e.g. *Hurry up mom or you will make me late and*

I will get in trouble with my teacher) are often built on self-limiting belief systems. Belief systems such as *I have to fight for what I want*, or *it is wrong to make a mistake* often support these kinds of behaviors. Parents can support their children by asking their child what they believe to be true. For example, "what do you believe will happen if you are late?" Once identified say to your child, "I give you permission to release (let go, or exhale) those thoughts." Explain letting go is like deflating a balloon or tire. Children often unconsciously hang onto thoughts because inside this may be a mistaken way of attempting to please their parents. They need your permission to let these thoughts go. It also allows your child to see how his own thoughts rather than what is true feed anxiety. Following are some additional communication techniques:

Using "I-Messages"

"I" messages are a basic skill that teaches children how to express themselves effectively with others. They are typically more productive than "you" statements as they are less likely to be received by others as an attack or threat. As your child learns to listen to his symptoms of anxiety it will be important for him to recognize how certain "I" statements give him energy (decreasing anxiety) while others may deplete it (increasing anxiety). Ones that increase anxiety are more likely to send mixed signals or shut down communication. Choosing "I" messages that boost energy illustrates to your child how taking care of himself (his energy) and communicating clearly go hand in hand.

"I" Messages that Boost Energy

"I" messages that are closest to your heart and how you truly feel tend to be more uplifting and anxiety free. *I am, I love, I feel, I appreciate, I need,* and *I see* whether said aloud or silently to yourself leave you feeling open, lifted, or lighter. Therefore, rather than focus on what you think you *should* say consider going with the "I" statements that feel closest to your sincere thoughts and feelings.

Your true thoughts and feelings are the ones you experience in the absence of anxiety. After all, if you did not genuinely love your child you would not be experiencing worry and concern for his anxiety. To deliver "I" messages in this way you and your child need to practice attending to your body first (exhaling, stretching, pausing) before speaking to others. Simply by bringing yourself into the here and now (through your body) you are able to speak from your truth to yourself and others.

"I" Messages that Deflate Energy

"I" messages that may deplete you or your child's energy are: *I can't, I don't know, I try, I'm tired, I'm busy, I am sick of,* or *I have had enough.* Again, when stated aloud notice the quality of energy that returns to you. Children sense and feel the difference between you speaking from your heart and when you are reacting from your thoughts and fears. By paying attention to your own energy you will begin to pause and speak in ways that are mutually beneficial to you and your child.

 Fact

When you speak in I-messages using a respectful tone with clear, brief language, you are communicating from a place of worthiness. This speaks volumes, as research supports that children learn more from your actions than your words.

"I" Messages Don't Blame

Another goal of I-messages is to focus on what you experience, rather than laying blame on another for making you feel or act in a certain way. Blame is similar to shame as it often debilitates one by connecting children to harsh beliefs rather than loving truths.

"I" statements maintain respectful means for communicating. Statements delivered with sarcasm, anger, or other negative nonverbals such as a clenched jaw or tightly crossed arms are reactions that control feelings rather than experience them. When children witness actions from truth they learn how to step into the authenticity of who they are.

Reflective Listening

Reflective listening occurs when a person acts as a sort of mirror for another, reflecting back what they observe, with just a bit of interpretation. This type of listening is actually the basis of most forms of psychotherapy, and recent research indicates that it can foster the development of new brain structures that mitigate depression and anxiety. Reflective listening validates the other person's experience and communicates empathy and understanding. It also opens the door for more and deeper communication, which is especially important with a child experiencing anxiety. Therefore, if your child says in a trembling voice, "I do not want to go to school today," you might say, "I see you are anxious about school. Is it because of your math test?"

 Essential

The practice of reflective listening (mirroring your child's experience) helps both you and your child. You get to experience and reinforce the discipline of attending to the moment, and your child gets to feel heard and valued. The key is to listen with nonjudgment, which means refraining from trying to fix, evaluate, or give unsolicited advice about what your child is saying.

Additional Ways to Open Communication

Parents can shut down opportunities to communicate with their child without realizing it. Most often this occurs when parents are stressed themselves. Therefore, it is important for you to implement some of the strategies for minimizing stress in this book in order to keep the lines of communication open. Stress narrows your perception in a way whereby you could easily miss or disregard opportunities for improved communication, seeing them more as work than freedom. Most importantly, remember that quality is more important than quantity. Let's face it, a long extensive conversation is pretty rare in the parent-child relationship. When you feel balanced and calm, you may open the door for communication through statements like "Tell me about your picture," or "What did you think of the movie?" Refrain from asking yes/no questions such as, "Are you hungry?" or "Did you have a good day?" Instead, ask open-ended questions, such as, "What was lunch like today, who did you sit with?" Be patient and watch for certain times of the day where your child may be more open for communication. Directly after school may work for you, but not your child.

Reframing

Your language, including the words, tone of voice, and expression you use, has the power to stimulate or lessen anxiety in yourself and others. Learning how to reframe your child's language is an essential tool for toning down stress and creating the possibility for higher thinking and inner growth. To reframe something means to say it in another way. It has been proven that positive statements signal the nervous system with messages of calm, relaxation, improved blood flow, and ease. Children and adolescents who are stressed or anxious tend to see things in a negative light. This is typically heard through their choice of words and seen through their irritability, or at times their disrespectful behavior. Anxious kids say things like "I can't" or "It won't work." You may reframe this by using the phrase "I look forward to figuring this out," or "This is difficult but I know it will work out." You may also encourage your child to reframe their thoughts themselves by asking a question such as, "What evidence do you have that it won't work out?" This challenges negative thinking, and helps your child to see how irrational thinking contributes to anxiety.

Teaching Kids *How* to Feel

Teaching children about their facial expressions and the labels (happy, mad, sad) is how young children are taught about their feelings. As an initial introduction this is fine, however when children and adolescents solely relate to their emotions from what occurs on the outside they may confuse feelings with actions. For example, if you ask them what anger *feels* like they might demonstrate yelling, or put their hands on their hips and point their finger. This is an opportunity to teach them feeling is not an action but rather an inner experience.

Feeling is the experience of your bodily sensations. One of the techniques you will learn about in Chapter 11 is progressive muscle relaxation. By having your child squeeze their fists tight and then release, they can tune into what sensation feels like when it is flowing. Increasing sensation is important because not only does it provide relief from emotions (energy) that has been sitting stagnant (fear, worry, anger) but also it circulates oxygen, glucose, and uplifting neurotransmitters such as dopamine, oxytocin, and serotonin. Breathing from your lower belly (expanding out on inhale, and contracting in on exhale) works in the same way. This circulation is what renews your child's perception allowing her to feel first rather than act first and skip feeling. Actions from experiencing feelings tend to be driven from love and compassion while actions from nonfeeling are more likely to be triggered from fear and control. Following are two steps to encouraging feeling:

1. Direct attention to your body
2. Notice your sensations

Direct Attention to Your Body

Body awareness is the first step to feeling your emotions. To do this, close your eyes and tune your attention to your body. Parents can help their children by encouraging them to close their eyes and scan their body parts with their awareness. Body parts with the most nerve endings such as your nose, fingertips, and face are often easier to tune into.

Notice Your Sensations

Sensations are experienced through your senses (touch, breath, temperature, light, and even sound). Some are tingly similar to having butterflies in your stomach while others are dull. Feelings that are heavy (anger, sadness, or guilt) are heavy with minimal movement while feelings that are light (joy, appreciation) are light with lots of movement.

It's a Family Affair

Anxiety tends to cluster in families. This means your child can be affected by someone in the family who lives with anxiety, or your child's symptoms can have an effect on the family. This section will highlight key elements in family involvement, which are important in your child's overall care.

Look for Patterns

It will be important for you and your partner (or your child's other biological parent) to look into the possibility that traits of anxiety have been traced through your family. Just like you can inherit eye color, families can also pass down mental characteristics. Research has shown us that Attention Deficit Hyperactivity Disorder, anxiety, and depression can run in families. This knowledge is helpful for the person who is exhibiting signs of anxiety, and any professionals who are supporting you.

If you suspect that there are family patterns that point to anxiety, gently explore them with your family members. Be aware of any chemical abuse or other addictive behaviors in your family, as these can be a coping mechanism for anxiety and depression.

Alert

Teens especially will need to know about possible chemical health issues in the family as they mature and make choices about alcohol or drugs. You might not want to have this conversation, but it is important. It is also a great time to set expectations and consequences regarding chemical use.

Developing Your Support Network

You and your child may also need support from your family. In addition to encouragement and emotional support, your family may be able to help you with the nuts and bolts of your child's care plan. Maybe your child could practice sleepovers or learn to be away from the immediate family for brief periods by spending time with aunts, uncles, or cousins. Perhaps a family member could visit your child's school for lunch, or bring her a treat as a show of support. Spending special time with grandparents is not only comforting for your child, it might even afford you and your partner a night out together. Allowing your child to sleep in a different environment allows her to be exposed to new routines and ways of doing things. This teaches your child about differences, tolerance, and how each family is unique.

Create a Support Team

Teams are a group of people that share a common purpose and commitment. Connecting and receiving support from others is essential to the human experience. Parenting is one of the most challenging jobs you will ever have. Some parents are fortunate to have built-in support from the start, meaning they feel connected to their child's teachers and school staff, other parents, babysitter, neighbors, family, and the child's doctor. Others may have to work harder at developing relationships with others, or it may vary year to year. If you feel unsupported by the individuals whom you expect to support you, this may be a sign to get some help yourself. Talking with a therapist or counselor can be extremely helpful. Your willingness to look into and accept help can make a world of difference.

Medical

Your child's medical team can be comprised of your child's doctor or nurse practitioner, and if necessary a psychiatrist. Alternative care providers like chiropractors, acupuncturists, nutritionists, or homeopaths can also be considered part of the medical team. Be sure to sign any releases of information so that they can communicate with one another, and to the school if necessary. It is especially important that your child's therapist and psychiatrist agree on the best plan of care, and this may take time if the providers do not work out of the same location.

 Alert

According to author and researcher Brené Brown, "Shame keeps worthiness away by convincing us that owning our stories will lead people to thinking less of us. [. . .] We all have it, and the more we talk about it the less it has control over us." When building your team, pay attention to the individuals that help you through without judgment. These individuals will be some of your best allies.

Spiritual Resources

A place of worship may be a source of support and encouragement for both you and your child. Spirituality helps your child view himself as being much more than his accomplishments. Look for spiritual resources that restore your child's faith in his capabilities, offer love, respect, understanding, and compassion. Sometimes children are turned off by certain beliefs. Some places of worship offer counseling that you can accept if it feels right. Be aware that the spiritual community does not always view mental health issues in the same way that the medical system does. You may need to seek support if the two appear to be in conflict.

Community Resources and School

Community resources include community education, after-school programs, park and recreation programs, libraries, and even local businesses. If your child is uneasy about leaving home, but old enough to do so safely, you might consider working with a local shop owner to assist your child in expanding her range. Perhaps your child could call you from the store or restaurant, or you could prepay for a treat she can collect when she arrives. Dance, music, theater, gymnastics, and martial arts can also provide great opportunities to practice social skills, build mastery, and learn self-reliance.

Connect to Truth

Being truthful may require tact and some self-awareness. Children experiencing anxiety can demand excessive time and attention, causing frustration and resentment to parents. Though you may need to express your feelings in order to set limits and help your child modify her behavior, it is important to avoid shame or blame, because this will only magnify your child's worry and anxiety. Expressing the attitude that "we are all in this together" can help minimize the possibility that your child will internalize blame for expressing her feelings in the way that she does.

Age Appropriateness

Explaining anxiety to your child will depend on developmentally appropriate terms and comparisons. Children tend to understand things better through real life examples. Younger children need clear, concrete descriptions, and may respond to a "story" about another child with similar experiences. Older children do well if they are able to ask you questions based on their fears or worries. Doctors and therapists are trained to give facts in a way that is geared toward a child's level. A natural time to mention worries and fears is during your child's annual well visit or checkup. Telling your doctor about how your child is managing stress is no different than updating how well your child is eating and sleeping. The more you discuss it openly and honestly, the less uncomfortable it will be.

 Fact

Dr. Paul Foxman, the director of the Center for Anxiety Disorders recommends a self-help program called The LifeSkills Program *www.chaange.com* as a resource for children and adolescents diagnosed with an anxiety disorder. The program is designed to increase the ability to cope with stress, build confidence, and utilize social skills.

Effects on Siblings

Siblings of children experiencing anxiety may have a wide range of emotional and behavioral reactions, and may not always be able to express resentment or disappointment directly. It is important to be honest, observant, reflective, and supportive. At times, it may be helpful to give a disenfranchised sibling a direct role in your child's care, such as a daily in-school check-in, homework helper, or companion on outings. Make sure, though, that you have a willing participant so that you are helping siblings to feel involved, but not responsible for your child's care. The goal here is to provide an opportunity for a sibling to feel like a valued participant, rather than an outsider. Be sure to offer one-on-one time and express interest in other siblings. Reassure them that what resides underneath stress and anxiety is love. Let them know you are learning and practicing strategies that will support the entire family.

Jealousy

It is actually quite common for siblings of children receiving attention and care to feel jealous of the amount of time and energy spent by parents on their sibling. They may feel their sibling is favored and receiving special treatment they themselves are not entitled to. Sometimes involving a sibling in the strategies, or in some cases therapy sessions, can help create a sense of inclusion and teamwork. It may help to remind your nonanxious child of times you went the extra mile for him, and to reassure him about how loved and appreciated he is. Be sure to emphasize how each child is loved uniquely for who he is.

 Essential

> Siblings may need reassurance that they will not necessarily face the same challenges, but that if they do, you will be there to care for them as well. It is also important to let siblings know that anxiety is not only treatable, but often gives people opportunities to learn skills they may have not otherwise been open to.

Frustration

Siblings of a child feeling anxious can become frustrated for a number of reasons. For example, if one child gets less homework or more breaks built into her day, her siblings might resent the special treatment. A sibling's anxiety may cause their plans to be altered, such as a special activity, bedtime, or family vacations. Clear, honest communication can go a long way to decrease frustration. A good sympathetic ear, without defensive responses, is necessary when supporting a frustrated sibling. Be honest, and try to emphasize the hope and expectation that your family will get through, feeling even better than before.

Isolation

Sometimes siblings will withdraw in response to the feeling that all of the attention in the family goes to the child with anxiety. This may be especially likely with teens or children who are quieter and more introverted to begin with. Watch out for long periods spent alone or for changes in the amount of time a sibling spends with his friends or activities. Because a sustained decreased interest in what used to be pleasurable for a child may indicate depression, you may want to watch out for the possibility that siblings of a child with anxiety may be having adjustment issues that also need attention. If your compassionate attempts to communicate clearly and reach out to your child do not seem to be helping, you may wish to consider family therapy, or implement the strategies in this book with the whole family.

You Are Special, Too!

As you can see, going through anxiety can be difficult on her siblings as well. It is extremely important to support other children while you are focusing attention on your child with anxiety. This may seem overwhelming at times, but there are often relatively simple options. For example, consider taking a sibling out for a treat after practice or game, or "just because." You can schedule one-on-one time with each of your children, even if it is a few minutes of homework support, asking for their company on a ride to the grocery store, an extra bedtime story, or a quick game of cards. Take care to let all of your children know that they are special and loved.

Effects on Partnerships and Marriage

Research shows an increased percentage of marital dissatisfaction in families with children who experience emotional setbacks. Because parents have varying levels of distress tolerance and coping, individual differences can be magnified when a couple is under stress. For example, an introverted spouse may become even more withdrawn when under stress, leading the other parent to feel unsupported or neglected. As you read the sections that follow, you may wish to identify talking points to share with your parenting partner.

Alert

Increasing your ability to see eye to eye and stand shoulder to shoulder with your partner, spouse, or co-parent will strengthen your marriage and family, and optimize your child's recovery.

Receiving a Diagnosis

Any time a family member receives a mental health diagnosis there is a natural sense of grief and loss that occurs. Some parents may experience a sort of "kicked in the gut" feeling, others may be sad and withdrawn, and still others feel angry with themselves, the child, the situation, or God. In fact, theory and research on the grieving process indicate that parents may have any or all of these reactions, and may alternate between emotional states. Regarding your marriage, the most important factor is that you are able to communicate with each other about what you are experiencing individually and as a couple, and that you allow each other the space and time to process whatever feelings you experience in response to your child's health challenge.

 Fact

Reframing how you see a situation impacts how you respond to it. If you see anxiety as an obstacle, problem, or illness, then it will be that. On the other hand, if you see it as an opportunity to practice techniques that deepen self-awareness, the possibilities are endless.

Parenting Style

The best fit parenting style for helping children and adolescents through anxiety is referred to as an *authoritative* style. Since your child may be experiencing self-doubt, fear, and insecurity this style of parenting has been found to be the best at building self-esteem. *Authoritative* parents are known to strike a balance between being clear and consistent with communication and rules while allowing some freedom and flexibility. In other words, some rules are negotiable while others are not. Mistakes are often seen as opportunities to learn and children and adolescents are permitted to have a voice as long as it is delivered with respect. Because the child is given some power to make decisions but has consistent parental input, he tends to foster self-reliance and self-regulation. In this style children learn skills such as cooperation, communication, respect, and to honor individual/family values and differences.

Standing Together

Because children experiencing anxiety often view things as out of control, it is especially important that parents be on the same page regarding how the symptoms are handled, whether or not they live under the same roof. Although it is typical for parents to differ in their approaches to childrearing, you can create a unified front by ensuring consistency in the following elements of family life:

- Keep negative or concerning conversations about your child or the other parent in private. Even if your child can't hear you he can pick up on your tone.
- Agree to provide time for your child to exercise, extra time to get ready (rushing increases anxiety), and to monitor foods that exasperate symptoms (sugar, caffeine).
- Let your child know ahead of time changes in the schedule, what to expect for the week, details such as who will pick them up from school, etc.
- Allow your parenting partner time for self-care and fun. Encourage each other to exercise, take a break, and get support when needed. Anxiety can be contagious and children often imitate what they learn.

CHAPTER 7

Parenting and Anxiety

Anxiety is all about letting go of expectations and preconceived notions, not only of your child, but also of how you might have expected parenting to be. Parenting often begins with a dream, compiled from illusions and greeting card images. Little did you know at that time that each and every birth comes with a journey of ebb and flow. Picture a beautiful maple tree in the fall, losing its leaves as it prepares for the winds and storms of winter. To be strong and withstand the dark days as well as the light, it must first let go. Once it loses its leaves it has less to carry and hold on to. It is no longer burdened, able to stabilize its roots into the ground, and bend its now flexible branches. Be the tree, and know the lessons you embark upon are gifts received via the reflections of your child.

The Parent's Role

Who you are matters more than what you do. As a role model for your children, your fears about either your own life, or theirs, will have an effect on your child's confidence and self-esteem. Through their relationship with you, and imitation of your choices and behavior, your child will make decisions about what life looks like, how she feels about herself in the world, and how capable she believes she is to manage that world. Letting your child see you experience some mild to moderate anxiety and resolving it effectively will be incredibly beneficial. Feelings of fear and anxiety are inevitable, and by watching you deal with it, when your child is faced with fear or anxiety herself, she will know that she too can meet difficulties in life head on. However, if your fears for your child seem to create chaos or conflict, your child will perceive her own anxious moments this way as well. The message your child hears is, "I do not trust you to care for yourself or think you will make good decisions, so I must worry," and the child can then more easily internalize beliefs such as "I can't" or "I shouldn't."

 Essential

When caring for an infant, a parent must do everything for him. Often, particular ways of doing things are developed as a means for coping with the ongoing tasks of raising small children. Over time, parents may hesitate to let go of these routines and orderly ways. As children grow, new ways for doing things develop, routines change, and schedules shift. This is the beginning of letting go.

Seeing Choices as Tools

You are a crucial element in your child's day-to-day functioning. The choices you make have the ability to stimulate or diffuse anxiety in the home. If you choose to divorce, separate, start a job, move, act abusively, try to be a perfect parent, use substances, or stress performance over experience, you are shaping your child. You are also shaping your child by exercising to keep fit, getting together with friends, taking a class to feed your own soul, or sitting down to relax and read a book for enjoyment. Even the rules you make in the house have the power to create anxiety or reduce it. For example, if the rule is "you must get an A in school because you are smart enough to do it" and there is a consequence for not making the grade, your child may be anxious about his performance. That might actually decrease your child's ability to concentrate and cause what the child is most afraid of: an inability to remember what he studied, and your consequent disappointment. If the rule is "you must do chores when you get home from school, and then do your homework before you can go out to play" and your child never finishes before dinner, your child may get frustrated and angry. Because your child loves you and wants to be seen as good, he may internalize his anger, and instead you will see an irritable, anxious, or depressed child.

Thriving Parents Equal Thriving Children

Since you are the cornerstone for your children's emotional and social development, your capacity to understand them will be a gift to them as they grow. This is also true when you show compassion for, and know how to interpret, their needs. Those qualities have been cited in studies as crucial building blocks in your child's self-concept, ability to cope, and school readiness.

Your Behavior Is Important

A group of American and German researchers studied 1,000 adolescent subjects, fourteen to seventeen years old, mostly middle class and attending school, and they found that more than genetics plays a part in a child developing an anxiety. Children who had parents with social phobia, depression, other anxiety disorders, who abused alcohol, were overprotective, or rejected by their parents were at a significantly increased risk of developing social phobias. Other researchers concur that social fears may be learned, at least in part, by parents who are shy and withdrawn. However, genetic behavior is not a life sentence. All it takes is one family member to become aware, open, and willing to try new behaviors to make long-lasting change. Science has now proven that human beings have the ability to change their own DNA simply through modifying thoughts and behaviors. You really are that powerful.

🅔❗ Alert

Fostering dependency in your child can inhibit his attempts to learn to do things by himself. When a child has the view that he is incompetent, without help from others he can become discouraged and see himself as stuck.

Parenting Triggers

Parenting children through emotional ups and downs can trigger feelings and behaviors embedded in your memory. Triggers are memories or experiences that get revisited by certain thoughts, sounds, feelings, sites, etc. Some triggers can be helpful such as seeing your child's backpack may remind you to ask if she has homework. Other triggers such as watching the clock or hearing siblings argue may trigger behaviors in you that generate tension in the household.

Changing behaviors that fuel rather than support your child through anxiety requires you to make a choice to pay attention to possible triggers (thoughts, feelings, sights, and sounds) that may be causing you to engage in counterproductive behaviors. Again, this could be a tone of voice, facial expression, or a pile of bills on your desk. To be effective identify one to two triggers that quickly come to mind. In the beginning choose triggers that are simple to work with. Over the next few days begin to pay attention to the feeling you may be pushing away when you come across that trigger, perhaps a feeling of helplessness, hurt, anger, or fear. Just notice, and see if you can allow yourself to receive even ten seconds of that feeling before responding to your child's behavior. Notice how just ten seconds of feeling what is behind the trigger alters the course you may take. Instead of yelling, you may speak firmly and respectfully to your child. Or instead of speaking at all you may remove yourself to a private area where you can support your breathing.

Thriving Parents

Thriving parents are open, disciplined, and yet flexible. They allow themselves to be vulnerable, as they realize the experience of their emotions offers them sustainable energy, insight, connection, and growth. They not only seek help when needed, but are able to receive it. Their connection to the moment allows them to sort out the tools and strategies that work well for them and their family. They believe in themselves, respect the journey of their child, and trust their own inner guidance. They recognize the beliefs, thoughts, and habits that hold them back. They take baby steps as they create manageable goals for themselves and others. They take time for themselves, keep their passions alive, and surround themselves with healthy friendships and support. Thriving parents seek a path of contentment, are willing to shed what no longer serves them, hug their child on a regular basis, savor moments that offer connection, and remember to say, "I love you."

Tips for Thriving Parents

Thriving parents have a mindset that taking care of themselves will help them become better able to take care and guide their children. It is difficult to teach children what you have not experienced yourself. For parents who are juggling schedules, jobs, and household tasks know that just by incorporating breathing into your life you are taking care of yourself. Create a habit of taking three deep breaths (inhale, exhale) three times a day. This will decrease the chances that you will absorb the fears of your child while increasing your ability to apply the following guidelines.

- **Keep the boundaries between parenting and friendship clear.** Refrain from treating your child as your confidant. When children and adolescents feel as if they have to carry your concerns and frustrations, this increases anxiety. Single parents may feel burdened by having to manage the emotional, physical, and intellectual well-being of their children on their own. Instead, find supportive resources such as a counselor, church group, support group, exercise class, friend, or family member you can speak to privately. Watch your behavior for signs of venting, as this is also something that exacerbates anxiety in yourself and children.

- **Allow your child to learn personal management.** This includes how to dress appropriately, remember his backpack, or how to handle arguments with siblings or friends. Let your kids discover how to be responsible to and for each other.
- **Allow your child to explore friendships. Unless your child is in danger, being bullied, or taken advantage of, let him make decisions about who he would like to play with.** It is tempting to want to steer children in a certain direction or to want them to play with the same familiar children. However, childhood is a time to learn about differences in individuals, relationships, and communication styles. Later, when your child is able to sort out on his own positive from negative influences, you will be able to see the benefits from the foundation you provided.
- **Give your child the opportunity to show he can be successful.** This is especially important, even if he tried an activity before and it did not go well. Treat each moment, each day, as new. Know that your child is growing and changing daily; to base every decision his past experiences and yours would negate the growth that is happening.
- **If your child is afraid to go somewhere or try something new, gently encourage or suggest small increments of engaging in the feared situation.** If she is afraid to sleep in her own bed, but you want her out of yours, begin by setting up an air mattress at the end of your bed. Each day, move it slightly. First move the mattress toward the door, and after

a night or two of success there, move it into the hallway, and eventually into your child's room.

- **There is no perfect balance.** There will naturally be times you and your child are more stressed than others. Notice if you strive for perfect balance in your life. This is an unrealistic expectation (often driven by anxiety) that requires a lot of energy to upkeep. You are better off embracing that life is a journey of ebb and flow. To do this focus on the flow of your breath (inhale, exhale) rather than attempting to control what is happening in your life.

Overprotective Parenting

Consider the following scenario: "Did you call Jimmy to play? Oh, okay, what time did you say you would be there? Don't forget to take your jacket just in case the weather turns cold, and don't forget to look both ways when you cross our street, and remember to say thank you to Mrs. Michael for inviting you, and if she offers you something to eat, remember to chew with your mouth closed, keep your elbows off the table, and say thank you when you are done. And, oh, don't forget to call me before you leave so I know you are on your way and can look for you as you make your way across the street."

 Fact

In 1946, Dr. Spock came out with his bestselling "baby bible," *The Commonsense Book of Baby and Child Care*. In it, he encouraged parents to give their children appropriate amounts of increasing independence as a way to ready them for leaving home as healthy, secure young adults. Overprotectiveness, he said, just makes for anxious children.

Overparenting or being overprotective tends to have very negative consequences. The message your child will hear is, "I have to worry about you so much because you are not competent to deal with things on your own. You need my supervision and decision-making or this will end badly." Commonly, your child will end up feeling angry and insulted by what will feel like a put-down. Alternately, a child may simply "quit trying" because she feels she has no control in the world. Basically, overparenting becomes the opposite of what a parent's most important job is, to encourage autonomy and foster a healthy self-concept.

What the Doctors Say

Harvard psychologist Jerome Kagan, in researching temperament, has shown unequivocally that what creates anxious children is parents hovering and protecting them from stressful experiences. He found that infants who were born "overexcitable" tended to cope better with life, and had a more positive outlook, if their parents gave them freedom to do, think, and make mistakes on their own. Nowadays, parents talk to their kids by cell phone or text message them continuously while they are gone from the house. It is the new way to hover over your child.

Michael Liebowitz, professor of clinical psychiatry at Columbia University and former director of the Anxiety Disorders Clinic at New York State Psychiatric Institute, believes parents can have well-adjusted children if they take the time to gently encourage their children to try new things, even if they are scared, so they can learn that nothing bad will happen. "They need gradual exposure to find that the world is not dangerous. Having overprotective parents is a risk factor for anxiety disorders because children do not have opportunities to master their innate shyness and become more comfortable in the world."

The general consensus is that when children are overprotected they never learn to modify or reshape the connections in their brain. It is important to allow your child to change his perceptions, by continuous modification of what is feared, so the anxiety does not become the pattern of her life.

When Parents Are Depressed

It has been said that a good therapist understands that when a child is struggling or having trouble with daily life, if you look to the parents, you will often find one who is depressed. Psychologists have also learned that even though the parents come to therapy and identify the child as the source of their distress, it is often more likely that the child has been reacting to the parent's depression.

 Fact

Depression may be the cause of anxiety, even if you don't feel depressed. Sometimes it shows up feeling numb or withdrawn. Stephen Cope, MSW, the founder and former Director of the Kripalu Institute for Extraordinary Living, observes that, "Depression manifests as our inability to be present for the experience of life."

How Your Depression Affects Your Child

Studies have found that depressed mothers have trouble with bonding, and are less sensitive, and more inconsistent in responding to a baby's needs. This in turn creates anxious, unhappy children that are difficult to comfort, have behavioral issues, are difficult to feed, struggle to go to sleep, and can experience more isolation socially. As they grow into toddlers, they can be very hard to manage; they fight authority (including parental authority) and can be negative thinkers. The distress the parent feels in response to this reinforces a sense of failure, and more depression ensues. Research has also documented that a child brought up in a home with a depressed parent is at a high risk for depression, substance abuse, and antisocial activities. Parents who are depressed often have counterproductive posture and breathing patterns. Gentle yoga classes that encourage correct posture and tune the parent into taking a long inhale and exhale can help lift mood. Exercise also helps boost mood, along with eating less sugar and incorporating healthy fats such as avocado, and increasing omega-3–enriched foods such as spinach.

When Parents Are Stressed

While periodic frustration with your child is inevitable, your child is counting on you to discover how to learn and grow from life challenges so you can help them concentrate on theirs. If you have difficulty dealing with stress, and your children experience you that way more often than not, this in turn makes their own challenges seem more difficult. In a study by the Institute of Education on life satisfaction, researchers found that children whose parents were stressed were also affected, especially if the father's distress level was high. Furthermore, the IOE claimed that a parent's emotional health, or lack thereof, has a long-term impact on the child's emotional health. Observing your child's anxiety can be a motivator to create small changes in your own behavior, for the good of you both.

 Essential

Your body has the ability to produce happy chemicals: dopamine, endorphin, oxytocin, and serotonin. According to author Loretta Breuning, PhD, confidence triggers serotonin. She states, "If you focus on your losses you will depress serotonin, even if you're a rock star or a CEO. You can build serotonin by focusing on your wins."

How Your Stress Affects Your Child

It is easy to forget that your children have ears. Even if they are not in the room, that does not mean they are not listening. When children hear you argue or yell, they may internalize your experience and make it their own. Research shows they will carry negative feelings around inside of themselves. This type of response may cause depression, anxiety, or mistrust in people and relationships. This is unlikely to occur immediately, instead unfolding over time. Children of stressed parents also feel the need to read their parents' moods and tone of voice as a way to judge how safe it is to be around them at that time, or to ask for what they need. This type of pattern teaches children to be preoccupied with fear and to instinctively want to control the future. As a result, assertiveness and the ability to handle confrontation may become underdeveloped.

 Question

My children are older, does that mean it is too late for me to turn things around?
Absolutely not. No matter how old you are or how old your children are, you can and will make a difference by implementing the information in this book. It may be delivered in a different way, however, less about the content and more about your awareness. To assume it is too late would mean that inner peace is solely dependent on external circumstances. Letting go of anxiety and interrupting the cycles is an internal journey.

Part of managing your stress is a willingness to watch your own behaviors. How do you handle stress? Do you unconsciously reach for food, a cigarette, a beer or glass of wine, or use foul language when you are under pressure? Or do you breathe, take a walk, read, spend time alone, exercise, think loving thoughts, go to bed early, eat healthy foods, take a bath, connect to people, ask for help, say "no" when necessary, allow yourself to cry, or do something you love? Your behavior is an example to your children, no matter what their age.

How Is Your Marriage?

You probably will not be surprised to hear that the state of your marriage can have a deep and lasting effect on your children. Arguments and issues to resolve are normal, and in fact can teach your child how to handle conflict appropriately as she grows. However, when yelling has no resolution, when you call each other names, and everyone walks away hurt, sad, or angry, negative connections get made. You and your spouse or parenting partner are role models for what your child will come to expect from relationships, so take a moment to ask yourself what you are really modeling. This may require you and your partner to take some time together to revisit what you value, engage in active listening, or to connect to the hobbies and interests that brought you together in the first place.

Questions to Help You Become Self-Aware

Because of the value modeling has on the growth of your children, your relationship with your significant other will certainly be something you want to think about, and/or make changes to. Parents have the ability to influence their child's anxiety for the better through their own self-awareness. Self-awareness allows you to be open and grow in an emotional environment of kindness and compassion. After taking three long deep breaths, reflect on the following questions. Ask yourself:

- Are you willing and ready to forgive and be forgiven?
- Are you willing and ready to let go of past arguments?
- Are you willing and ready to treat each day as new?
- Are you willing and ready to truly listen without distractions or interruptions?
- Are you willing and ready to honor the wounds of the past as teachable moments?
- Are you willing and ready to accept your human nature, to make mistakes safe, and to keep your expectations of each other realistic?
- Are you willing and ready to see the good rather than focusing on the not-so-good in each other?

- Are you willing and ready to take responsibility, to own your own anxiety, and to give self-love strategies a fair chance?
- Are you willing and ready to accept that your needs, wants, desires, and dreams are equally important?
- Are you willing and ready to thrive, rather than survive, during your parenting journey?

In this sacred partnership of parents, together you are one. Whether you are living together or not, you both impact the experiences of your child. Your children serve as reflections for your current state of mind. You have the power to influence these reflections. It is never too late. Focus on the times you do this well rather than the times you let yourself and others down. This will build resiliency and help you develop your ability to be and live peacefully.

Separation, Divorce, and Blended Families

There is as much conflicting evidence about the effects of separation and divorce on children as there are studies. There are books that say children of divorce or separated parents will suffer more from depression and anxiety, have lower self-esteem, and tend to tolerate or exhibit more abuse and neglect in their own relationships. There are also books that tell you if you stay together in a high-conflict marriage that will cause exactly the same issues. Some researchers have said that low-conflict marriages where the parents just do not love each other anymore and divorce anyway will cause the most anxiety and depression for a child. Research on blended families has also yielded lots of conflicting evidence.

Researchers have found that adolescents find it the most difficult to adjust to the blended family arrangement. Although young children want to engage with a stepparent if that parent is seen as warm, engaging, and available, they still have considerable anxiety over how to be loyal to their own absent parent. Adolescents, because of their age, developing sexuality, and establishing autonomy, can find the presence of a stranger in the house disruptive and anxiety-provoking. These studies have suggested that because of this anxiety, about one-third of adolescent boys and one-fourth of adolescent girls choose to disengage from their stepfamilies and spend their time with friends, outside of the house, instead.

 Essential

Some studies caution parents not to remarry until the children are gone from the house because it creates too much anxiety and stress for them. Other researchers believe that a family can be blended, but that it takes approximately three to five years to mold into a cohesive family unit, and not uncommonly up to seven years.

Your Child's Age Makes a Difference

If your child is in preschool, research confirms he will miss the parent who has moved out of the home and have a greater need for safety and security. He might, because of his anxiety and fears, regress in his most recent developmental accomplishment. He might have difficulty sleeping, be fearful, irritable, aggressive, demanding, or depressed and withdrawn. It is suggested that children ages five to eight can be more self-blaming and verbal about their sadness, be scared you will find another family to love instead, have difficulty understanding what "permanent" means, may be forgetful, seem to lose time, or seem to be in a dream state. Children ages nine through adolescence tend to be more vocal, angry, resentful, blaming, and often act out in a more hostile way.

Warning Signs

If your child has several of the following symptoms persistently over time, either because you have divorced, separated, or blended your family with another, it is important to look into therapy:

- Does not want to go out and play or call friends
- Has become negative, fearful, anxious, or clingy
- Is unwilling to go to bed, has difficulty falling asleep, is waking up in the middle of the night, has nightmares, recurrent bedwetting, refusal to wake up or go to school
- Is angry, fighting with friends or siblings, or yelling at you with greater frequency
- Experiments with tobacco, medications, household substances, drugs, or alcohol
- Inflicts physical pain, or takes excessive physical risks that could or have resulted in injury to herself
- Talks of suicide, or hating her life

Although children, tweens, and teens can be dramatic as a way to get you to hear them, if your child's behavior seems overly exaggerated following a change in the family dynamic, you should give it further consideration.

 Fact

According to Jane Nelson the author of *Positive Discipline for Blended Families*, "Young children are especially sensitive to non-verbal messages adults send them. They can 'read' energy long before they can speak words. And when an adults' words and non-verbal messages don't match, they instinctively trust the non-verbal part."

Parenting Tips for Divorced and Blended Families

To lessen the anxiety your child will feel during separation and divorce, here are some key points to remember: First, let your child be a child. The best you can do for him right now is to keep him out of your business, keep what happens between you and your partner private, and do not put him in a position of parenting you or being your emotional caretaker. Some kids may attempt to do this even when you try to prevent it. They are merely trying to have some sense of control over their situation. Give them some other way of having control, like choosing when they do their homework—either after school or after dinner. Maybe you can let them choose how many books they want you to read them before bed, or allow them to decide which chores they feel they would be best at, instead of telling them which ones they will do.

 Essential

To lessen a child's anxiety, no matter what their age, it is very important during a time of change to keep your promises, be consistent, and have a routine. While blending families together, the most important element of the process is communication. That means you communicate to your children and allow them to communicate to you. Having a family meeting once a week is an excellent start.

Keep in mind that the new stepparents, and possibly stepsiblings, are *your* choice, not necessarily your child's. It is important to have compassion for how this might feel for them and realize that it can take years to work out. That does not mean your kids are being difficult, or that something is wrong with your family. Lastly, to reduce both anxiety and conflict, it is best to let the biological parent remain primarily responsible for control and discipline of their own children until the children feel they have developed a strong bond with the stepparent. This often means after a few years, not after weeks or months. This rule is especially important for adolescents, who may already be struggling with authority and independence issues.

Fact

> Families come in all different shapes and sizes. According to the American Psychological Association 40 to 50 percent of marriages will end in divorce.

So, the bottom line is this: As a parent, your child will look to you as a gauge for how he forms his perceptions about acting and being in his own life. If you are anxious, stressed, or depressed, your child will most likely be as well. When adjustments are going to occur for your child that are out of his control, help him feel he is being taken into account by communicating with compassion and by being your best self. This will allow him to feel safe as he is struggling to navigate through the change. Being your best self means taking an inventory of your ability to live with stress, your emotional life, and your marriage. Looking for ways to find balance in these areas benefits both you and your child.

CHAPTER 8

Parenting Pointers

L earning how to live with tension can be at times frustrating, demanding, and stressful. That is not necessarily your child's intent, but when children are acting out of fear the irrationality of their symptoms can feel overwhelming for those around them. Although the common saying is usually "misery loves miserable company," in this case it should be "anxiety creates anxious company." This chapter will give you pointers, strategies, and tools to help you and your child work through anxious moments.

Consistency and Follow-Through

To a child with anxiety, missing the ball in a soccer game or having a homework assignment due at school can be opportunities for disaster and the final proving ground for how ineffective she feels in her life. Providing stability, security, and consistency can increase your child's sense of self-worth and ease negative thoughts. When life feels tenuous and out of control, having clear rules, consequences, and order are best.

Consistency

Being reliable and predictable is potent medicine for an anxious child. Children need to know what and whom they can count on. It is not to say spontaneity won't be of value to your child;

however, on a day-to-day basis, an organized lifestyle with fairly predictable routines is best. Routines are like anchors: they minimize worry. Children don't have to figure out daily when dinner will be served, when to do homework, and what time you will be home. Busy families can post calendars on refrigerators or in an area that your child goes to every day, with everyone's schedule spelled out.

 Alert

If the day includes a new activity, or a change in time for pick up or drop off, explain beforehand why the pattern is different. If your child is too young to read, use pictures on the calendar so he can see where he is going or what he is doing that day.

To foster consistency, the rules you make for the household need to remain constant until you have a family meeting or other opportunity to sit down with your child and identify the new expectation and related consequence. Because children with anxiety can become overwhelmed easily, anticipating and averting unnecessary triggers is helpful. With that in mind, it might be important to set a specific time to do homework, have a set time for meals, plan and organize projects for school with a timeline, and consistently reward your child if he sets a goal and accomplishes it. For children with anxiety, consistency can equal stability. Therefore, when you think about how to bring consistency into your family, you can also ask, "What can we implement to make life feel more stable?"

It is best to have clear rules early on, with you, the parent, making the decision about what is best, while honoring your child's desires and changing abilities. As children grow older you can offer small choices and see how they do with them, limiting their choices to two specific options at first. If they struggle with that choice too much, you'll know you took this step too early. That's fine. Stop for now and try again in six months.

Follow-Through

Like consistency, follow-through for children can translate to security and trust. Creating an environment at home that optimizes your child's ability to count on you doing what you told them you would do, even if it means a consequence for their behavior, is important for anxiety reduction. The foundation parents instill with follow-through in the home can increase a child's ability to have trust, and decrease worry in relationships outside the home.

 Question

> I thought the right way to parent was to give my child options, letting her have more control in her life, yet she seems more anxious and irritable now. Why?
>
> When parents give choices, the child then has to make a decision. That is a big task for kids with anxiety who do not trust themselves. They end up agitated out of a sense of fear, seem to be procrastinating when they are actually unable to make a choice, and they then feel worse about themselves. It is therefore best to limit choices and to avoid language such as *"go figure it out yourself."*

The same holds for building an environment where children feel they can work through a hurtful communication with a parent or sibling, and in creating a home where they feel accepted exactly as they are. Telling your child you care that he is struggling with anxiety is one thing; showing him by helping him succeed is how he will *know* you care. Follow-through also means keeping your commitments. A child with anxiety already has enough questions about life and people, and when parents or caregivers do not keep their word, or use threats to manage situations, the world is reflected as unstable, and the parent loses credibility in a child's eyes.

Changing your mind, breaking a promise, or being arbitrary with siblings and rules gives a child mixed messages. Besides undermining trust and security, these events might create anger and resentments. Not just with you and your child, but between the anxious child and his siblings as well.

Being Active and Proactive

Most children, especially when young, usually do not plan ahead for a situation that creates anxiety. That means your child will likely approach an issue in the same ineffective way time after time. Understandably, this can perpetuate a sense of failure and an inability to trust herself. If you know from experience that allowing your child to be in charge of herself in the morning creates havoc and anxiety, step in and offer support.

In addition, if you know that time and organizational skills are areas needed for growth, be proactive. Identify the source of stress and set up a plan to create opportunities for success without everyone having to go through the stress of failure first. For example, say your son is invited to a birthday sleepover party. He is especially excited because it means some of the boys at school like him enough to want him there. However, when you get there he freezes at the door, grabs your leg, and refuses to go inside. At first you gently encourage and coax. When that does not work, you plead. Finally, you scold him and shake him off of you with embarrassment and irritation as the other boys and moms watch. Walking away, you are frustrated and perplexed that an exciting, fun event turned into a disaster and feel terrible for how you left him. This situation gives you and your son an opportunity to develop a plan, proactively, for the future. The next time a new situation comes up, you two can sit down the day before to discuss it. You can talk about how he feels about being invited, what the most fun parts of the party might be, what he thinks they might all do, what he might be nervous about, and what his greatest fears might be. You also might suggest that you do not mind staying for a few extra minutes until he is settled in with his friends, or picking him up early if the sleeping over part feels the most scary. Most kids will agree to go to a party if they know they have a way out of what they fear most, and when the scary part comes they often are having so much fun they do not want to leave after all.

Building an Effective Plan

At the heart of every well-constructed plan is a clear intention. Intentions come from inside, typically drawn from what you love and care about. For example, you may have the intention to create opportunities for your child to experience his capability, worthiness, and strength. Next, before building your goals and the steps you will take to achieve them, focus on what it is you are looking for. Ask, *What is the purpose of my plan? What do I hope to see as the result of these actions?* Once those questions are answered you can begin building the plan. The steps are outlined again here.

1. What is my intention? (e.g. To provide opportunities for my child to feel worthy)
2. What do I hope to see as a result? How will I know if the plan works? What behaviors might I see? (e.g. My child will be able to complete a task without reassurance or direction)
3. What is one goal that will help me move in this direction? (e.g. Delegate tasks that my child is capable of)
4. What is one possible intervention to achieve this goal? (e.g. Refrain from hovering over my child, instead allowing her to learn from her own experiences)

Fact

A 2003 study had participants write down five things they were grate-ful for, each week for a period of ten weeks. Results showed that when compared to people in control groups who wrote down their day's frus-trations or simply listed the day's events, these participants were 25 percent happier, more optimistic about the future, and participated in one and a half hours more exercise per week than those in the control groups.

Patience Really Is a Virtue

Although a medication can be helpful, there is no quick fix for anxiety sufferers. A large component of anxiety is fear based and personal, so there is no "one size fits all" solution. What worked for another child and family may not work for yours. As a caregiver, it will not be uncommon to have some intense feelings yourself. A thoughtful approach with a plan may take longer to set in place and execute, but will probably be a lot more effective and help-ful than any "quick fix." Quick fixes sound easy and provoke an eagerness to have a "normal" life back. Avoid comparing your situ-ation to others. You and your child's journey are unique and with patience you begin to see the lessons and skills that unfold from it.

Watch and Encourage

It is important to be patient, even if it means a job will not be done completely or in a timely fashion, and allow your child to have the experience of doing it for himself. Some children need to feel their anxiety, without parental intervention. As stated in Chap-ter 6, learning how to respect and experience your emotions is a foundational practice for building a supportive home environment. Part of the development of internal motivation comes from feeling stress. For example, say your daughter tells you she has a project due at school in three days. You have already helped a number of times with setting up a plan, establishing a timeline, and seeing her accomplish the project. Out of your own fear because of how projects have gone in the past, and the irritability it caused for both of you, you might want to jump right in and say, "Okay, let's get started; first, why don't you . . . " Try instead, "I trust you have all the tools needed to do a great job with that. You did such a terrific job on the last one. Why don't you get started, and I'll be by after the dishes to check it out." When you go to see how far she has gotten, be patient with whatever situation you walk into. Encourage, but do not take over, even if it took her an hour to get her materials together. Ask what she has decided her next step should be and gently guide her if she is off track. It can be a slow process, but necessary if you ever want her to be able to have a healthy sense of self-confidence and to work on her own. Being anxious about how long she is taking or initiating the well-intentioned rescue just sets you up to have to rescue her again next time. Your job as a parent is to help your child learn how to help herself.

Procrastination

It helps to realize that most children with anxiety do procrastinate. They can have a hard time thinking things through, and if they are stuck in a ritual or familiar process of self-doubt, they will not get very far with whatever their task was. Procrastination is a form of self-sabotage; it blocks your child from feeling a sense of accomplishment. Children who procrastinate often feel stuck, inside they may know they need to make changes but are unsure about what changes to make. Many times they hang onto what is familiar (procrastination) out of fear of feeling what is unfamiliar. As a parent it will be important for you to encourage your child to slowly shift her ways. Perhaps encouraging her to start her homework thirty minutes rather than one hour earlier is more realistic. Also, it is important for parents to notice if they are taking their child's procrastination personally. For example, notice if you feel disrespected, ignored, or challenged in any way. Procrastination may be a trigger for some parents and typically what fuels this trigger is an underlying fear that your child will fail or that you have somehow failed as a parent. Once you allow yourself to own that truth and take a moment to feel your fear rather than react to it, you and your child can begin to go about making changes that work for everyone.

 Alert

Remember that lectures, repeating commands, yelling, and interrupting fuel your child's anxiety. Less is more. Also, be sure to ask questions that give you more than a yes or no answer. For example, "At what time will you be starting your project?" rather than "Are you going to start your project?"

It is common to have strong feelings when your children are having difficulty, so talk with a friend, your spouse, or a therapist instead of directing frustration at yourself or child.

Use Mirror Neurons to Defuse Situations

Mirror neurons are one of the newer discoveries in the field of brain science. They play an important role in helping scientists learn how we empathize with others. According to recent research, what parents should know is that the same regions of the brain become activated whether you are observing a specific gesture or expression or making it yourself. This means your facial expressions and hand gestures can have an impact on the brain of your child. Think about the times when your child became upset because you waved your hand to move him away. Perhaps you did not say anything verbally; however, the gesture itself was enough to change the experience (i.e. the resulting brainwaves) of the other person. This speaks volumes regarding how important it is for parents to take full responsibility for their actions. It also indicates how the power of a smile, gaze, or similar gesture of love sends out positive, uplifting energy that can affect the brainwaves of both the sender and the receiver.

 Essential

> Handling yourself in a steady, composed way is what will be most helpful to your child with anxiety. Even if you get stressed or feel overwhelmed, modeling how to collect yourself and work through a tough spot shows your child that she can learn to do the same thing.

Part of being calm is to exude an air of knowing or confidence. Verbal statements like "I know you are upset; I trust you can do this," or "I know this feels hard for you; you are strong though, I've seen it," can be very calming and helpful. Your children need to feel your confidence in them. They count on you when their emotions are too big for them to handle and logic is lost to them. If your child is misbehaving, it is best not to argue or debate with her. Quietly remind her of the rules and consequences of her behavior and ask if she would like to engage in some calming behavior, or take the consequence. If your child chooses to use tools to de-escalate, praise her with confidence: "I knew you could do this; I am so proud of you," or, "Wow, look at you; I love your creativity and strength."

If your child has a meltdown, do not assume falling apart was her choice, because sometimes, just as with a tantrum, the anxiety is so big that your child cannot figure out how to get on top of it anymore. Follow up with your child after a struggle or meltdown. When your child is calm, ask why it went too far, and use the information to discuss and understand how all experiences help us grow and prepare for the future. Most of all do not be afraid of your child's feelings. They are just emotions and with awareness will pass.

Routine Is King

Regular patterns and routines tend to diminish anxiety and increase the supply of confidence and peace. Much like consistency and follow-through, it is an essential ingredient to raising children. Children or adults experiencing anxiety feel calmer in daily life when it is predictable, when they know what is expected of them, and they are on a schedule. It is best to set specific times for meals, playtime, homework, quiet time, and bedtime. However, while an established routine is beneficial, you will want to avoid rigidity so that your child can practice flexibility from time to time.

Bedtime Routine

Help your child establish a bedtime routine. This means you do the same things in the same order and at the same time every night. For example, at 7:30 P.M. your child takes a warm bath, then brushes his teeth and combs his hair. By 8:00 P.M., he is in his bed and it is story time until 8:15 P.M. He then gets to choose to read for an additional fifteen minutes by himself, or chat with you about his day. Lights are out at 8:30 P.M. If you have a child who finds it difficult to fall asleep, quiet music, a story, or recorded relaxation exercise work well. It is important to keep in mind that new routines can take several weeks to establish, so hang in there.

Co-Parenting

It is especially important, no matter if you are living together, blended, separated, or divorced from your child's other parent, that you engage in healthy conversations about parenting and managing your child's anxiety. Agreement concerning the child can give your child one less thing to be anxious about, and the consistency of your approaches gives your child the structure he needs. For example, bedtime schedules and routine need to be the same even if one parent is not at home for the evening. If you live separately and choose different routines, that is okay, but you still need consistency. Each house has a particular routine your child can count on when she is at that house.

 Fact

An overnight retreat is an excellent way to replenish the relationship with your partner and get a new perspective on an old issue. Every now and then you need some distance to see possibilities, and the space to discuss them. Besides, a night away can also give you an opportunity to miss the kids.

If you find that your partner is not following through on an agreement, it is best to let the other know without doing it in front of the children. Maybe a tap on the shoulder as you walk by, or a squeeze of the hand could be just the reminder your partner needs. It is best not to discuss frustrations or react angrily in front of a child with anxiety. The guilt and esteem issues they have already will only be complicated if they believe you are upset with each other because of them. You can be honest with your children and let them know that it is okay to disagree; how you resolve the issue is what is most important.

What Affects You

Be as honest as you can with yourself and your partner or co-parent about your own childhood and how it might be influencing you now as a parent. Rather than judge, or criticize yourself, or feel guilt because you are struggling, be open about your issues so you can get support. For example, if you were taught that "good" children were seen and not heard and now you have a child who breaks down emotionally, you might react negatively, or even over-react to your child. If the co-parent knows this and your child starts to act up, he can take over and give support to both of you. It does not mean you are entitled not to grow in that area; it does mean, though, that your child's emotional health is important and you both recognize you still have work to do in that area. That is what collaborating is about.

Parenting Tips

Good tips to follow are to create one voice when parenting and to openly listen to your co-parent. Listening does not mean you agree, it just means you respect that the other parent has a thought or opinion they want to share. In addition, watch what you say, talk over disagreements in private, and make your home a safe haven.

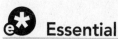 **Essential**

Most divorced couples find that the issues they had while married follow them into the divorce. Therefore, if you had communication issues prior to separation, you likely will still have these. Divorce does not change or solve the problems you experienced in the relationship, so you will have to work on communication if you want your kids to flourish.

Educate Yourself

Creating a resource of information about anxiety and the professionals in the community who specialize in this field not only supplies you with tips, tools, advocacy, support, and validation, it also creates a feeling of self empowerment.

The more you understand, the less fear you have; knowledge then equals power and movement. Also keep in mind that learning a new tool, like how to breathe properly when anxiety begins, might be just what your child needs to help him get on top of his anxiety without having to see a doctor or take medication. The worst feeling in the world is not knowing what to do, or how to help your own child. Packing your toolbox with skills and knowledge for handling anxiety is half the journey.

Help Yourself

You can find information on the web, at bookstores, the library, at your child's school, from your doctor, and through friends and family. Although there are hundreds of websites about anxiety, some are better and more complete than others are. There is a list of recommended resources for you in Appendix B. If you go to a bookstore, look in the self-help section and the children's section for books on anxiety and mental health. When visiting your local library you can talk with a librarian or use the computerized catalog to find books, journals, recordings, and magazine articles. Finding a support group online or in your community is also a great asset. You need to know that you are normal, even when you are upset with your child with anxiety, and that will happen when you find others with similar journeys.

CHAPTER 9

Parenting Makeovers

Just like you can make over your hair and outfit, you can also change or renew the ways you handle your parenting. Like designing a new outfit, you can get quite creative in your parenting. This means you can play with different language and redefine traditional ways to meet the current knowledge of what scientists now know about the brain. Most importantly, it provides another avenue for helping children and families to live with stress. It indicates you and your child have a choice in whether stress moves into a state of anxiety or not. Your willingness to see and try something in a different way may recruit the interest and willingness of your child. This chapter will get you started.

Rule Makeovers

Commands like the word "no" used to be parenting mainstays. But today new science is giving parents an incentive for relinquishing the word (unless, of course, it is used to keep your child safe, like preventing him form running into the road). This creates an opportunity for making over how you prepare and state your rules. Taking the time to remove your "nos" can truly make a difference in the way your child responds to both your written and verbal rules. Following are guidelines for transforming your rules into empowerment tools.

Fact

Authors Mark Waldman and Dr. Andrew Newberg, *Words Can Change Your Brain*, 2012, labeled the word "no" as "the most dangerous word in the world." Through brain scans, they were able to identify the release of stress-producing hormones in response to the word, which impaired logic, reason, communication, and language processing. Science now proves overstating, repeating, or even writing the word "no" can trigger a flight-or-fight response in others.

Transform Your Rules Into Empowerment Tools

To begin transforming your rules you must first review the purpose of them. For most parents the purpose is to create a safe, cooperative environment conducive to learning and living with each other. Rules often reflect family values such as respect, hard work, and/or cooperation. The research shows that focusing on what you value sends a signal to your body that it is safe. Information that is interpreted by the body and brain as safe is more likely to be received in a calm way. This insight provides incentive to parents and educators to watch how their rules are stated. Following are some steps that will help you shift gears from enforcement to empowerment:

1. Change rules to values
2. Rather than state your rules, create them
3. Rather than enforce, embody

Change Rules to Values

Renaming "rules" as "values" does two things: one, it prevents you from overusing the word no, and secondly, values are nonthreatening to children and adolescents. Values promote a sense of belonging, connection, and inner strength. For example, if you were to write your rules on a whiteboard, rather than phrasing the rule as "No name calling," you could state it positively as "We value respect for self and others."

Instead of State, Create

Rules are not random; they are set deliberately to create a context for certain behaviors, and restating them is done in response to a specific misdemeanor. On occasion a parent might take the time to sit with their child at their level (meaning face-to-face, eye to eye) to discuss the rules, but usually in response to the rules being broken in some way. If your goal is to tone down stress in the family environment, it is a good idea for you and your child to create the rules together. To do this, you have to ask your child to tap into their imagination. You might ask, "If our family were being respectful to one another, what would that look like? How would we do it?" You and your child can then come up with a mental image and describe it to each other. You may even have your child draw a picture of it. This creative process of personalization helps the child internalize and understand the values.

 Essential

> Rules are important. However, follow-through is what distinguishes an effective rule from an ineffective one. Needless to say, logical consequences do have their place; still, it is recommended that the dinner table be a place for connection. Therefore, if you need to deliver a consequence for something, do it in private, away from an audience. Meting out consequences in a public setting will only increase anxiety.

Rather Than Enforce, Embody

You might be asking yourself why anyone would want to personalize rules. To truly own something, you must embody it. Think about it: Why wouldn't you own and embrace self-respect, patience, individuality, and cooperation? To do this well, you must be willing to feel what you value. Learning how to feel can be reviewed in Chapter 6.

Example of a Rule Makeover

Following is an example of a rule moving through the three steps of transformation. Notice the difference between the way it is stated on the top and on the bottom. Notice the difference in feeling and how it may promote peace and harmony in your home.

1. Rule: No phones at the table.
   Value: We value time to connect.
2. State: No phones at the table.
   Create: How will we behave if we value this meal as time together? What does our behavior look like if we are connected?
3. Enforce: You just lost your phone.
   Embody: I appreciate everyone putting away their phones for dinner.

Reframe Language

In addition to the reframing techniques you learned in Chapter 6, this section offers further ways to make over what you say and how you say it. Your words are powerful, and new science suggests they can trigger a response in someone else's amygdala, the part of the brain that signals fight or flight to the body. Reframing language is worth exploring as it not only impacts the response of your own brain, but also of your child.

To reframe your language, there are three words to be aware of: "should," "no," and "don't." *Should* is a word that implies your child is wrong. It sets her up for feeling bad before she can feel good. This is a counterproductive pattern that is unnecessary and makes life appear so much harder than it is. The word *no*, as already stated, triggers fear or acts as a signal to your child's brain and body that it is unsafe. Again, there are times you will have to use the word "no," but in most cases you will choose an alternative. The third word to reframe is *don't*. *Don't* is dangerous because it often points to behavior you do not want to see. For example, "Don't touch that." Particularly for small children, it is more beneficial to redirect them to the activity or appropriate behavior that you do wish to see. By changing your words, you can influence the neurocircuitry in your brain as well as your child's. This makes it more likely that you and your child will activate other parts of your brain that promote harmony. Here are some examples of how to reframe your language:

Rather than:	Reframe to:
You should pick up after yourself	Please pick up your plates and trash
Don't touch your sister's things	Ask before you touch
No whining	Use a clear voice

Specialize Routines

Routines benefit all children, particularly ones sensitive to anxiety. This section is not about changing your routines, as reliability and consistency are the backbone of their success, but rather about stylizing or making them a little extra special. Let's face it, routines can get a little mundane and boring. To liven them up, add some special touches. For example, place a note in your child's lunchbox, cook a loved one's favorite meal, have your child read to you rather than you read to her, eat breakfast for dinner, eat outside on a picnic blanket, make hot chocolate for homework time, or allow your children to help cook dinner. Specializing routines offers positive attention and stimulates connection.

Change a Habit

If there is one habit you could change, and you believe it would serve you and your child well to do so, what would it be? Changing the way you parent often has less to do with your child and more to do with you. Parents who choose to quit smoking or decide to start exercising are often surprised to see other areas of their life improve. Could a certain habit be preventing you from implementing some of the strategies in this book? Changing a habit takes time, and in some cases you may need support. For something like quitting smoking, you have a huge opportunity to be an example to your child. Solicit family members and ask for their support. Let them know what you will need. Love and encouragement may be two things you could ask for. Changing a habit is one of the most powerful ways to illustrate to your child how anyone can successfully work through things that are challenging.

 Essential

If you weren't busy worrying about your child, what would you be doing instead? It is time for you to pick up your passion again, or embark on a new one. What do you like to do? What excites you? Reading, writing, photography, fishing, exercise, painting . . . what have you put on the back burner in the name of love and commitment to your child? Doing what you love helps you to be the parent you hope to be, and an excellent example for your child.

Work Out Your Right Brain

The human brain has two hemispheres, referred to as the right and left brain. The left brain tends to live in the past and in the future. It helps you remember to go to your doctors appointment, do your laundry, and pick up what you need for dinner. Your right brain helps you connect to the present moment through your consciousness and awareness. It is the part of you that promotes feeling before thinking. The right brain is strengthened through experiences that engage the senses and emotional self through activities that promote creativity, mindfulness, movement, meditation, sound, and prayer. Strengthening your right brain lowers your reactivity. It does this because the right brain lives predominately through the present moment (where anxiety does not exist). The present moment is where you and your child are most clear and resilient to the pressures and fears around you.

 Essential

Each time you choose to be compassionate to yourself or others, you are strengthening the right side of your brain. Parents who are mindful about media choices can stimulate compassion in their children. Viewing films such as *The Blind Side* are great tools for teaching and feeling empathy.

Children with anxiety tend to have overdeveloped left brains, the hemisphere that lives in the past and the future. Teaching children tools for redirecting their right brain to the present moment will be essential to increasing their wisdom and ability about how they can decrease their own anxiety. It is helpful if you teach them how to think in pictures and utilize their imaginations. Remember the body and mind does not know the difference between a real or imagined threat. It responds as if everything is happening right now. This is valuable information; if your child's body does not know the difference between a real and imagined threat that means it cannot tell the difference between a real and imagined nonthreat. Therefore, by having your child imagine a calm and peaceful scene or image (sun, tree, ocean, mountains) your child's body (and brain) acts as if that image is happening right now. The same thing occurs when your child hears an inspirational or heartfelt story. When done consciously you can engage and strengthen your child's right brain through storytelling and visualization.

Keep in mind if your child is exposed to fearful images, stories or if they are constantly plugged into the television and/or computer this weakens their ability to utilize their built-in abilities to overcome anxiety and instead be in the present moment. However, by slowly incorporating choices that develop your right brain, you show your child how human beings are not fixed. You can learn, grow, and change at any age. The best place to begin is with you. As you go about your day notice the peaceful images around you, rain dripping on the window, trees blowing in the wind. Later when you begin to feel stress, close your eyes and imagine these same images in your mind. Even if it is for a second or two or if you find you cannot see the image but rather sense it or hear it that works just as well.

Create a New Day

Many parent's supporting children through stress and anxiety wake up to a new day expecting that the challenges of yesterday will still be present. Expectations are powerful and if you expect that you and your child will continue to struggle and be plagued by anxiety most likely that is what you will get. Part of the process of helping your child will be in your willingness and ability to create a new day.

Think of creating a new day as clearing the slate or erasing the chalkboard. Imagine wiping away the stories and fears of yesterday to better able you to focus on today. Wash away the stories that start with *what if*, or the language you associate with your child (moody, irritable, difficult, etc.). Also, consider washing away your responses of yesterday for example, the constant reminders you gave your child, advice or instructions. It may be helpful for you to do this while taking a shower. Imagine all of the responses of yesterday washing off your body down into the drain. Take some deep breaths and allow yourself to receive fresh thoughts, feelings, sounds, and images. Do this daily and notice how this in itself makes a tremendous difference on you and your family. Following is a technique that you can do privately at home and work. Teachers could even do this with children at school.

Rub your hands together vigorously together for thirty seconds. Close your eyes and lay your palms over your eyes and state, *I choose to see things in a new way*; lay your hands over your ears and state, *I choose to listen with open ears*; lay your hands over your throat and say, *I choose to speak clearly and wisely today*; lay your hands on your heart and say, *I choose to feel deeply*, and finally your hands on your abdomen and say, *I am safe*. At the end visualize the sun or a clear blue sky.

CHAPTER 10

Disciplining Children with Anxiety

Disciplining children with anxiety is tricky because parents may already feel as if they are on shaky ground. A child's self-esteem may appear frail and his threshold for stress low. Small steps are key with a child who has anxiety. Planning and preparing in small pieces allows your child to reap better results and achieve his goals without becoming overwhelmed. Often when a child takes on too much or disregards his responsibilities, things build and explode into perceived problems and roadblocks. This can lead to disrespectful behavior such as a bad attitude, talking back, or teasing others. This chapter reminds parents that when used well, discipline is a tool, not a punishment. Therefore, the intent of discipline is to build your child's ability to manage his life by permitting carefully guided natural, logical consequences to actions.

Self-Regulation over Self-Control

Self-regulation is the ability to calm yourself down when you are upset. Self-control, on the other hand, may be misconstrued by your child as needing to control (stop) his feelings. This sends conflicting messages about how to live with stress and anxiety. Research indicates when the molecules which make up the energy of your emotions travel through the body you feel better, are able to think more clearly, and respond in ways that not only benefit you but also the individuals around you. Explain to your child that stopping or suppressing feelings is like building an internal traffic jam. It creates inner conflict and sends mixed signals to the nervous system. On the other hand, self-regulation uses self-awareness as a way to move through that traffic. For example, when you cross a street you have to judge the situation by noticing the sounds and sights, and decide whether danger is present. In other words, you have to rely on your sense of awareness of the external situation and how your sense of self-awareness interacts with it to get to the other side of the road safely and, hopefully, without triggering fear and anxiety.

To encourage the development of self-regulation, watch your use of language. One word that needs careful management is "stop," as in, "Stop doing that." If you observe your own reaction to the word, you will notice "stop" momentarily gets your attention, but also may change your breathing pattern from slow and rhythmic to short and shallow. Unlike the dead-end "stop" command, true discipline teaches or suggests the appropriate behavior. For example, instead of saying, "Stop complaining," consider asking, "What do you need to feel better?" or redirect the child's attention by asking, "What is going well?"

 Essential

> Discipline enables your child to learn something from his actions. If your child is preoccupied with feeling unworthy or ashamed, this will overpower what he learns. Therefore, to be effective, your words and body language must be delivered with respect. Respectful body language is not something you do; it is a way to feel. In order to feel respect for others you must first learn how to respect yourself. To do this you will need to honor all of your feelings even the ones that are uncomfortable (frustration, anger, and fear). Once you honor those emotions you create space inside for their movement and when lifted you are able to feel the emotions that foster self-respect and compassion for others. Honoring is breathing.

Once you do this you will be able to hear counterproductive language more clearly. For example, "You drive me crazy," is a signal that you may be going down a path of disrespect. Instead, keep your phrases framed in more positive I-messages like "I feel," "I am," or "I need."

A Balancing Act

Your child's ability to build self-reliance is a balancing act. Encouraging independence and freedom to think endorses your values about respecting others and/or established family rules. By offering your child enough independence and freedom to explore, you can decrease dependency, fearfulness, and insecurity in your child. It will be important to constantly assess your child's changing age, developmental ability, and skills to find that balance. It is usually different for each child, and therefore important to honor individual temperaments.

 Question

My children are upset because they say I have different rules for each of them. Am I doing something wrong?

Rules usually are different for each child, especially if one is experiencing challenges. Continually assess your child's changing age, developmental ability, and skills as you make rules. Consider a family meeting to discuss the differences, and talk about how you can build self-reliance with each child in the family. Teach children how two people can participate in the same exact situation and each have a different experience.

Using Logical and Natural Consequences

Natural consequences are the automatic results of an action, and the parent usually plans logical consequences in advance, sometimes together with the child. Allowing logical or natural consequences to occur helps your child develop an internal understanding of self-regulation. You want your child to feel empowered and capable, which is difficult to do when you jump in and rescue your child, preventing them from experiencing their own emotions. This occurs when you make decisions for him, or resort to punishment out of fear and frustration. Choices are more hopeful and positive if you allow your child to make a decision and be responsible for the consequence for that choice. The choice then becomes a structured learning opportunity that preserves the dignity of the child, because there is no punishment or shame attached to the outcome; there is just an opportunity to take baby steps and grow in trial and error.

Doing Too Much

Parents often stumble into overcompensating for their child. This can significantly affect and discourage the development of skills necessary to overcome anxiety and thrive. Although your desire is to help your child, especially when she is stressed or anxious, see it as a moment to pause. This is particularly important for tasks you know she can do for herself. Yes, sometimes it is easier to clean up for her if she is already running late, cover up her mistakes to save her self-esteem, or do her homework for her because she's having a meltdown. Children really do learn best from natural and logical consequences. Trust that this is in your child's best interest.

Logical Consequences

Logical consequences are ones that you create, based on and specifically related to an action. Three tips that help your child get the most out of logical consequences are:

- The consequence is explained ahead of time (before the behavior occurs)
- The consequence is related to the behavior

- The consequence is geared toward your child's development level

For example, if your child yells at her brother, taking her computer privileges away is a consequence that has little to do with the action that triggered it. Instead, the logical consequence would be to escort or ask your child to go to a place where she can calm down. The child may yell back or argue, and it is easy to want to respond by slipping into behavior that defends your rules and consequences. Instead, take a deep, calming breath and verbally repeat the action you wish to see the child take. In this case, you want the child to learn how to calm down, self-regulate, and to be respectful—ideally, values that you have already laid out and agreed upon. Later, when the child is calm, encourage her to apologize, or ask her to tell you what she could have said or did instead of the reaction she chose to make. Handling the situation like this teaches the child much more than lectures and quick demands do. Also, reactions such as yelling increase the likelihood that you might deliver a punishment that increases shame and blame rather than teaching a constructive lesson.

Some additional examples of logical consequences include: if your child is dawdling during dinner, she does not get dessert; or if she plays with the dog instead of picking up her toys before bed, the toys are put on a shelf for a specified amount of time.

One alternative that many parents and children find positive is to engage the child in the consequence. This makes your child a part of the problem-solving process and feels a little less controlling. You can say to your child, "You seem to have difficulty getting yourself to bed on time; what do you think the consequence should be?" This does not mean you will do what your child says, but you can take his thoughts into account. "It feels like you are pushing for a later bedtime, which is not an option; can you think of a consequence?" Depending on your child's response, you might say, "It sounds like you feel a consequence would be to turn off the

TV fifteen minutes earlier so you get yourself moving. That sounds reasonable to us."

Natural Consequences

A natural consequence is exactly what it sounds like: the natural outcome of your child's choice of behavior. Natural consequences for your child's actions are most effective when used to teach a child about responsibility. For example, when a child does not do his homework, a natural consequence will be a zero for the assignment given by the teacher, and falling behind in the class. Another example might be that if your child insists on going outside without his coat in winter, he will be cold and learn that he needs to wear the coat in order to remain warm. A natural consequence is not life threatening, and it avoids a power struggle between parent and child. These consequences allow the natural course of events to become the teacher. An example for an older child might be that if your teenager gets a speeding ticket, he will have to pay for it himself and demerit points will be assigned to his license.

The exceptions for using natural consequences as teaching moments are if the consequence is dangerous, the consequence will be delayed for a long time (consequences work best when immediate), or the consequence causes emotional, legal, or physical problems for other children or adults.

 Fact

The best you can do as a parent is to provide opportunities for growth that are realistic, supportive, and educational, while not sacrificing responsibilities and values. When you allow your child to experience logical and natural consequences, you are doing just that.

Natural and logical consequences allow your child a voice, provide a tone of mutual respect, and still reinforce firm and clear guidelines.

How Consequences Are Different from Punishment

Logical and natural consequences differ from punishment in that punishment does not teach any skills. Its intent, whether conscious or unconscious, is to make the child feel bad enough so he will never do it again. This mindset increases behaviors such as lying, avoidance, withdrawal, and anxiety. It also decreases healthy communication and the development of worthiness and capability. Punishment-related phrases sound like "You always," "You will never," "You are such a," or "Don't you ever, or else." If you were raised by punishment and find yourself going down the same path with your own children, it is strongly encouraged that you get support from a parenting class and/or therapist. Parenting classes are often available through schools, Early Childhood Family Education classes, libraries, and churches. Your local newspaper or school department will likely be able to assist you. If transportation or time is an issue, you can also find support online. Check the resource section at the end of this book for links and suggestions.

Parenting Dos

Following are some areas you want to strengthen, as they are known to guide children in a way that increases their autonomy and independence.

- **Present two choices for problem solving and decision making to young children, and three to adolescents.** Teach your child that choice is one of her greatest tools. Children experiencing anxiety often have an "all or none" mode of thinking. Through discipline, you can teach them they always have more than one option. For example, you can take ten extra minutes to study, or decide against it and take the chance that you will do fine. Ultimately, natural consequences will play themselves out. Most often children learn on their own through natural consequences; however, if they repeat the behavior after receiving the consequence you may need to have a discussion with your child to help him make the connection between the action he took and the consequence he received.

- **Deliver consequences after you calm down.** Give yourself permission to say to your child, "I am really upset right now. There will be a consequence, but first I need to calm down." Once you remove yourself from the situation, consider sitting up straight, closing your eyes, and do some slow, deep breathing. As you inhale through your nose, drawing the breath deep into your lower belly, think of the word "let," and as you exhale, think of the word "go." Do this at least three times.

- **Follow through on whatever consequence you choose.** Your consequence should be based on the one you are most likely to follow through with. If you say you will ground your child for three months, it is highly unlikely you will follow through with this. Avoid consequences that place a burden on you. Consider temporarily suspending one of the child's privileges. For example, if the child spends too much time on the computer, they lose the privilege of using the computer for a day or two. In some cases, computers, cell phones, and other electronic devices might have to be physically removed from the room and put out of reach to reduce conflict.

- **Intervene early.** Conflicts escalate when parents step in too late. That means the behavior goes on for quite a while before parents tend to it. Refrain from developing a habit of finishing something of your own (e.g. e-mails, texting) before attending to your child. Children notice when you are distracted, and may see it as an opportunity to get away with things. You are better off attending to the behavior in the early stages (e.g. whining) before it escalates (e.g.

yelling). This increases the chances that your child will grow and learn from the experience.

- **Give your child space to grow.** When you stand over children, they will feel as if you are waiting for them to fail and do not trust them to complete the task or get through the situation alone. Persistent instructions about the right way to do things may be torturous to your child. Set realistic, obtainable goals and expectations. Most discipline is centered around teaching responsibility, but long lists of responsibilities can create pressure, anxiety, and frustration. In the beginning, focus on only two or three things. Keep them small, and gradually work on new responsibilities once the initial ones are mastered.

 Essential

According to author Mark Robert Waldman, focusing on negative words and thoughts in your speech not only releases stress hormones in your brain, but in the listener's brain as well. A simple shift in what you choose to pay attention to loosens the grips of anxiety.

Positive Reinforcement

The foundation of positive reinforcement is to catch your child when she is doing something that pleases you, and then give her positive feedback about it. It was developed based on the premise that a child's feelings of esteem and confidence are connected to, and influenced by, their relationship with their primary caregivers.

At first it may seem like a lot of work, because you need to be constantly attuned to your child's behavior in order to catch her doing something right and downplay what she is doing wrong. Research shows that, when used correctly, positive reinforcement will inspire confidence in your child and help her adopt that important "can do" attitude.

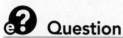 **Question**

> **I told my son that if he faced his fears and went with his class to the waterpark, I would get him the new bike he wanted. Is that positive reinforcement?**
> No, that would be considered a bribe. A reward happens after the fact. Let's say your son is doing the best he can to get through his fears and chooses to go to the waterpark. He is not going to the waterpark for the reward; he is going for the pleasure of achievement. Your reward is an unexpected bonus, whereas a bribe is used to motivate a child in advance. Bribes typically are not recommended, and often muddle what exactly it is you are trying to reinforce and teach.

When you use positive reinforcement, you shift your focus from reminding your child of (and reprimanding him for) what he is doing wrong, to acknowledging his successes and showing him that he is loved, appreciated, and valued. Watch for the desired behavior to occur and then reinforce it with praise, a pat on the back for a job well done, and/or follow up with a special privilege. "Looks like your studying paid off; great job." Keep in mind that praise works best when it does not place a value on the person. There is a difference between "You are awesome" and "Great job." "You are awesome," implies the person's awesomeness is due solely to his accomplishments. Studies have shown that overly praising kids can have the reverse effect. Children and adolescents know when your comments are warranted and genuine. Adolescents in particular may feel as if you are being fake, or trying to manipulate them to act a certain way. Be genuine and matter of fact. A high five, smile, thumbs up, or verbal praise goes a long way.

Encouragement

Encouragement differs from praise, but is equally effective. Rather than saying "Good job," you might say, "Thank you for taking out the trash," or "I appreciate you taking the time to help your sister." Encouragement places less of a value on the person, and is a wonderful way to increase cooperation in the home environment. The bottom line is everyone likes to be noticed and appreciated for what they do, no matter how small or big it is. Parents can model appreciation through encouraging statements by supporting your parenting partner. Children learn most from what you do, as opposed to what you say.

Rewards

Rewards are based on classical conditioning. They are often used in schools and workplaces to motivate employees to go the extra mile. When using rewards, be sure the focus is on effort rather than outcome. For example, you may offer a small allowance if your child completes chores such as folding laundry and/or vacuuming. Know that it will take time for your child to master these skills, and remember that encouraging the child during the process is positive reinforcement. Also, remember that no money or item could ever replace the time and attention with you.

 Essential

Rewards do not need to be material or cost money. Consider rewarding your child with a homemade favorite meal, trip to the park, playground, playing a game such as hide and seek, inviting a friend over for pizza, or a gathering around a fire pit.

The Resilient Child

Resilient children see their emotions as sources of energy, motivation, insight, and understanding. With the support of respectful discipline and encouragement, they are able to recognize the choices that support them. They learn from their mistakes instead of being crumbled by them. They possess the belief and attitude that they are worthy enough, in spite of their mishaps and stumbling blocks. They trust that they possess the ability to influence how they view the events in their life. They recognize that their feelings, thoughts and actions matter. They take responsibility for their mistakes, and ask for help when necessary. They break down tasks into manageable steps, focusing on the process rather than over-focusing on the outcome. They feel the rewards of their effort, rather than search for validation through external things. They choose to allow themselves to experience their emotions rather than push or shove them away. They measure their accomplishments according to their own abilities, rather than by comparing themselves to others. They see their stress and anxiety as windows of opportunity to coach their bodies and move back to the present moment.

 Fact

According to *Psychology Today*, research shows that optimistic people tend to be happier, have more friends, and, in some cases, have more money.

I Have, I Am, I Can

A helpful exercise that connects your child with his ability to grow in resilience is to ask him to write down three to five endings for each of the following queries: *I have, I am,* and *I can.* If he cannot write, you can brainstorm possibilities with him, write out his answers or draw them, and hang the list somewhere in his bedroom. This list can be updated as often as he likes, but at least

once a month. This exercise fosters a continued ability to see himself in a positive light and be reminded of his accomplishments. For
example:

I have . . .
Many people who love me
I am . . .
Stronger every day
I can . . .
Ask my parents for help if I need it

How Parents Can Help

One of the most important qualities you can instill in your children is resilience. Every child and every family is resilient. It is how
well they are able to maintain their resiliency that truly makes a
difference. By encouraging your child to feel and allow the experience of his emotions you are building resiliency. Remember emotions are not actions. As you begin to feel your own emotions this
will be easier for you to teach to others. It is then that you will be
able to observe the energy of your emotions moving through your
body and breath without judgment. Tools applied with nonjudgment have the potential to soothe anxiety.

CHAPTER 11

Self-Love Strategies for Parent and Child

L ove and anxiety cannot exist together. You cannot think and, more importantly, feel loving thoughts and be anxious. Self-love strategies are lifelong tools that help bring you into the present moment. Each time you, the parent, use one of these strategies, you strengthen your ability to support you and your child's mental, physical, emotional, spiritual, and neurological faculties that sustain wellness. As you utilize them you will gain the knowledge and ability to teach them to your child so that she will also strengthen her toolbox for the times you are not with her.

Meditation

Meditation is a way to train the mind to calm down, focus, and pay attention. It allows you to access your higher consciousness, which is the part of you that is able to trust and make choices that are in your best interest as well as your child's. When your mind is busy with mental chatter your body is not able to optimally utilize its resources that promote healing, attention, and connection. Busy thoughts keep your brain on alert and future focused. Meditation also creates an alert brain, yet accomplishes this by focusing on the here-and-now. The difference is in how your body responds. When you are future focused your body can become tense, tight, and distracted. Present focus, on the other hand, allows you to relax, feel, and sense what is happening without taxing the body, keeping it in emergency (anxiety) mode when there is no pending threat.

 Essential

Meditation not only reduces fear and anxiety, but teaches you how to intentionally engage and disengage your senses. For example, you might choose to close your eyes and focus on listening to the sounds around you without judgment. Notice which ones are near and which ones are far. This increases your ability to concentrate while decreasing tension. It does this by bringing you into the here and now.

Beginning Meditation

In the beginning, your meditation practice may be a few minutes long. Duration of practice is not as important as frequency. Therefore, it is better to practice a few minutes daily, rather than for thirty minutes once a week. Many people associate meditation with religion or sitting on the floor. Meditation can take on many variations and can be applied while moving or sitting still. You can learn how to meditate while walking, drinking tea, biking, or even while you do the dishes. Anytime you are observing your breath and body through consciousness and loving awareness, meaning your intention is to support yourself in a kind way, you are meditating. Your intention is not to get rid of or stop your thoughts. Your thoughts are part of being human; they will continue, however, as you breath and focus on the sensations in your body, which is delivered through your sense of smell, touch, hearing, sight, temperature, and balance. In time you will find the amount of your thoughts decrease. You will also find that the quality of your thoughts will change from fearful to compassionate-based.

It is recommended that you practice meditating yourself before attempting to teach it to your child. To begin, start by applying it to something you already do. For example, doing the dishes or folding the laundry. As you begin the task notice your eyes. Begin to soften your gaze (as if you had sleepy eyes). You may have to close them for a few seconds and reopen them. Next, relax the corners of your mouth and separate your back teeth. Notice if your lips are pursed, and if so separate them slightly. Relax your jaw and forehead. This may take up to thirty seconds. Then place your two feet on the floor either while sitting or standing. Begin to notice yourself balancing between your two feet. Press them into the floor until you feel securely grounded. As you take these small actions know you are already in the process of meditation. It is when you go about your day with mental awareness that meditation is activated. Now, while folding the laundry you might notice the texture and smell of the clothes and how they feel on the palm of your hand. You may gaze out the window and watch the birds or hear the wind, or you may choose to simply focus on breathing in and out without judgment. Just by noticing you are breathing you are meditating.

 Fact

Children can learn to start meditating by the age of five, and sessions can take as little as two minutes. Children do not need special equipment and can meditate with others or practice alone.

Teaching Meditation to Your Child

The best way to teach meditation is to be a model. Using the steps just given, when folding the laundry you may say out loud, "This laundry smells so fresh, and the sun is so bright I can almost feel its warmth from inside." You may also choose to say nothing instead and allow your child to observe and see how you choose to begin and end your day. For some it could be sitting with a cup of coffee for a few minutes while closing your eyes (rather than surfing your e-mails); for others it could be lighting a candle and gazing at it for a few minutes at the end of the day. Do what works for you. Once you practice on yourself and become a role model you can begin to guide your child. In the beginning, you may need to sit with your child alone and simply breathe together. Some children do well lying in bed while listening to relaxing sounds. Getting outside in nature and taking a walk without trying to occupy the space with conversation also works. Just allowing your child to feel, breathe and be free is one of the natural ways to invite meditation into your life.

Benefits of Meditation

Meditation decreases stress, pulse rate, blood pressure, metabolism, and muscle tension while enhancing mood and helping you feel more peaceful. You become more in touch with your body, which helps you to get an honest and accurate read of your stress and anxiety levels. It also increases memory, improves circulation, the ability to pay attention, and supports the overall immune system.

Breathing

Breath work is an excellent and effective technique that you can practice anywhere and at any time. These exercises are wonderful for children of all ages once they are able to follow along, because they can be learned in a matter of a few minutes and create immediate benefits. There is also an interesting dual nature to breath work: on the one hand, breathing is automatic, and on the other hand, you can control it. For people who have anxiety this is important, because their anxiety creates a tendency to freeze, or hold one's breath, increasing the feeling that things are out of control. This easy technique is a great tool and an ideal way to self-regulate.

Breathing Basics

Studies show a very effective way to calm oneself is to prolong your exhalation in a slow, controlled manner. Keep that in mind when practicing the exercises that follow. Here is an example of breath work. It can be done for two to ten minutes.

1. Sit cross-legged with your back straight. If you are on the floor or outside, you might want to sit on a pillow for comfort. If you and your child would rather sit on a chair, it is best to keep your feet level on the floor in front of you.
2. Allow your hands to rest comfortably on your lap and let your thumb touch the middle fingertip of the same hand.
3. Close your eyes if you would like, or focus on one point.
4. Begin to breathe easily and evenly, in and out, prolonging the exhalation by slowing it down.
5. Silently count each breath as follows: Inhale: 1, 2; exhale: 1, 2, 3. Inhale: 1, 2; exhale: 1, 2, 3. (Make your exhalation last one count longer than your inhalation.)
6. To finish the meditation put your hand on your heart and take a deep breath in and slowly release your exhale.

 Essential

"Chronic anxiety and tension powerfully condition the breath, so much so that sometimes, even when we sleep, our breath doesn't return to optimal breathing" (NurrieStearns, *Yoga for Anxiety*, 2010). Taking time to take deep breaths, drawing it into the lower abdomen, is as important as remembering to brush your teeth.

Alternate Nostril Breathing

Alternate nostril breathing is an ancient technique that ties directly into your child's nervous system. The right nostril has been proven to correlate with the sympathetic nervous system, which increases alertness and arousal (similar to a cup of coffee). The left nostril corresponds with the parasympathetic nervous system, which increases relaxation (similar to a warm bath). If your child is not sick, or does not suffer from allergies or respiratory conditions, teach her to block off the right nostril with her thumb and breath exclusively through the left (inhaling and exhaling) several times, slowly. By doing this she will learn how her own respiratory and nervous system are designed for both relaxation and alertness. Follow these steps:

1. Sit up tall, close your eyes.
2. Block off the right nostril with your right thumb.
3. Inhale and exhale through the left nostril, while relaxing your jaw and shoulders. Take three or four breaths, slow inhales and exhales with the right nostril closed off; they should be somewhat even in length.

 Fact

Most people engage in upper chest breathing when going about in their daily life. To access the calming qualities it is essential that you practice breathing from the lower belly. On inhalation, the lower belly (below the navel) blows up like a balloon. On exhalation, it deflates, pushing the air out. Teaching your child to breathe deeply in this way helps him to stimulate the vagus nerve in the lung area, which promotes physical calming. If your child gets dizzy, encourage him to exhale or take a break and resume normal breathing.

Signs that Breath Work Is Working

When practicing breath work, it is typical for both adults and children to experience some bodily discomfort. It is important for you to know that these are signs that what you are doing is working. Some of these bodily signs include shifting in the seat, looking around the room, restlessness, and difficulty concentrating. When the brain is introduced to something new, it initially moves through some discomfort evidenced through the body. Stay calm, be patient, and trust that the breath and body know what to do.

These experiences may be similar to the edginess your child feels when he is anxious. As your child experiences discomfort in meditation or breath work, he becomes familiar with how to move it in daily life.

 Question

My daughter is very anxious before she goes to sleep. What can I do?
Reading and listening to stories before bedtime is very calming. Books that teach young children about relaxation can be wonderful guides (for example, *Relax* by Catherine O'Neill). Adolescents and children may enjoy listening to a relaxing CD or app. *StressFreeKids.com* provides CDs and books for children, teens, and adults.

Playful Breathing

There are many fun ways to present breathing techniques to children. A simple way is to get a bottle of bubbles from a toy store, or have your child pretend to blow bubbles. The breathing required is the same as for the calm breathing technique, but you can have fun trying to see who can blow the biggest bubble. This takes long, slow, steady breaths, which increases relaxation. You can then tell her that any time she feels anxious, she can say to herself, "I do not need to worry, I can do pretend bubble blowing and feel better!" Other creative ways for teaching young children how to breathe in a controlled, relaxed manner are to imagine they are blowing on hot food or blowing out a candle.

Progressive Muscle Relaxation

This widely used technique has been around since the 1930s. Progressive muscle relaxation, or PMR, is a two-step process of deliberately applying tension to certain muscle groups, contracting them, and then releasing the muscle and observing it as it relaxes.

The object of this technique is to help you and your child quickly learn to recognize what a tensed muscle and a completely relaxed muscle feel like. You can do this with any body part, such as the hands, feet, and facial muscles. PMR works well when your body is craving physical stimulation. For example, children who feel like they are crawling out of their own skin, wiggly, or distracted often do well with PMR and breath work together.

How to Perform PMR

It is best to practice PMR in a quiet, comfortable place, wearing loose-fitting clothing and no shoes. You can lie down, but as is common with these types of exercises, it increases the chance that you or your child may fall asleep. Therefore, unless that is the goal, it may be better to sit in a comfortable chair. This is the process:

1. Starting with your toes, tighten the muscles in your toes and hold for a count of five. Then let go, and observe and enjoy the release for 30 seconds.
2. Tighten the muscles in your feet and hold for a count of five. Again, relax through the release for a count of thirty.
3. Continue by moving slowly up through your body: contracting and releasing each leg, your abdomen, back, neck, face, and eyes.
4. With each body part, breathe through the muscle work deeply and slowly.
5. You can even have your child lift his arms over his head and squeeze his fists tight, and then release them by his side. Have your child imagine the tension is in the palm of his hand, squeeze it tight, and then exhale and let it go.
6. After you have finished with your entire body, relax with your eyes closed for a few seconds, then get up slowly and stretch.

Visual Imagery

Physician and author Martin L. Rossman says there is enough evidence to make the case that "the human imagination is the most powerful force on earth." Your child's imagination is one of her greatest tools. By visualizing calming or empowering scenes, she has the ability to change her current state of mind from the experience of fear, dread, or feeling overwhelmed to feeling tranquil, lucid, and peaceful.

 Fact

According to Guided Imagery, Inc., a company that produces relaxation recordings, research has concluded that stimulating the brain through imagery may directly affect both the endocrine and nervous systems. They feel this can lead to changes in how the immune system functions, can decrease pain, and reduce anxiety by 65 percent.

How Imagery Works

This technique is based on the same concepts discussed previously: that your mind and body are connected, and if you use all your senses, your body can respond as if what you imagine is real. The more deeply you fantasize about the imagined place, the more relaxing the experience can be. Here's an example of how imagery works: Imagine yourself one year from now. You have completed reading this book and have already incorporated many of the self-love strategies into your daily life, and both you and your child have benefitted from it. See yourself in a calm, peaceful setting. It may be the beach, a meadow, the woods, or perhaps in a garden. In this calm, peaceful setting, see yourself taking deep, lower belly breaths. Notice the soothing sounds around you. On the next inhalation, see yourself lifting up your arms and squeezing your hands into fists as if you were trying to grab and hold tightly the fresh air around you. As you exhale, you let your arms fall by your sides and you feel your muscles and tension release. This release provides you with a rush of feel-good hormones, while circulating healthy neurotransmitters around your brain and body. Share this guided visualization with your child to help set a positive goal using imagery.

Guided Imagery

Guided imagery uses a more formal method to direct your thoughts and guide your imagination toward relaxation. Guided visualizations can be found on iTunes or may be purchased as an app to be played on your smartphone, on DVD, or on CD. Clinically based relaxation and guided visualization MP3s and apps may also be found at online shops such as *www.heartmath.com*. Imagery works well for children because they do not have to think; they can just sit back, close their eyes, and let a soothing voice take them to a calm, relaxing place, through a gentle story. Guided imagery has also been useful with children who have difficulty falling asleep, or staying asleep, because of anxiety. It allows children and teens to turn off their minds and fall into a deep and peaceful sleep while listening to beautiful music, the sounds of nature, and a calming, affirming story.

 Essential

Imagery may aid in healing, increase learning and creativity, and enhance performance. By using imagery, your child can embrace his emotions and the positive thoughts in his head, increasing self-efficacy.

Self-Talk

In education as well as in parenting, a great deal of attention is given to how to talk to other people. This section focuses on teaching children how to talk to themselves in a way that diminishes anxiety. People generally don't share the thoughts that are going on in their head, particularly if they are stressful in nature. When your child tells you about a fear, stressful situation, or event, consider asking, "What were your thoughts telling you in that moment?" Some children may not let you know what is going on inside of their head because they do not wish to disappoint or burden you. Also, if they are always hearing how stressed or anxious you are, they may be more in tune with your words rather than their own.

Cognitive therapists believe that anxious self-talk leads to anxious thoughts, which lead to anxious feelings, which lead to anxious behaviors. Since self-talk is not tangible and is an internal experience, it is important for parents to model modifying thoughts by externalizing them. To do this, you will need to speak out loud in front of your child. For example, you might say, "When I think about my work project, I can feel my breathing get shallower, my neck gets tight, and I start chatting inside my head. I ask myself 'How am I going to do this, I have no time, what if I don't finish?' This makes me feel tense, afraid, and more thoughts come. I make a choice to breathe more deeply, from my chest down into my belly; this slows my thoughts down, and helps me change them to ones that can help me such as, 'I can do this, it will all work out, and I am capable.'"

Here is the technique laid out in easy point form to share with your child:

1. To help change your thoughts from a negative cycle to a positive one, shift from breathing shallowly to deep breathing (move your breath from your chest to your belly).
2. Take three long deep breaths (remember that one full breath cycle is one inhalation and one exhalation).
3. At the end of the third breath, focus on positive I-statements: "I am," "I can," and "It is."

Questions You Can Ask Yourself

When addressing your child's negative self-talk, it is important to incorporate questions that encourage open discussions and reflective thinking. These reflections (reflecting back to your child and what you hear her say) help your child to process and sort out how and when he might apply the strategies to his daily life. Some of these might include:

- What makes me think this is true?
- If a friend told me this, what would I say to them?
- How many times has this happened before?
- What is the worst that could happen if it were true?
- If it happened, how would I cope through it?

Another trick to repattern old ways of thinking is to concentrate on *what* you say about the worrisome situation and *how* you say it. You can use this approach yourself, or with older children. Imagine telling this worry to your best friend. Observe the exact words you use. What would that friend say in response to those words in order to be caring and validating? What might this person say to help you feel better about yourself, and how would she say it? What you imagine this friend would say or do for you is what you need to do for yourself; that is, to be compassionate with yourself, which increases confidence and decreases the impact of negative thinking.

Truth Statements

Truth statements acknowledge what is happening in the moment while creating a hopeful future. They tend to keep expectations simple and realistic. Some examples of truth statements are:

- I expect to feel some worry over this, but I know I will cope through it.
- This may seem hard now, but it will become easier and easier over time.

- When this is over, I will be glad that I did it.
- I have more influence over these thoughts and feelings than I once imagined.
- These feelings are uncomfortable. They will be over with soon, and I will be fine.
- Learning how to live with stress shows how capable I am.

Remember, when you or your child are making your list of positive coping statements, keep in mind that these statements are like affirmations. The objective is to reprogram the computer in your head to fit the life you want, and create the momentum needed to be the person you know is hiding inside.

Exercise

Exercise and physical movement will be a critical part of managing your child's anxiety. The key is to find something your child enjoys. Activities that build your child's self-esteem, a strong body, and a positive outlook will accomplish this well. Some of these include: yoga, tai chi, karate, swimming, hiking, and biking. Some children and adolescents also thrive in a team environment, through organized sports. It will be important for parents to weed out activities that create more stress than is necessary; ones that avoid inner conflict or messages of perfection. Most often you won't know this until you have given it a try. Also, in most circumstances the value of the experience is more about the quality of teaching, encouragement, friendships, and/or coaching than what sport your child chooses.

 Fact

Ample scientific evidence exists to prove that stretching and yawning can reduce stress and provide an emotional release in the body.

From Worrywart to Worry Warrior

Children or adults with anxiety are sometimes called "worrywarts." Names like this prevent children from seeing themselves in another more positive way. These types of labels are often a reflection of parental anxiety, or in some cases used by siblings who think that feelings are something you make fun of or push away. The term worrywart is typically applied to someone who overreacts to small mistakes, is doubtful, and dreads outcomes he cannot control.

Worry Warriors

Worry warriors are able to see their thoughts as something that can be managed by their breath and body. To help your child see herself as a worry warrior, it is important to refrain from messages that indicate you are trying to get rid of the worry. You don't get rid of worries; you *recycle* them. This means that through body awareness and breathing, worries get converted into beneficial emotions that serve your child well. You cannot recycle what you don't want or have. Each time your child pauses to observe his body and breathing, he is sending that worry through a process of change.

Press Delete

Just like you can reframe or change the cover photo on your phone, kids can be taught how they can do this with their thoughts as well. Younger children may relate to this technique more through drawing. For example, you can write or draw your worry and then practice erasing it. Have your child exhale while erasing it so he can actually feel the thought leaving his body. Worry warriors understand that they can change their cover photo, meaning that when they hear a voice in their head that says something negative or fearful, they have the power to change it. All they have to do is take a breath and speak to that fearful part of self, saying something like "change," "cancel," or "delete." Encourage them to use a warrior tone of voice when they speak to themselves. Say it like a command, and the thought will be canceled. When they do this, they are making space for their positive voice to surface and be heard.

 Essential

> It is difficult for a young child to understand the difference between a thought and a feeling. An explanation of that difference might sound like: "A thought is something that happens in your head, like all of a sudden when you see your toothbrush and you think, 'Oh, Mommy said to brush my teeth!' A feeling is something that might happen in your stomach or heart, like the feeling of butterflies in your belly because you forgot you were supposed to brush your teeth, and you worry that I will be upset."

Helping Young Children to be Worry Warriors

Young children may find it hard to understand what you mean by "recycle your worries," and therefore will not be able to comprehend how to apply the strategy. A fun approach to try would be to play a question game. As you read a book with pictures together, stop and ask at each picture, "Hmm, I wonder what he is thinking? What would be your guess?" If your child struggles at the beginning, help her work it through by examining different aspects of the picture. "Well, let's see if we can tell by her eyes, or her face," you might say. "What do you think her arms are telling us, crossed like that?" This allows you the opportunity to help your child identify possibilities, positive ones as well as negative, in an effort to understand his own feelings better. Then talk about how to say a keyword like "Stop" or "Erase" and replace the negative thought, with something like this: "Yes, her eyes do looked worried. Do you think she is worried her dad will miss her game? Maybe she can say 'Stop' to herself and remember that he has never missed a game yet, and he helps her practice all the time, so he either is on his way or has a very good reason if he does not show up. What else do you think she could say to herself to make herself feel better?" This approach is also a great way to help children identify feelings and separate out the difference between a thought and a feeling, which can be difficult for younger children.

Self-Soothing Strategies

It is essential that you and your child learn how to care for yourselves with techniques that can calm anxiety. Meditation, breathing exercises, prayer, physical exercise, a warm bath, unstructured play, getting involved in a hobby you enjoy, and getting together with friends all soothe the busyness of the mind. Pre-teens and adolescents often report music being one of their most popular forms of stress relief. Be sure your child's music includes positive, nonviolent lyrics and messages. Connecting to nature is also a natural way to reset the rhythm of the body. Interacting with animals is a great source for stress relief, as well as creativity and laughter. When weather keeps you indoors, consider playful activities such as a balloon toss, dancing, fine motor activities such as building with Legos, and arts and crafts. Here are some additional well-researched and -documented self-soothing strategies.

Chanting

Chanting is an ancient technique that uses specific sounds made with your own voice, or listening to the chanting of others, to alter the neurochemistry of the brain. Since your body is made up of 80–90 percent water, certain sounds repeated can impact your body on a cellular level. According to *The Healing Power of Sound and Overtone Chant,* chants such as *sat nam* create "higher rate of vibration which creates large spaces between cells, making us less dense and preventing negative intrusive energy from sticking to us easily." (*Sat* in Sanskrit means truth and *nam* means name (truth is in my name)). You can also have children practice and feel the benefits of sound by chanting vowel sounds. Chants are available for downloading online or for purchase on iTunes, and playing chant music can be an effective way to break up any negative energy in your home.

Chimes, Bells, Crystal Bowls

Tibetan singing bowls, gong, wooden chimes and/or crystal bowls reverberate when struck, creating a long-lasting sound wave that can release tension in the body. You can also purchase these sounds in an app and adjust them to ring randomly on your phone or at certain scheduled times of day to remind you to take a deep breath and refocus your awareness on your body. Children and adolescents are often curious about sounds, and may be more interested than you expect.

Tapping

Tapping (also referred to as EFT, Emotional Freedom Technique) is a healing technique partially based on acupressure, and done using the tips of your fingers. Specific points in the body are tapped with the fingers to increase and promote the circulation of energy. Often tapping is accompanied by statements that allow your child to reframe a feeling. For example: "Even though I feel frustrated, I completely love and accept myself." More information regarding tapping points can be found online, and also in Nick Ortner's book, *The Tapping Solution*.

Mudras

Mudras are a position of your body (often the hands and fingers) that have been found to direct energy in a specific direction. Different mudras have been found to correspond to different energy centers in the body often referred to as chakras. Chakras are areas in the body where energy pools together. For example, if you want to stimulate peace there is a specific hand position (incorporated with breath and awareness) that will help stimulate the flow in certain areas of the body such as the abdomen, heart, and throat.

When this energy is flowing in these areas, physical and emotional well-being are found to be impacted in a positive way.

The tips of your fingers have more nerve endings than any other part of your body. They can connect to your body via engaging in deep breathing. According to Amy Weintraub, author of *Yoga Skills for Therapists*, "After centuries of study, it is understood that each finger, the pressure applied, and the direction it faces, correspond to different areas of the body, the brain, and the emotions. Certain mudras lift mood, while others calm it." One mudra that promotes calm is pressing the pad of the uppermost joint of your two middle fingers, two inches above your navel, with your palms facing up. You can even add the sound of *ahhhhhh* while pressing them. Hold the mudra for a few rounds of breathing. Marsha Therese Danzig's book *Children's Book of Mudras* is a resource for parents looking to use this technique with their children to help manage anxiety.

Mantras

Mantras are words or phrases used when your mind is quiet or during meditation. *Man* means mind while *tra* refers to what frees the mind. They can help you and your child shift from a state of fear into love. Studies show when repeated for several minutes mantras balance the right and left brain. Parents can also state mantras for their child. Some examples of mantras are: *peace radiates through me, I am love, let go,* or *So hum* (I am that). You can also create specific mantras to help your child through situations. Some examples are: *good grades come easily, taking tests come with ease, making friends comes naturally* and/or *studying strengthens me.* Mantras work best when repeated nine or ten times in a row in the morning and at night.

Reiki

Reiki is another ancient technique that you can do on yourself or your child. You can use the palm of your hand to move congested energy in the body, creating a sense of peace and inner balance. Parents can do Reiki on their children before they go to bed to help promote a good night's sleep. While breathing deeply, move your hand in a circular motion, clockwise a few inches above your child's heart or belly. This is best done in a dimly lit room, away from distractions. Reiki classes are offered frequently in communities by yoga studios, massage therapists, and nurses.

Energy Medicine

Energy medicine has been around for thousands of years. Psychologist David Feinstein and energy healer Donna Eden have been among the pioneers who have brought this incredible tool to modern life. Like acupressure, it involves tapping and tracing pathways (meridians) of energy. One of the ideas behind this technique is to get the blood flowing between hemispheres of the brain. This can be achieved by exercises such as having your child march in place while slapping the hand to their opposite knee. You can also have your child rub their hands together to create friction. This is a form of energy. Next, have them bring the palm of their energized hand to their forehead and take some deep breaths. This stimulates blood flow while sending calming signals to the nerves. Parents interested in learning simple practices might consider reading *The Little Book of Energy Medicine* by Donna Eden.

Time In

It is likely that your child has been exposed to what it means to take a time out. Self-love strategies are less about taking a time out, and more about taking time to go in. Practices such as meditation, breathing, and mindful living are ways to prepare for the outside pressures of the world by first going inward. Yes, there are times when you want to challenge yourself to hang in there and prove that you can cope, but there are also times when you need to care for yourself by going for a walk. You can tell yourself and others, "I am going to my room for an hour; I need some 'me time,'" or, "I am going to read a book or take a bath." As you do this, you are modeling that working through stress and anxiety requires acts of self-love.

 Essential

Consider keeping an individual and/or family journal of all the positive moments you have experienced. Teach children early that journals are not just for venting. In fact, the research shows venting teaches the brain to revisit the same patterns. Instead, encourage your child to write down reflections, gratitude lists, hope, dreams, milestones, insight, record good days and joys, or even accomplishments inside his journal.

Warmth and Smell

Similar to when you soothed your child as an infant by swaddling her or wrapping her in your arms and drawing her close, wrapping yourself or your child in a warm blanket fresh out of the dryer can help soothe the nervous system. Making sure your child is exposed to natural sunlight for at least ten minutes daily is also essential as light supports the production of vitamin D in the body and vitamin D helps regulate the absorption of calcium in your bones and supports cell-to-cell communication, which is essential to the nervous system. Yummy, homemade soup can also ease and warm the nerves in your child's tummy.

Smell is one of the quickest ways to soothe your mood. The benefits of aromatherapy are discussed in the next chapter. It is equally important to monitor harsh or toxic smells that may bother your child. Some household products can cause headaches and irritability, some examples being harsh cleaning products, laundry detergent, deodorant, and perfumes.

Volunteer Work/Mentoring

Recent research shows that acts of kindness and generosity not only boost neurotransmitters such as oxytocin in the person you are helping, but also in the individual doing the volunteering. Children who are offered mentor or volunteer opportunities feel as if they are serving a greater purpose. This takes the edge off anxiety, allowing your child's perspective to broaden. This is particularly helpful to children experiencing anxiety as stress narrows their perspective and gives the impression that life is a burden rather than life as a purpose. Through helping others children gain a sense of significance, and belonging to their community. Ask your child or adolescent what their passion is and use this information to help you find organizations that are in need for support. If your child loves animals perhaps they can volunteer or collect supplies for a local shelter. You could also take part in community clean-up projects, feeding the homeless, church or school causes, etc. Part of normal healthy development is to want to contribute to society in some way. By providing your child these opportunities you are helping to highlight their innate goodness.

CHAPTER 12

Self-Love Living: Exercise, Nutrition, and Sleep

Proper nutrition, sleep, and adequate physical exercise are a large part of self-love living. Anxiety is what happens when stress is left unattended, creating a disconnect between the mind, body, and spirit. Unhealthy habits such as overusing technology and mindless eating contribute to making it difficult for your child to pick up on her internal cues. Creating healthy habits to replace them steers your child back on track with a deeper understanding of her own bodily needs.

Simple Ways to Curb Anxiety

There are several easy antidotes for minor or temporary anxiety, which are effective for children at almost any age. These remedies, many based on traditional systems of healing, are noninvasive, largely inexpensive, and easy to implement. Also note that yoga, massage, and aromatherapy are excellent ways to reduce anxiety and are described in detail in Chapter 13.

Maintain Blood Sugar

According to nutritionist Jack Challem, author of *The Food-Mood Solution* maintaining stable blood sugar levels through regular meals or small snacks that are rich in protein and mood-enhancing nutrients (omega-3 fats) helps decrease levels of anxiety.

To do this, consider making foods for breakfast that you might typically eat for lunch, such as a slice of low-salt turkey, vegetable soup, tofu smoothies, or whole grain or gluten-free bread with coconut butter or almond butter. Include an extra snack for when your child rides home on the bus or in the car.

Examine the Dairy/Wheat Dilemma

Some children are sensitive to the way dairy is pasteurized. If your child sounds congested or struggles with allergies, this compiled with stress can contribute to overall anxiety levels. Consider substituting with nondairy alternatives such as almond milk, coconut milk, or soy. These are also rich in vitamin B, which is a mood-enhancing supplement.

Consider having your child tested for gluten or wheat intolerance. According to Dr. Stephen Wangen, "It has been well established that a gluten intolerance can dramatically affect the skin, nervous system, musculoskeletal system, immune system energy level, joins, teeth, and even behavior and mood."

Tea Time

Tea has long been used worldwide as an herbal and social remedy for calming the mind, improving digestive problems, and other positive effects on the body. Chamomile is one of the most popular teas for encouraging sleep; passionflower, lemon balm, and jasmine are also purported to have soothing effects. The warming sensation of the tea, enjoyed in a quiet environment, is a healthy way to wind down and reconnect to yourself at the end of the day. It is also a nice accompaniment to reading or doing homework. Even the ritual of preparing the tea can be grounding, if it is done mindfully. Just remember to check to be sure that it does not contain caffeine!

Bath

Bathing has been used for millennia in many cultures to promote health, hygiene, spiritual purification, and even socialization.

The calming effect of the warm water, especially when combined with aromatic soaps and oils, music, and soft lighting, can alleviate anxiety and help with insomnia. Many parents use bathing as a part of the bedtime ritual. For younger children especially, bath time can be excellent for bonding, a time to incorporate massage, or even breathing and visualization. Use your intuition, though, to make sure combining more than one approach at a time is not overly stimulating. You can encourage older children to use bathing independently for calming purposes, and also to reduce insomnia.

Shake and Dance

This technique uses the body's activity to help the mind let go of tension, anxiety, and worry. All it requires is music, a few minutes, and the ability to let go of self-consciousness. To start, find some lively music with a good beat that you think your child would enjoy, or, depending on age, ask your child to pick a piece of music to "get the jitters out." Play the music, and begin to very deliberately shake your body (do this with your child). Shake your hands, feet, arms, legs, head, torso, eyes, tongue, hair, and anything else you can! Do this for at least a minute or two; it's okay if you can't do the whole song. If you like, after shaking, you can then switch the music to something soaring, happy, uplifting, or calming. You and your child will both be surprised at how different you feel after this exercise, and the laughter that can result is good medicine in itself! Make it a regular part of your routine and older children are less likely to resist it.

❓ Question

What if my child won't eat at dinner?
Young children have little bellies and tend to love snacking. The rule of thumb with small children is try to put healthy choices into their snacks, so by the end of the day they have had a variety of fruits, vegetables, proteins, and whole grains. That way, if they eat very little at dinner you will know that their nutritional needs were met through snacking. Pairing carrots and celery with dips such as ranch dressing, cream cheese, almond butter, or hummus makes vegetables more interesting.

Foods That Can Increase Anxiety

Just as a healthy diet can relieve symptoms of anxiety, some foods can worsen mood symptoms because of their effects on the body's biochemistry. If your child feels anxious, you may wish to restrict or eliminate sugar, caffeine, some starches, wheat, and processed foods.

Caffeine

Most people know that caffeine is a stimulant that can cause jitteriness, irritability, and anxiety, but many do not know about hidden sources of caffeine. Many sodas and sports drinks contain caffeine. Energy drinks, even if advertised as natural, may also contain caffeine. Caffeine is also present in cocoa, chocolate, and some teas. If your child has trouble sleeping, be sure to limit sources of caffeine at least four hours before bedtime. You may wish to eliminate caffeine entirely from your child's diet when anxiety is a concern.

Sugar

Many parents are familiar with the hyperactivity, and possible energy and emotional crash, which results from your child's excessive sugar consumption at Halloween, Valentine's Day, parties, or other occasions when sweets are center stage. Sugar in and of itself has no nutritional value other than simple calories. When ingested, it can cause a quick surge in energy, which can then be followed by a "crash" marked by tiredness, lethargy, or even emotionality and irritability. Also, look at labels closely. Many yogurts have the same amount of sugar as a can of soda. Greek yogurt typically has half the sugar compared to regular yogurt. Also, you can purchase plain yogurt and teach your child how to sweeten her own food with natural honey and organic sugar. Teach your child how to read nutritional information labels (e.g. serving sizes) closely.

 Essential

> MSG is common in processed foods like soups, boxed or frozen dinners, side dishes, fast food, and other restaurant food. It can cause gastric distress, headache, nervousness, and general malaise, so read nutritional labeling carefully, especially if your child has anxiety with tummy troubles.

For some, the energy surge can mimic a panic attack. You may wish to limit your child's sugar intake to help with anxiety. To sweeten foods more naturally, with a more gentle effect on mood and energy, consider fruit juice, stevia (an herbal sweetener available at most health food stores), or honey, if your child is over two. Remember that fresh fruit is a natural, healthy, and satisfying option for dessert. Be alert to "disguised sugar" in the form of high-fructose corn syrup and sucrose, which are common in many processed foods. Also, be aware of added sugar in foods we think of as nonsweet, like breads, crackers, and spaghetti or other sauces.

Carbohydrates
Carbohydrates are essential for the production of energy, and all people need some carbs to be healthy. In fact, taking carbohydrates out of your diet completely can interfere with your

intestinal tract. Carbohydrate intake can be increased when physical demands increase; take, for example, the athlete who eats a huge spaghetti dinner or pancake breakfast before a competition. However, if your child's diet is too high in carbohydrates, he may experience extreme fluctuations in mood and energy, and may be prone to periods of anxiety. This is because carbohydrates quickly metabolize into the sugars (glucose) the body uses for energy. When the sugar burns off, a crash in energy, with accompanying malaise, distress, irritability, "spaciness," or moodiness, can occur. Conditions like hypoglycemia or diabetes are dependent on good management of carbohydrate intake. Starch alternatives such as brown rice pasta, quinoa, or gluten-free products may be easier to digest, easing the highs and lows.

Protein

Increasing the amount of high-protein foods in the diet has been found to stabilize and elevate mood, and increase energy. Remember to use lean sources of protein such as fish, turkey, and chicken, and avoid meats high in fat, sodium, nitrates, or other additives. Adding protein to a meal or snack heavy in carbohydrates slows the metabolization of glucose, and prevents a "crash." If your child has trouble staying asleep, this may be due to a carb crash signaling her body that she needs more calories. Try offering a small serving of protein (nuts or nut butters, meat, cheese, yogurt) before bed to see if this helps.

Vitamins and Nutritional Supplements

There is much controversy about the safety and efficacy of vitamins, herbs, enzymes, and nutritional supplements. The 1994 Dietary Supplement Health and Education Act (DSHEA) restricts the FDA's authority over supplements, provided that companies do not claim their products treat, prevent, or cure disease. As such, the FDA views nutritional supplements as foods that contain ingredients intended to supplement the diet. Most studies available use adult populations, and with rare exceptions (such as teen girls with low calcium intake, or those eating large amounts of fast food), many professionals, including the American Association of Pediatrics, warn against using supplements in children to make up for an uneven diet, as well as women who are pregnant or nursing, who should source their nutritional needs through food. However, individuals low in vitamins and minerals such calcium, magnesium, and vitamin B can show signs of anxiety. You can find accurate and useful information on supplements at the National Institutes of Health (*www.nih.gov*) and the National Center for Complementary and Alternative Medicine (*www.nccam.nih.gov*).

 Alert

It is extremely important that you check with your child's doctor or a qualified naturopathic or homeopathic physician before starting a supplementation program. The doctor will help you determine proper dosing for your child's age, and check on potential medication interactions, side effects, or other precautions.

Herbs

Herbal (or botanical) supplements are dietary supplements that are used for a medicinal purpose. They generally support a specific aspect of the body's health, such as the heart, bones, or digestive system. However, just because a product is labeled as "natural" does not mean that it is safe or without side effects. In fact, many herbal supplements can produce strong effects in the body, particularly if taken improperly or at high doses. People with anxiety should be especially careful when using herbal formulas. Remember also that the levels of standardization in dosing, labeling, and added ingredients are not regulated by the FDA in the same way that pharmaceutical products are, and can be dangerous to infants and children. Herbs that have been safely used with children include: St. John's Wort, hops, L-theanine, holy basil, passionflower, skullcap, valerian, and oat straw. Research also shows that kava, L-theanine, and holy basil can reduce anxiety. However, it is important for you do to some research before administering herbs, to check dosages, interactions, and possible side effects. Again, consulting with a medical professional can be a good idea before beginning an herbal course of treatment.

Vitamins

Vitamin supplements provide extra supplies of micronutrients the body needs for growth, digestion, and mood regulation. Different food sources contain different vitamins and minerals, and a wide and varied diet is the best way to make sure you and your child get enough of them. Supplements can be used in special conditions, under the care and advice of a qualified physician. Vitamins and minerals that are especially important in managing mood and anxiety include:

- **B vitamins:** Effective in helping maintain adequate serotonin levels, which improve mood and combat the effects of stress. These vitamins lessen the body's tendency to become overstimulated by adrenaline, such as might occur in panic attacks or prolonged states of anxiety associated with PTSD. A good B-complex supplement should contain the essential B vitamins, which are thiamin, riboflavin, niacin, vitamin B_6, vitamin B_{12}, and pantothenic acid. Generally, B vitamins are found in meat, fish, garlic, sunflower seeds, grains, legumes, liver, bananas, and some dairy products.
- **Vitamin D:** Supports normal levels of calcium and phosphorus; found in cod liver oil, fish (salmon), fortified dairy products, eggs, and sun exposure.
- **Vitamin C:** Antioxidant that supports the health and growth of connective tissue, nervous tissue, and mitochondria,

and is plentiful in citrus fruits and green veggies (e.g. Brussels sprouts). Over-the-counter products like powders and chewable tablets are convenient and kid-friendly.

Mineral Supplements

Mineral supplements provide micronutrients found extensively in bone and teeth. In addition, minerals help the body create new cells and enzymes, distribute fluids, control nerve impulses, and bring oxygen to cells while taking away carbon dioxide. One important mineral to help regulate anxiety is magnesium. Magnesium can relax nerves and muscles, and is a natural sleep-inducing element found in legumes, dark leafy vegetables, almonds, and whole grains.

 Fact

Check with your alternative health care provider or local health food store for powdered calcium/magnesium products, which can be mixed into tea or hot water at bedtime to aid sleep. These blends are easy to take and help relax muscles, soothe nerves, decreasing pain and creating deeper and more restful sleep. Be sure the one you choose is safe for children.

Essential Fatty Acids

Essential fatty acids (EFAs), sometimes referred to as omega-3s, are natural nutrients that improve communication between brain cells. Their importance in cardiovascular health has been clearly established, and there is good research supporting the use of EFAs/omega-3s to manage anxiety, depression, and bipolar disorder. EFAs are available in cold water fish such as salmon, tuna, trout, and others, as well as in avocado. Flaxseed oil contains alpha-linoleic acid, which converts to the EFAs found in fish oils. There are many health benefits to increasing fish in the diet, and flaxseed oil is easy to incorporate into the diet as well. The size of the capsules can be daunting for children, so you may have to add the oil to a food. Some products (especially flax) need refrigeration, and many people can't take fish oils without other food, due to stomach upset and "fish breath." If either occurs on a regular basis, consider changing your child's supplement or switching to flax.

Exercise and Yoga

Exercise, including yoga, alleviates mental stress, increases blood flow to the brain, improves mood, energy, and sleep, and can create an overall sense of well-being. It can provide distraction from emotional distress, help your child tune into her body, and enhance her sense of physical strength, endurance, mastery, and confidence.

Exercise Guidelines

The 2008 USDA and Department of Health and Human Services guidelines recommend that all children six years and older should get sixty minutes of moderate to vigorous exercise on most, if not all, days of the week. Exercise should include the components of endurance, strength, and flexibility, and should involve both structured and free play. Encourage regular exercise to help your anxious child optimize mood-boosting brain chemistry, and to "blow off steam." However, if your child has trouble sleeping, she should avoid exercise within two to four hours before bedtime because it can be overly stimulating.

Buddy System

Your child will be more likely to enjoy exercise and adopt it as a life habit if your family engages in physical activity together. Easy ways to accomplish this are to toss a ball in the backyard, shoot some hoops at a local park, bike, hike, walk, skate, swim, or ski. Gardening, yard work, and housework can also be good exercise, and provide opportunities to enhance your child's sense of belonging in the family by making her work efforts important.

It Needs to Be Fun

Nobody really likes exercise if it isn't fun. Help your child enjoy exercise by being positive about physical activity and modeling how much fun it can be. Be creative, dance, jump rope, make an obstacle course in the backyard, create your own ball game, or turn on some lively music for your child if he uses a treadmill or stationary bike at home. Create your own triathlon by walking or running, swimming, and biking, all in the same day. Find out what your child likes to do, and encourage him: If she likes to skateboard, or inline skate, make sure she has the proper safety equipment and help her hook up with some buddies. Take smaller children to the playground so that they can climb, slide, swing, run around, and just plain have fun.

Yoga

This is an ancient meditation practice with Eastern roots that involves quieting the mind and using various body postures to attain a greater sense of balance and control and create a sense of well-being. One of the best postures you can learn from yoga is the standing mountain pose. This pose teaches your child how to become centered and grounded into his body, which is important as children experiencing anxiety are often caught up in their thoughts. To do the pose, stand up tall with your two feet parallel on the floor and your arms by your side. If you are leaning forward into your knees gentle shift yourself between the ball of your feet and heels, roll your shoulders back and down and have your chin parallel to the earth. Engage your legs, soften your eyes so you feel like you are gazing at the sky and open your palms so you can receive your breath.

A second posture to encourage is child's pose. Have your child get down on the floor on all fours, knees down (like a table) and then move her hips back until they land on her heels, place her forehead on the floor or a pillow. Run your hand down her spine. As you do this imagine fluid moving freely up and down the spine clearing the mental toxins from the day.

A third posture is to have your child lie down on her back and place her legs up a wall. Have her be far enough from the wall to lie comfortably (several inches). With her arms down by her side, ask her to close her eyes (maybe put an eye pillow on her eyes) and feel her breathing rising and falling. On inhale her belly blows up like a balloon and on exhale it deflates toward her spine. Have her do this anywhere from three to ten minutes in a space that is relatively quiet. She could even listen to relaxing music on her iPod while doing this.

Many communities have yoga centers that offer classes for children and/or families. Check your local bookstore or library for children's yoga tapes, CDs, and DVDs.

These three basic yoga poses can help to alleviate anxiety. One or all three poses along with slow conscious breathing (two or three long inhales, followed by three long exhales) can make a huge difference when practiced daily.

Sleep Routine and Ritual

It is very common for children with anxiety to have trouble transitioning into sleep, sleeping independently, and falling and staying asleep. One of the purposes of sleep is to help your child recover from the stressors of the day. Children who are sensitive to anxiety are known to easily absorb the tension and the emotions of others from their surroundings. It will be important for your child to recognize, accept this about herself and create rituals that support her in letting go before attempting to go to sleep.

Letting Go of the Day

At the end of the day before bed or even when she gets home from school encourage her to create her own ritual for letting go. Many times children and adolescents associate completing the day with tasks (e.g. homework, chores) or activities such as practicing a sport. Most parents would agree the days are filled with physical, emotional, and mental demands. Having your child create a letting go ritual is a way to teach him how to let go of the demands and at times lingering thoughts and feelings of the day.

The most important part of a letting go ritual is the intention. An intention is a way to determine how you will act or what will take place in the moment. It is different than a goal in that a goal is future focused while an intention focuses on the present moment. For example, while performing the ritual of washing her hands your child might imagine all the toxins (negativity, stress, pressure) are being washed away. She could state a mantra to herself out loud or silently (while washing her hands), *I choose to keep all the positive energy and let go of all the negative* or *letting go of what I don't need and appreciating what I do comes easily.* Allow your child to be creative and incorporate it into something they might already do. For example, your child could go outside and shoot hoops. Each time he gets the basketball in the hoop he could imagine dunking the stressors of the day. Some children might like a Post-it on their mirror that simply states, *I am choosing to let this day go.* Keep in mind it is the intention of letting go that makes this a powerful ritual rather than getting the words right.

Winding Down

It is important to help your child find ways to ramp down his level of physical, mental, and emotional stimulation so that he can drop off to sleep easily and naturally. One hour or more before bedtime, you can help your child to wind down by having him finish homework and computer gaming time, lowering the volume on music, shutting down screen time, and dimming the lights. Avoiding TV, computers, or video games maximizes the production of sleep hormones. Reading and music can be good transition activities, but make sure that your child avoids watching or listening to anything aggressive.

Bedtime Snack

Another part of the bedtime ritual for many families includes a bedtime snack. For optimal sleep, your child's snack should include a bit of protein and carbohydrate, possibly including milk or other tryptophan-rich foods, which encourage melatonin production. An example of a good sleepytime snack might be a bit of cottage cheese or Greek yogurt and some canned, fresh, or dried apricots, or a slice of turkey on a piece of bread with a glass of milk, herbal or decaf tea. Avoid cocoa at bedtime; most contain too much sugar and caffeine, and may prevent your child from naturally drifting off to sleep.

Check In

You may wish to use snack time to check in with your child at the end of the day. That is, take a few minutes to review with your child how her day went. Try to focus on what went well for your child, and set up positive intentions for tomorrow. After your child has had a snack, you might want to incorporate positive visualization along with breathing and relaxation so that you can send your child off to sleep feeling relaxed and confident, rather than worried and overwhelmed. A gentle side stretch (arms overhead, stretching side to side) before bed can also help muscles to relax more easily into sleep.

Creature Comforts

Help your child let go of the day's anxieties by creating a calm and nurturing environment for sleep. Research indicates that people sleep better when a room is slightly cool (about 60–65°F; slightly warmer for babies) and when their bed is supportive, but comfortable. Smaller children do especially well with cozy blankets, and may feel more secure if their stuffed animals, or "lovies," are with them in the bed. Use nightlights in your child's room if he is afraid of the dark, and provide additional nightlights in the bathroom and near your room so that your child feels secure once everyone goes to bed.

Managing Insomnia

Insomnia is usually seen as a nighttime problem, involving trouble falling or staying asleep. However, insomnia causes daytime problems as well, such as tiredness, lack of energy, difficulty concentrating, and irritability. If your child is not sleeping well, she may feel out of step with the world around her. Prolonged sleeplessness can cause health troubles, depression, and can even increase the potential for accidents and injury. Interestingly, the experience of insomnia has as much to do with one's perception of not sleeping well as with the actual amount of sleep. It will be important for your child to recognize that she may have a belief that sleep is difficult for her. Use the Letting Go of the Day ritual described earlier in this chapter and have your child associate its effects with sleep.

Get Up Early

One of the simplest ways to reduce anxiety is to get up earlier. Moving up your "start time" will help your body to be more ready for "quitting time" when the day is done. Depending on your child's age, you can adjust the time he gets up by fifteen to thirty minutes each day, and see how he responds after a week or so. Remember to factor in the amount of sleep your child needs by his age when balancing bedtimes and rising times. An additional bonus of awakening earlier is that the extra time can be used for exercise or yoga, meditation, organization, and ensuring a good breakfast.

Increase Activity

Regular exercise boosts serotonin, making melatonin more available. It also tires and relaxes muscles, provides an outlet for stress, regulates blood sugar, and supports other bodily processes important to sleep. It is best to avoid exercise for several hours before bedtime, and some experts feel that morning activity boosts mood the best. If your child has insomnia, make sure she has some time to be active each day.

 Alert

Melatonin, a readily available herbal supplement for sleep, may have applications for older children with insomnia (for example, in adolescents receiving steroids for chemotherapy). Even though melatonin is a naturally occurring hormone, it must be used with caution, and with a recommendation from your child's doctor.

The Bed Is for Sleeping

Most sleep specialists agree that it is best to reserve the bed (and even the bedroom, if possible) for sleeping. If your child uses her bed for reading, studying, drawing, or play, the sheer power of behavioral patterning may make it more difficult for her to turn her mind off and fall asleep easily. Make sure your child's bed is comfortable (try lying on it yourself) and that she has cozy blankets, pillows, and other comfort items that create a nighttime oasis. Most of all, make bedrooms free from screens including phones, computers, and television sets.

Stories and Music

Many kids find the distraction of music, books, or stories on tape an invaluable tool in falling asleep. The external focus gives busy minds something other than worry to attach to, and, if the themes or images in the audio promote serenity and relaxation, the body will respond to these cues. Guided imagery for sleep can also be very helpful, but make sure you choose a program your child will use only for sleep, and have another for general relaxation. Make sure the volume is at a comfortable level. Some children find they can go back to sleep on their own if they awaken during the night simply by turning their audio selection back on.

Fact

In the Ayurvedic (Indian) system honey promotes sleep, and may be a natural and palatable cure for insomnia. The general ratio is one teaspoon to one cup of water, or you can add the honey to warm milk or a calming tea to enhance its effect. Remember, never give honey to children under the age of two due to the risk of botulism.

White Noise

Adding ambient sound such as a fan, fountain, or white noise machine can help your child turn down the volume on anxious thoughts and create an external reference point which helps him to drop off to sleep. There are inexpensive sound machines available at many drug or department stores that can be set to any number of natural or created sounds. MP3s or CDs with ocean waves, crickets, or running water can also be helpful. If you are working on decreasing bedwetting, you may want to avoid water sounds, which might subconsciously affect your child's urge to urinate.

CHAPTER 13

The Case for Natural Healing: Alternative Therapies

This chapter covers therapies that have been around for centuries, in some cases thousands of years, passed on through a teacher-student lineage as ways to restore and renew the body's internal systems. These systems include your nervous system, respiratory system, immune functioning, endocrine system, and more. They can be used on their own or in conjunction with traditional medicine. An added bonus for some of these therapies is that through their experiences, children begin to value and learn about their own body's abilities. Taking your child to a professional who specializes in these therapies supports you as a parent, as you no longer have to be the only one educating and reinforcing these approaches.

Massage

The ancient art of massage as a healing agent has come a long way. Its humble beginning of artistic hand strokes on the body to restore the soul, rejuvenate the body, and decrease stress has now become a nationally certified health care option. Traditional health care systems are recognizing the therapeutic effects of massage in the healing process. Employers, doctors, chiropractors, even hospitals recommend and offer massage for wellness as a viable and beneficial therapy.

The type of touch used on a baby or child does differ from that used on an adult. The massage will be more gentle and tender, and the length is determined by your child's age and sensitivity to stimulation. When choosing a massage therapist it is very important to make sure the practitioner is certified and has expertise working with children.

It is also important to avoid sensitive or injured areas, to refrain from massaging a child who is ill or has a fever, and to avoid the stomach area for at least twenty minutes after your child eats. Keep in mind massage can be done in a chair or strictly on your child's hands and feet. It is good practice to always ask your child permission before placing your hands on her.

Benefits

Massage has been found to decrease anxiety and slow down the heart rate. It can also increase attachment and bonding in the parent-child relationship when it is the parent who is giving the massage. Because massage can help children feel a sense of letting go, warmth, and care, your child's experience with massage may help her be more open to therapy. It may increase her ability to discuss issues related to why she feels anxious and increase the ability to trust in the helping profession. Physical advantages of massage include lowered blood pressure, slowed breathing rate, increased sense of comfort, improved circulation, and enhanced digestive functioning.

 Fact

It is believed that touch reduces anxiety because it promotes the growth of myelin. Myelin is the insulating material around nerves that makes nerve impulses travel faster, causing babies to be less fussy, and feel calmer.

What the Research Shows

In separate studies at the Touch Research Institute at the University of Miami School of Medicine, adolescents who received two chair massages over a month's time had decreased aggression, and those with ADHD had reduced anxiety levels, improved behavior, and rated themselves as happier. Massage therapy reduced anxiety and depression in children who were diagnosed with post-traumatic stress disorder after Hurricane Andrew in 1992. Infants whose parents gave them a massage before they went to bed slept better throughout the night and fell asleep more peaceably. Because massage stimulates all of an infant's or child's body, studies show it stabilizes heart rate and respiration, and increases the ability to cope with stress. Researchers also found that the level of cortisol, a stress-related hormone, decreased after a massage. Other research has shown that massage releases oxytocin in both the giver and receiver. The release of this hormone creates a "warm, fuzzy" feeling and may in part explain why bonding is strengthened during massage.

 Alert

According to AskDrSears.com, a study was done with premature infants in a "grower nursery." A grower nursery is a specialized hospital setting designed to help babies gain weight. This study showed that premature babies who were massaged had 47 percent more weight gain than those who did not receive extra touch.

Chinese Pediatric Massage

This type of massage is also call pediatric Tui Na. It is said to influence a child's energy flow, much like acupuncture. The difference is that Tui Na uses gentle massage to activate energy meridians or blockages instead of needles. Treatment can start at birth, and is quick and effective until age six. After age six, regular acupressure can be used. In most cases treatment only takes one to two sessions for symptoms to abate.

How to Find a Massage Therapist

To find a massage therapist, check out websites such as the American Massage Therapy Association (AMTA) at *www.amta.massage.org*, or The International Association of Infant Massage (IAIM) at *www.iaim.net*, which is a nonprofit national directory of certified infant massage instructors. They can help you find a massage therapist in your area, help you make decisions about what to look for in a massage therapist, and connect you with journals and research. Local breastfeeding centers may offer infant massage, and if you have a massage therapy training school in your area you may be able to receive chair massage for half the price. A few questions IAIM suggests you ask when looking for a massage therapist are if the therapist is certified or licensed, how much training she has done with children, and what the treatment method will be.

Acupuncture

This ancient system of healing was developed over 3,000 years ago in China, and over the years has become recognized as an effective healing agent by Western health professionals. Today, acupuncture involves the use of fine needles placed in carefully chosen points, or meridians, once the practitioner has identified the disharmony within a person's body and mind. Most people associate needles with the pain of injections or having blood drawn. The needles used in acupuncture have no resemblance to those needles, however; they are much finer, solid instead of hollow, and tiny. Treatment can be one or two sessions or take a few months, depending on the target condition. As with all treatment options discussed, make sure you or your child are treated by a licensed acupuncturist (LAc).

Benefits

The Chinese believe that there is an energy flow called "qi" (pronounced *chee*) running throughout the body, and that acupuncture restores the balance of this energy flow, therefore eliminating symptoms of a disorder. With children and teenagers, acupuncture seems to be helpful in reducing anxiety, attention deficit disorder, addictions such as smoking, alcohol, food, or drugs, arthritis, asthma, circulatory problems, depression, general aches and pains, menstrual problems, sciatica, and skin conditions.

How Pediatric Acupuncture Works

This form of treatment can be a safe and noninvasive option as compared to the possible side effects of medication for anxiety. Typically your child can sit in your lap during treatment, which enables you to be a part of the healing process, and helps your child feel safe and supported. It is important that you ensure the individual administering treatment has a license and comes recommended.

 Essential

Traditional Chinese medicine includes herbs, and many acupuncturists may include herbs as a part of your child's treatment. Although the needling techniques have resulted in very few negative side effects, some herbs have been connected to more serious and frequent side effects.

Shonishin

Shonishin originated in Japan in the seventeenth century. It is literally translated as "children's acupuncture" or "acupuncture for children." It differs from standard acupuncture because the practitioner does not pierce the skin, but instead uses an assortment of metal implements to gently stimulate the meridians and acupuncture points to move qi. This form of acupuncture, as with the standard kind, moves energy to unblock and strengthen the qi where it is weak, restoring balance in the child's body and a sense of calm. It is most useful for children from infancy through age five, although older children up to age twelve can benefit from this technique.

Aromatherapy

The use of essential oils and aromatic plants to affect mood or health dates back thousands of years to cultures including China, India, and Egypt and in fact receives several mentions in the Bible. The use of incense in Catholic and other religious services, while often primarily for other purposes, is also an example of aromatherapeutic effect.

 Fact

While not aromatherapy, the Bach flower essences are another form of vibrational healing. By the time Dr. Edward Bach died in 1936, he had developed thirty-eight wildflower remedies. He created most of these remedies by testing them on himself first.

Two men are primarily responsible for bringing the use of flower and oil essences into the twentieth century. French chemist René-Maurice Gattefossé, who coined the term "aromatherapy" in the 1920s, was convinced that essential oils had antiseptic properties and began working with them in his laboratory. Edward Bach, who was a medical doctor and homeopathic physician in London, left a lucrative practice and went on to develop the Bach flower remedies.

How Aromatherapy Works

Essential oils can enhance the mood, alleviate fatigue, reduce anxiety, and promote relaxation. It is believed that when inhaled, the essence works on the brain and nervous system through stimulation of the olfactory nerves. Basically, when a child breathes in the scent of an essential oil, electrochemical messages are sent to the emotion center of the brain, the limbic system. The limbic system then triggers memory and emotional responses, which send messages to the brain and body. If the oil smelled is a calming one, (e.g. lavender, vanilla) aromatherapy can trigger the parasympathetic nervous system, which is responsible for relaxation.

 Fact

Peppermint oil is useful for nausea and upset stomachs. To use, place two or three drops on a tissue, hankie, or natural cotton ball, or under the pillow (be sure not to put it right under their nose as it might be too strong; you can hold it about 6 inches away). Avoid getting the oil on the skin.

Because children's skin and systems are delicate and sensitive, you must be very careful when using essential oils with them. It is also important to research the company ahead of time to make sure the oil is organic and does not have added chemicals. Although some practitioners agree that essential oils are not recommended for use on children at all, some believe that children over the age of six can use a short list of oil blends that are one-third to one-half as potent as what is recommended for adults.

Lavender, chamomile, and mandarin are generally considered safe for children. Chamomile and lavender both calm anxiety. Chamomile has the added bonus of soothing digestion and is great with babies who struggle with colic. Lavender has a dual effect: it not only helps alleviate anxiety, it also lifts the spirits and is great for easing insomnia. In addition, lavender is known to have antiseptic properties and may help with headaches.

You can also massage your child with commercially prepared lotions, or use diluted oils in her bath. Be careful to use only essential oils; synthetic blends can cause allergic reactions and are unlikely to provide the same benefits as the original source. Also, be sure to carefully research the recommended percentage dilution of essential oils in carrier oil.

 Question

How do you use aromatherapy with children?
One of the best ways to bring aromatherapy into your home is through a diffuser. That allows the smell to diffuse slowly into the air. The company Young Living is a great resource for purchasing essential oils as well as the tools for using them (e.g. diffusers). You can also visit the website *www.sheriannaboyle.com* to purchase NYR oils, which are highly regulated essential oils.

Cautions for Children

You should also be aware that many "carrier oils" with which the essential oil is blended for dilution are nut-based, such as almond, macadamia, or hazelnut. So be aware that if your child has a nut allergy, these should absolutely be avoided. Many parents do not know that even baby oil contains almond oil. Nut-free oil alternatives commonly used include olive, sunflower, grapeseed, and avocado. It is best not to use aromatherapy on babies. Always consult with an expert, and never try to blend a potion on your own.

Biofeedback

Biofeedback evolved out of laboratory research in the 1940s to become one of the earliest known behavioral medicine treatments. The word *biofeedback* comes from *bio*, which means life, and *feedback*, which means "returning to the source." Years later biofeedback is commonly practiced by physicians, nurses, psychologists, physical therapists, dentists, and other professionals in private and hospital settings to treat adults and children with anxiety, and to address chronic physical conditions like pain.

How Biofeedback Works

Biofeedback is a painless, noninvasive technique that monitors the body's functions such as muscle tension, blood pressure, or heart rate, and "feeds back" the information to the patient. During a biofeedback session, your child will sit in front of a computer monitor with sensors on his skin that will measure one or more of the bodily functions listed here. This will happen as he looks at animated games, cartoons, or stories, or listens to tones or melodies. The images and sounds on the screen change as your child learns to change his physical state and the associated feelings. As he becomes more relaxed, opening up a channel of communication between himself and his body, he learns to regulate his anxiety and stress. The doctor or therapist will monitor the results on a separate screen, and give you and your child feedback on how he is progressing. Biofeedback can be an excellent self-help discipline, with each session lasting between thirty to sixty minutes.

 Fact

Deepak Chopra, MD, and Dean Ornish, MD, created a software program called *The Journey to Wild Divine*, a biofeedback "game." Children can use this game at home to help learn about deep breathing and guided imagery in order to reduce anxiety.

EEG Biofeedback

EEG biofeedback, also referred to as neurobiofeedback, uses an electroencephalograph (EEG). This is a device that detects, monitors, and records the electrical activity in the brain, called brainwaves. Through the biofeedback machine, your child will learn how to increase or decrease brainwave levels. In general, the focus is on slowing brain waves to foster greater focus and calm attention. The most typical application for this technique is in treating ADHD, and it has also been found useful in treating anxiety and addiction.

What Biofeedback Can Help

Biofeedback treatments can help a variety of medical concerns in children such as headaches, panic disorder, asthma, abdominal pain, sleep disorder, ADHD, stress, and addictions. As you can see, many of the conditions for which biofeedback is helpful also have anxiety as a component.

Biofeedback has two lines of benefit; on one hand, it can help your child become calmer and alleviate anxiety, chronic pain, insomnia, or muscle spasms. On the other hand, it can help your child become more alert, focused, and energetic, improving attention, concentration, schoolwork, or athletic performance. Biofeedback can enhance creativity as well as mental flexibility and emotional resilience.

 Alert

Providers, even if they have advanced degrees such as MD, PhD, or RN, must still undertake additional training to use biofeedback. Providers are not required to be licensed to administer biofeedback, although there are certification programs available. That means you will want to specifically ask about training and experience, and about whether the type of biofeedback your child is receiving will be effective.

Energy Work

Many people, when hearing the words "energy work," will immediately feel put off as if they are delving into something mystical, or on the edge of reason. What they do not realize is that they already use energy therapy every day. Think about it—your child can't sleep, so you go into her room, sit down next to her, and gently talk to her, rubbing her back—that's energy therapy. Or your child falls off his bike and you go to him, hold him in your arms, kiss his hurt knee, and hug him until the tears are gone—that's energy therapy, too. In each of those instances, you have passed your calm, loving energy to your child. That is also why you are the first person your child wants when he is hurt, you are the one he gives the harshest attitudes to, and you are the one he calls when he is scared. Your energy is what your children are seeking. It is unconditional, safe, and gives them comfort and strength.

 Fact

In the early 1800s, Phineas Quimby was considered the intellectual father of New Thought, a philosophy and spiritual movement based on metaphysical beliefs. He posited a link between the body and mind's natural, internal powers and the ability to heal oneself. Since then many have used his basic tenets to form their own types of energy healing.

What Is It and How Can It Help?

Energy therapy is a healing process that creates environments, philosophies, and therapies to support children who hurt inside. Much like acupuncture, it is done by correcting the imbalances in their internal energy. Most of the techniques are easy to learn and can be self-administered. Some examples of practices involving the use of energy to heal include the following:

- **Reiki and Johrei** are Japanese techniques for stress reduction and relaxation that many believe can promote healing. These are based on the idea that an unseen "life force energy" flows through all people and if it is low, then you are more susceptible to feeling anxious or getting sick, and if it is high, you can attain a sense of well-being.

- **Qigong** is based on the Chinese principle of "qi" energy. It is believed that different breathing patterns, when accompanied by certain motions and postures of the body, can enhance and create a sense of balance and calm, and release emotional and physical blocks. A tremendous amount of positive research is being released about the practice of Qigong and how it is being used in cancer therapy.
- **Healing touch** occurs when a therapist identifies imbalances in your child's body and then corrects the energy. To accomplish this, the practitioner passes his hands over your child, without actually touching her.
- **Prayer.** Praying for the healing of another or praying for love and support has proven to have many benefits to both the person stating the prayer as well as the receiver of it.
- **EFT (energy field therapy) or TFT (through field therapy)** occurs when certain meridians on the body are touched to release an emotional or physical problem. EFT and TFT can be done anywhere, can be self-administered, are portable and efficient ways to calm the mind, and give a person a greater sense of control over anxious or distressing feelings.

Energy healing is a process that requires you to look beyond a symptom of illness, like the fact that your child is afraid to leave your side after a trauma, and instead look into your child's inner being to quiet her mind. The intent is to release the fear that created a blockage so your child can feel free again.

Blocks in energy are viewed as an attempt by the body and spirit to protect itself. Essentially, once your child stores the trauma or fear, she internalizes it, takes on the negative energy associated with it, and establishes a "new normal" so she can go on with life. Energy therapy can be used alone, or as a complement to any traditional or holistic treatment methods. Many believe it can reduce stress and anxiety, increase energy, improve physical health and wellness, and help your child feel more content.

 Question

My child was bullied at school. We have talked to him many times since the incident. He cried, we came up with a game plan for future incidences, and he seems happy again—isn't that enough?

No, because he has not released the trauma internally. It is believed that energy blocks can remain with you for years or a lifetime if they are not treated. In this belief system your child can become susceptible to disease, emotional or mental disorders, and spiritual disconnection because he is internalizing his fear.

CHAPTER 14

If It's Not Anxiety, Then What?

B ecause anxiety can be subtle and pervasive, it can either mimic or overlap with other disabilities. It can also be brought upon by normal childhood characteristics, changes, and transitions. In this chapter, learn how anxiety moves through development and in some cases overlaps with pre-existing conditions such as Attention Deficit Hyperactivity Disorder. The most common conditions that anxiety is a symptom of, or can be confused with, are reviewed. It is not uncommon for other conditions such as learning disabilities to become less pronounced and therefore less of a struggle when strategies for relieving stress and anxiety are applied.

Overlap with ADHD

Attention deficit disorder (ADD) is a neurobiological condition that interferes with a child's ability to focus attention, stay organized, resist impulses, and follow through on tasks. Author of *Healing ADD* and physician, Dr. Daniel G. Amen identifies seven types of ADD, one of which he calls *Anxious ADD*. In his book *Healing ADD* he describes Anxious ADD as "inattentive, easily distracted, disorganized, anxious, tense, nervous, predicts the worst, gets anxious with timed tasks, social anxiety and often has physical stress symptoms such as headaches and gastrointestinal symptoms." His book provides solid research with SPECT imaging (brain imaging) evidence that supports a range of treatments including: visualization, hypnosis, supplements, and utilizing affirmations.

A child with ADHD may feel an internal sense that the world is moving too fast, and he may have trouble paying attention because his mind is wrapped up in his multiple thoughts and worries. Children with anxiety can also suffer from thoughts and worries that seem unstoppable, and they may appear inattentive as a result. Similarly, children with ADHD may experience depression or anxiety because it is so difficult for them to meet the demands of their world.

 Alert

Because ADHD can seriously affect your child's ability to learn, socialize, and develop the confidence, organization, and self-management skills he will need in adulthood, it is especially important to address this factor. The LifeSkills Program at *www.chaange.com* mentioned earlier as well as self-awareness practices (meditation, exercise, and guided imagery) can improve emotional and social functioning as they train your child to be more aware of himself and the world around him.

Academic Concerns

Most children with ADHD show signs of their distractibility and/or impulsivity in the school setting. They may be unable to stay at their desks, focus on the teacher, or work for more than a few minutes without needing redirection. This applies to doing homework as well. It is typical for students with ADHD to have trouble managing assignments, and completing and turning in homework. You or someone close to your child may see this as laziness or underachievement, but it is not. Children with ADHD have physiological differences that prevent them from focusing. The overall effect is often reflected in poor grades or failure to progress in subjects. Children with anxiety often show restlessness and inattention as well, and may have trouble with homework if they feel overwhelmed.

Your child's teacher can usually tell you whether she suspects that ADHD, rather than anxiety, is at the root of your child's trouble with schoolwork, or is an issue in the classroom. Keep in mind that ADD, because it lacks the behavioral component of hyperactivity, can be difficult to detect and may be more likely to mimic anxiety.

 Essential

ADHD children benefit greatly from energy medicine, which is explained in Chapter 13. By having them rub their hands together to create friction and placing the palm of the hand on their forehead they can create a pulsation of blood flow in their forebrain. When done regularly, this technique teaches children and adolescents how to self-soothe while simultaneously increasing their ability to learn and remember.

Behavior Concerns

Children with ADHD or anxiety may have behavioral concerns at home or school because of high levels of frustration. Typically, children with both disorders have more trouble transitioning between activities. For a child with ADHD, it might be because it is so difficult for him to organize and sequence his thoughts and actions. Many times finding a tutor, ADD coach, or teacher that can teach basic organization skills can make a world of difference. For a child with anxiety, it is due to fear, anticipation of failure, or feelings of being out of control. What you will see behaviorally is tantrums or meltdowns.

Social Problems

Children with ADHD can have trouble making and keeping friends because of their impulsivity, which others see as odd or immature. Children with anxiety can also have unusual habits or ways of relating to others that can seem puzzling or unacceptable to their peers, as shared previously. For children who struggle with either, the rejection they feel can cause low self-esteem or depression, which leads to a sense of isolation and hopelessness about the future.

 Essential

> If your child's anxiety has obsessive qualities, he might spend hours writing one paper and not be able to complete any other work. This can look like laziness, procrastination, or ADD-style disorganization to you. However, it is important to realize that, in this instance, your child's anxiety is driven by a need for perfection and the fear that whatever he does is never good enough and must be redone. Teach your child the value of making mistakes. Thomas Edison made 9,000 attempts when he invented the light bulb. When he was later interviewed by a young reporter, he stated, "I now know 9,000 ways a light bulb does not work."

Temperament

Temperament consists of your child's inborn characteristics such as: shy, active, slow to adapt, adapt easily, sensitive to stimulation, etc. Most children have several traits that represent their temperament not just one. It is important to note that these characteristics have been with your child since birth and most often can only be reported by a parent or caregiver. Children with sensitivity to their environment (e.g. stimulation, sounds, texture), slow to adjust, or who tire easily may be more susceptible to symptoms of anxiety. The earlier you recognize and accept your child's temperament style for what it is the easier it will be to provide your child with tools that support their growth. It is the parents who want their child to change that may find themselves challenged by the symptoms. Temperament is not a life sentence, meaning that with compassion and tools such as the ones in this book your child can and will learn how to work with their traits in a way that serves them well.

Overlap with Depression

Depression is a mood disorder that can cause your child to feel tired, sad, lonely, bored, hopeless, or unmotivated for an extended period of time. In order for a clinical diagnosis in children, a depressive episode must last longer than two weeks and must interfere with daily functioning and/or be a change that is observable by others. Some researchers view anxiety and depression as two sides of the same coin. This is in part because both conditions involve disruption to the same neurotransmitters in the brain. In addition, symptoms of depression and anxiety overlap and may imitate each other. For example, many people with anxiety experience periods of depressed mood or other depressive symptoms such as guilt and feelings of worthlessness. Conversely, those with depression can experience states of agitation and worry that are very similar to the symptoms of anxiety.

The Irritability Factor

Because children and adolescents aren't always capable of identifying and communicating their feelings and internal experiences to others, they are more likely than adults to show irritability when they are depressed. Irritable children and teens can be very difficult to be around as they never seem content, and may be negative or argumentative. Irritability is often contagious, and may snowball into conflict if it is persistent or extreme.

Feelings of Guilt

Persistent feelings of worthlessness or excessive and unwarranted guilt can be very intense in both children and adults who are depressed. Guilt is also a strong component of anxiety, particularly if a child is old enough to feel she does not measure up to the expectations of peers, parents, and teachers. To help your child through these darker heavier emotions it will be important for you to model and teach them how to feel their emotions (Chapter 6). Children and adolescents tend to focus on their primary feelings (sad, mad, and happy). Help them to explore the range and variety of their emotions by getting them outside, connecting to nature, and disengaging from the busyness of life. Teach them to notice how grief sits heavy on the shoulders, and guilt is expressed through dropping our heads. By noticing their body's response, they are experiencing the physical manifestation and feeling of the emotion.

 Fact

Dysthymia is a sub-type of depression, which is experienced much like a "low-grade fever." That is, it can linger on and cause a person to feel just a bit ill at ease or raw around the edges. Some theorists say that dysthymia may even occur because a person's senses and emotions are overly sensitive and prone to overload.

Physical Considerations

When depression and anxiety are more serious, they can affect your child's ability to sleep and eat regularly. Children suffering from depression can experience loss of appetite, marked weight loss, or failure to make expected weight gains, while children with anxiety may also have trouble with their appetite and weight loss. Insomnia involving both the ability to fall and stay asleep can occur in both anxiety and depression, as can a diminished ability to think clearly, concentrate, and make decisions. Children with anxiety are more likely to show agitation, while depressed children are more likely to experience fatigue and lethargy.

Substance Abuse

People with depression and anxiety are at risk for developing alcohol or drug abuse. The use of chemicals to alleviate emotional distress is referred to as "self-medication." Teens with anxiety may be especially vulnerable, particularly if they use alcohol or drugs as a "social lubricant." Talk frankly with your children about your values and expectations regarding chemical use, and be alert for sudden changes in sleep, eating, energy level, and choice of friends, as these can all be indicators of chemical abuse.

Adjustment Disorders

It is common for children to experience changes in behavior and emotional upheaval when the world around them changes suddenly, as in a divorce or change of schools. In a child with anxiety, these challenges can be especially difficult because both her inner and outer world feel out of control at the same time. Both children and adults can experience adjustment disorders, and they are among the most commonly diagnosed mental health issues. In an adjustment disorder, there is a specifically identifiable stressor, which must have occurred no more than three months before the onset of emotional or behavioral symptoms. Adjustment disorders are generally short-lived, resolving in about six months after the original stress occurred. An adjustment disorder can involve depression, anxiety, or both. Behavioral disturbances can be common, especially in children who are more likely to "show" their feelings through their behaviors. Common events that might cause a child to experience an adjustment disorder are outlined next. If you are concerned that your child is having more trouble adjusting to change than she should, use the tips provided to help her cope, so that her anxiety does not become problematic.

Moves

Moving to a new home is stressful for all families, and can be especially troubling if a child has to leave good friends or change schools. These transitions can be especially difficult in the middle-school years, when kids are working so hard to define who they will be and choosing a solid base of peers. For children with underlying anxiety, a move can be highly traumatic. If your child has anxiety, do your best to give him all the information you can and familiarize him with the new neighborhood. If the move is not long distance, maybe you can take a walk through the new neighborhood, especially when a school bus is picking up or dropping off other children, or drive around and visit a nearby park and restaurants. After the move, be sure to take the time to go back and visit old friends. Above all, let your child know that moving is not easy and listen to his fears. Validate the losses he will experience, and find ways he can be included in the familial team to make it a success.

Illness or Death in the Family

Both sudden and chronic illnesses are highly stressful for families, and of course, the loss of a loved one is among the most stressful events a person can experience. When family life becomes upset or unbalanced, this can be very destabilizing for a child with anxiety. Children who spend excessive amounts of time away from their parents, because of lengthy hospitalizations for either themselves or a family member, can develop symptoms of anxiety and have more difficulty with developmental transitions.

Illness and death are mysterious and scary, especially for younger children. Experts say that it is best to give your child whatever information is available, but in a form that fits his level of development. There are many great books and other resources that can help younger children grasp serious life events at a level they can understand. Medical providers, places of worship, friends, and family are also great resources and support, and can buffer both you and your child from the anxiety inherent in managing illness and death.

Birth of a Sibling

Though the birth of a sibling is a new beginning for all families, it can be an especially difficult time for older children, particularly if they are already anxious. They now have to share Mom and Dad's attention, and they can sometimes feel alone and isolated when the rest of the world pays too much attention to the new baby. Children with anxiety may show increased trouble with separation, or regress (lose skills) in managing their emotions and behavior. Helpful tips include making sure you continue to spend one-on-one time with your child, and include him as much as you can in the new daily routines you are establishing. Consider giving your older child a special mother or father's helper job that includes him in the daily tasks. Avoid making older children responsible for the care of their younger siblings on a regular basis, as this can cause resentment and tension between the siblings.

 Fact

Research has also shown that because higher expectations are placed on the oldest child in a family, first-borns experience more guilt, anxiety, and difficulty in coping with stressful situations.

Blended Families

Divorce, separation, and remarriage are events that naturally create a wealth of feelings for children, including anxiety. Sometimes even positive changes, such as a parent marrying a person the child really likes, can cause stress. General fears of the unknown, or uncertainty of where a child "fits" in the new family, are often undercurrents in children with anxiety. Blended families need time to adjust; be patient and remember to give your children special attention. Blended families who respect each other's backgrounds and outside family members, meaning they avoid negative, reactive comments or gossip, tend to adjust best. There are multiple resources on the Internet, at bookstores, through places of worship, or through community education to assist blended families.

Other Points to Consider

The following are additional concerns that can relate to children with anxiety that deserve mention, either because they have anxiety as a central component or because they can produce anxiety in children. Understand that the more you know, the better—it will help you realize the path you need to take with your particular child.

PANDAS

PANDAS is an abbreviation for pediatric autoimmune neuro-psychiatric disorders associated with streptococcal infections. Though rare, this term is used to describe children who develop obsessive-compulsive disorder (OCD) and/or tic disorders such as Tourette syndrome. These symptoms worsen following strep infections such as strep throat and scarlet fever, and often have a dramatic or "overnight" presentation. Moodiness and separation anxiety are also common in PANDAS.

Oppositional Defiant Disorder

ODD stands for oppositional defiant disorder. A child with ODD resists or refuses the demands of authority figures, and is generally negative, hostile, and defiant. Children with ODD can be argumentative, prone to losing their tempers, blaming, resentful, and spiteful or vindictive. In addition, children with ODD sometimes deliberately annoy others and can be touchy and easily annoyed themselves. Though it is clear that the general presentation of ODD is an angry one, anxiety sometimes lurks below the surface. Children with ODD can also suffer from depression or other mood issues, which should be thoroughly evaluated as a possible cause of acting-out behavior. For example, children with anxiety may refuse to go to school, which can look like defiant behavior when in fact it is fearful behavior.

Differently Abled

Children with physical disabilities or disabling medical conditions (severe allergies or asthma, diabetes, and so on) are prone to anxiety because the demands of the physical body both tax and are overtaxed by the emotional system. Additionally, some of the medicines used to treat chronic conditions can produce the side effects of anxiety or depression.

Social rejection can be common, and socializing can be difficult given your child's specific needs. Group therapy or church groups that emphasize cooperation and respect can often be a way for kids who feel different to feel sense of belonging and support, which helps them reduce anxiety or depression related to their condition. Also, some children do better socializing one on one, slowly working up to small group settings. Check with your child's physician to see if he knows of groups or organizations that might be helpful to you and your child.

Is My Child Gifted?

Giftedness, like creativity, is complex and troublesome to measure because it is multidimensional, affecting many areas in your child's life. Generally, if your child is gifted, he may show many of the signs of active-alert children. He may complain of being bored or get in trouble for being restless at school. He may refuse to do "busywork" that requires little creative effort. He may sleep little, and read, draw, or want an opportunity to be more creative while doing projects or homework. Gifted children can sometimes be anxious or perfectionistic as well, and may show a low frustration tolerance when their abilities do not always match what their minds create. There are many resources for gifted children at school and in the community. At home, try to provide opportunities for both focused work and unstructured time, and remember to help your child put on the brakes if she seems to be overly focused, overly stimulated, or overly perfectionistic.

Developmental Transitions

Your child is consistently learning, growing, and changing. This is hard work, and sometimes children can become snagged at particular stages in their development. The following sections detail some especially difficult times for children. Look back to the section on adjustment disorders for reference if you feel your child has more trouble in a particular area than most children her age. If your child does not seem to adjust well after four weeks, you may need to focus on strategies geared toward decreasing anxiety.

Day Care

Going to a new day care, especially if it also involves a new home or school, can cause anxiety in even the most well-adjusted children. Certainly, dropping a child off at day care for the first time can be one of a parent's most difficult days. To ease transition, try to check in with your child each day after you pick her up, and send some small comfort items, depending on your child's age. Examples might be a picture of you and your child together, pocket-sized toy, stuffed animal, or blanket. Be sure to keep in regular contact with your day care provider to track your child's adjustment and discuss any concerns either of you may have. Generally, if your child appears happy when you pick her up at the end of the day and is excited to return the next, you can be assured that she is doing well in the new setting. If your child continues to appear anxious, continue to make note and observe your child's behavior. Trust your gut and speak to your child's pediatrician if your concerns continue. Also pay attention your own levels of anxiety; if you are anxious dropping your child off, they will pick up on that. Stay calm, focused, and reassuring.

Preschool

Preschool can be nerve-racking and exciting for children and parents alike. If your child has not been in day care, it may be among the first times you and your child are apart for more than a few hours. It can be unsettling to leave your child with strangers, even when you have chosen your child's preschool with confidence. To minimize your child's anxiety, expose your child to the school ahead of time and consider a playdate or two with some children who will be in the class beforehand. Keep routines both before and after preschool consistent. This includes bedtime, meals, and pickup and drop off time. It helps if you drop off and pick up your child a few minutes early so your child does not have to feel rushed or nervous during these transitions. Be an active listener during times when you ask about your child's day. Children need to feel heard by you through your undivided attention. Get on your child's level so you can establish eye contact and communicate reassurance through your smile and gaze.

 Essential

Transitional objects are meaningful personal items that represent a parent or caregiver for a child when the caregiver is absent. A classic example is the teddy bear, toy, or blanket a child takes to bed with her each night. For a child with anxiety, it can be important to use transitional objects when she is away from home, such as at Grandma and Grandpa's or summer camp.

Kindergarten

The transition to kindergarten can be full of anticipation and nervousness for both you and your child. The "official" school experience represents more time away from home, larger groups of kids, busing, and more adults to tell them where to be and what to do. Children with separation anxiety can be especially vulnerable at this time. Try to keep your routine the same at home, and talk to your child regularly to support and encourage her. It may be helpful to check in with your child's teacher or offer to help in the classroom if your child is struggling with separation. When you do part from your child, it is best to keep goodbyes short and sweet. Consider a goodbye ritual, such as the way you kiss, hug or give a high five. The book *The Kissing Hand* by Audrey Penn is a wonderful book to read to children who are looking for ways to stay connected when they are not with you.

Middle School Transition

Many children transition to larger schools with other unfamiliar children during middle school, and the demands for responsibility and self-motivation increase academically. The results are often frustrating, painful, emotional, and even comical at times. It is utterly important, however, not to minimize your child's interests in and struggles with friends, choice of leisure pursuits, dress, or music. Many anxious children at this age benefit from a mentor, older sibling, or therapist with whom they can entrust their trials and tribulations. Keep connected through mini talks, inquiring about your child's interests, hugs, smiles, and through active listening or sitting in receptive silence. Your adolescent's physical changes create some biological anxiety. Hormonal shifts coupled with huge growth spurts create a need for a healthy diet, exercise, and lots of rest. It is normal for your adolescent to move away from things she was previously interested in. Try not to take your adolescent's behaviors personally. Take breaks to restore and replenish your patience.

High School

As your child moves into the high school years it will be important for you to pay attention to the times your adolescent appears resistant, critical, lazy, or unmotivated. Sometimes these are subtle signs of an underlining anxiety signaling that your child may be feeling the enormity of the pressures and responsibilities on his plate. It is during these times your child needs to feel as if you are there for him through thick and thin. It is not that you won't expect your child to complete his responsibilities; rather, you will respond to your child differently. For example, instead of assuming he is lazy, treat him as if he is temporarily off balance. Consider connecting through open communication such as, "You seem off, is everything okay?" You can also encourage your child to get back on task in a more compassionate way rather than through sharp demands and critical observations. Remember, setting boundaries and limits with your teenager is an act of love. Discipline helps children feel safe, yet allows them to test the waters without being left to experience severe consequence.

 Alert

Middle-school age (grades five or six through grade eight) can be one of the most tumultuous periods for children, even for those children who do not have anxiety. Puberty brings on physical changes involving surging hormones and developing brain and emotional systems, and life brings new demands for personal and social awareness and responsibility. Proper sleep, eating habits, and exercise will be essential during this period of their life. Remember that it is a myth that children can make up sleep. Keep bedtimes fairly consistent and technology out in the open (out of the bedroom), particularly in the evenings.

Shyness and Introversion

Introversion and shyness are temperament characteristics. Sometimes it is difficult to determine whether a child is shy, introverted, or truly has anxiety. Consistent avoidance of activities or chances to meet new people may signal that you need to look into your observations more carefully to rule out debilitating shyness or underlying anxiety.

What Is Shyness?

Shyness is a term often used to describe those who avoid (shy away from) contact with others. A shy person may want to be social, but may experience physical symptoms of anxiety, which makes interaction with others uncomfortable. Shyness is actually a personality trait, and it can have many positive qualities. People who are shy often make good listeners who are sensitive, empathic, and are easy to be around. To sort this out, watch your child or teen in social settings and see if she is able to make eye contact and listen politely. If she seems happy with herself, and others feel comfortable around her, she may simply be introverted. In most cases, when provided with tools and social opportunities children learn to overcome their outward shyness. They may always feel a bit of inward shyness, but through tools and techniques learn to adapt and grow from it.

What Is Introversion?

Introversion is closely related to shyness, but introverts do not generally feel physically uncomfortable in social situations. Instead, introverts simply prefer to spend time in solitary pursuits, and "recharge" by spending time alone. Like those who are shy, introverts are often highly observant and introspective. It is typical for adolescents to appear quite introverted at times, as they may spend hours in their rooms gaming, grooming, or connecting with friends. Many gifted children can be introverted because their drive for learning and creativity pulls them inward. If you suspect your child's introversion is related to anxiety about social or other demands, this trait may need further exploration.

What Is Extroversion?

An extrovert is a person who delights in being in large groups of people and recharges by connecting with others rather than being alone. Extroverts can sometimes appear to be the life of the party, but they can also simply need a higher level of social contact than their more introverted peers. Even extroverted children who appear confident and savvy on the outside can develop anxiety. If your child has frequent meltdowns after social gatherings, or if you suspect she is a "great actor," anxiety may be something to look further into.

The Overextended Child

Professionals and parents today are concerned that their children are overextended. Though researchers agree that some structured activity is good for kids, the goal is to balance structured time with free time. If your child has anxiety, you'll want to be especially sensitive to how he seems to handle the demands of his schedule to help him from becoming overwhelmed. Conversely, some children with anxiety have trouble with unstructured time because they have difficulty making choices and initiating activity. As such, you may need to coach your child a bit on how to create structure for himself. The tips that follow will help you determine if you or your child are over programmed.

 Fact

If, as you watch your child interact with others such as teachers, friends, and family, he seems to be overwhelmed, unfocused, or "not himself," this may indicate that it is time to start assessing your child's schedule and ability to cope. The same can be said for your own responses to the demands of your schedule.

Signs Your Child Is Overextended

Signs that your child might be over programmed include frequent fatigue, resistance, or refusal to attend activities, complaints about or lack of enjoyment of activities, aches and pains, frequent irritability, persistent feeling that there is not enough time, frequent illnesses, and worry. If your child regularly experiences more than one or two of the things on that list, it may be time to have a sincere talk with her about how to cut back on activities.

Signs You May Be Overextended

If you as a parent are overextended, you may experience any of the things on that list, too. Some additional questions to ask yourself include: Do I feel like I spend my life in the car, going from one activity to the next? Do I skip meals or eat them while driving? Do we have time to be together as a family? Do I create time for hobbies and leisure? Am I getting enough sleep? Depending on your answers to these questions, it might be time to consider reducing the amount of activity you and your child are involved in. Sometimes eliminating even one obligation can reduce stress dramatically and help everyone to breathe a bit easier. Allowing your child to make her own choice about what she would like to let go of is an act of self-love.

CHAPTER 15

Types of Anxiety in Children

According to the American Psychiatric Association and the American Academy of Child and Adolescent Psychiatry, there are seven groups of anxiety. This chapter will concentrate on panic disorder, phobias, general anxiety disorder (GAD), obsessive-compulsive disorder (OCD), post-traumatic stress disorder (PTSD), selective mutism, and separation anxiety disorder. It will not review anxiety disorder due to a general medical condition or a substance-induced anxiety disorder. Additionally, you will find information on night terrors here, because they are so common in children. If you find your child meets the criteria for one of the disorders listed here, remember that it is not a diagnosis; it is a guideline to let you know if it is time to see a doctor or qualified therapist. Keep in mind that each and every one of these disorders is treatable and will improve if parents are willing to seek help, create a support team, and adopt strategies that support healthy living.

Separation Anxiety Disorder

A young child who is scared of new people and places is normal. However, if a child has continued intense fear that something is going to happen to someone he loves and he stops normal activities, this could be a sign of a larger issue. Separation anxiety disorder affects about 4 percent of children ages six through twelve, and research shows treatment is often successful.

Factors to Consider

Environmental and temperamental factors that seem to characterize children who suffer from separation anxiety disorder are an extremely close-knit family, a fearful or extremely shy temperament as an infant, shyness or passivity in girls aged three to five years old, or an insecure parent who found it difficult to attach in infancy.

The Developmental Process

When your baby was born, you might have noticed she easily adapted to new surroundings and people, which is typical of babies six months old or younger. Actually, with infants, it is usually the parents who have more anxiety than the child when being left with a babysitter or in a new environment! A peak in separation anxiety is expected between the ages of eight months and one year, although some children experience it later, between eighteen months and two and a half years old, and some may never experience it at all. During this time, you may find you cannot leave the room for even a moment without your child becoming agitated and upset.

 Essential

Separation anxiety can be considered developmentally normal until around age six. Many times, such as in a preschooler, it is a sign of healthy attachments to loved ones, an example being a five-year-old that clutches your leg for several minutes before you leave. However, if the distress continues beyond your child's same-aged peers, and increases in duration, frequency, and intensity, you will want to seek help from a professional.

Consider speaking to your pediatrician, who will most likely ask you questions about your child's school experience. As always, trust your gut. If you feel the present situation may not be a good match for your child's needs, you may need to seek another program. Some children thrive in a smaller, less stimulating environment while others do better where there is more movement. Parents discover a great deal about their child's learning styles in these early years.

Stranger anxiety is also something to be aware of during early childhood. It is evidenced when your child clings onto you for dear life, her huge, panicky eyes looking like you are going to feed her to a dinosaur if you even try to give her to another person. As time goes by and your child learns to feel safe and secure in the knowledge that you really are going to return, and she really will be given back to you, the anxiety usually fades. It is if she continues to experience excessive fear that seems out of proportion at the start of her elementary school years that you will want to seek support from a qualified professional.

Symptoms

Separation anxiety disorder has a variety of physical and behavioral signs. Your doctor or therapist will look for at least three or more of the following symptoms that must begin before the age of eighteen, be present for at least four weeks, need to cause significant distress in the child, and/or must interfere with social and/or academic functioning. The symptoms also cannot be due to another medical diagnosis:

- Excessive distress when separated from you
- Worry about losing you, or harm coming to you
- Ongoing worry that some awful event such as kidnapping will separate her from you
- Recurrent reluctance to go anywhere, even out to play with friends, or to watch TV in a room if you are not present

- Ongoing distress about being alone at home or outside the home
- Reluctance to go to sleep without you nearby
- Difficulty falling asleep without you, or waking from nightmares about separation from you
- Repeated physical complaints, such as stomachaches, nausea, and headaches when separated from you or expecting to be separated from you

Risk Factors

Separation anxiety can look like or develop into depression because your child might be withdrawn, seem irritable, have difficulty sleeping, or experience difficulty concentrating. Symptoms of separation anxiety may be prompted by a scary experience or something your child heard about, such as child abduction or a fire in the community. For your child to be able to resolve the feelings of separation anxiety it is important he develop a sense of safety in his world, trust people other than parents, and be able to understand that even though his parents have left, they are coming back. When a fracture in the ability to bond or attach in infancy through adoption, illness, or return to work has occurred, it can predispose a child to develop this disorder. Some studies suggest children and teenagers who live in dangerous neighborhoods might be inappropriately diagnosed with separation anxiety disorder, even though it is reasonable for them to have fears about leaving their homes.

Panic Disorder

To be considered as a panic disorder your child must have abrupt, intense fear that comes intermittently, unpredictably, and is recurrent. A panic attack happens very fast, is intense, and will reach its peak within ten minutes. Panic disorder is not common in young children and affects most people beginning in late adolescence, up to midlife.

 Question

Does your tween or teen feel anxious when she is supposed to visit someone else's house?
Agoraphobia is the pattern of avoiding certain places or situations in an attempt to control one's anxiety. It occurs when your child has an inability to go beyond known and safe surroundings because of intense fear and anxiety that she will not be able to get help or escape. Panic disorder can develop into agoraphobia. Your child's irrational fear of being in places he might feel trapped in or unable to escape from may cause him to feel like he has to stay at home so he can keep the panic away. Left untreated, this avoidance can build on itself and become quite debilitating.

Physical Symptoms

An experience of at least one episode that is followed by one month of persistent worry about future attacks is something doctors look for when considering this diagnosis. The attacks must be experienced as having an apparent onset and reach a peak in ten minutes. There needs to be a sense of imminent danger as well as four or more of the following symptoms:

- Pounding heart rate or chest pain
- Trembling or shaking and/or dizziness
- Shortness of breath
- Nausea or stomachaches
- Choking feeling
- Fear of losing control or dying
- Numbness or tingling
- Chills, sweating, or hot flashes
- Feeling of unreality

Learning disorders may coexist with panic disorders and should not be overlooked. If your child is having a hard time with school, it might not be just about his panic. If, after you see a doctor and the panic disorder is treated, your child is still upset about going to school, this may be an indicator of an undiagnosed learning disability. In either case, it is often a sign your child could benefit from additional support as well as a stress relieving practices. Very often, a visit to the doctor helps you and your child to initiate such changes in your routine.

Risk Factors

While 10 percent of children will have at least one panic attack, only 1 to 2 percent will develop panic disorder. However, the experience of panic is so scary that your child or adolescent may live in dread of another attack. He may also go to great lengths to avoid situations that may bring on another attack. This can cause him to want to stay home from school and have anxiety when separated from his parents. Another risk factor is school avoidance. As seen in Chapter 3, school avoidance can be complicated and difficult to treat, so it is best to intervene in the early stages rather than wait to see if it occurs again.

 Fact

> As with other anxiety disorders, there is a genetic component to panic attacks. Researchers have concluded that when a parent has a panic disorder, her children will be four to seven times more likely to develop one as well.

Of those adolescents who continue to have panic disorder as they go into adulthood, many will develop other difficulties. This disorder can also cause your child to believe he is unhealthy, go to the doctor often, and show significant social impairment. The random nature of panic attacks is powerful and confusing. Since there is no reason outside her body for the worry, your child could start thinking there is something wrong inside her body. Once again research shows if left untreated it could cause your child to stop most activity, especially outside the home, out of fear the panic will reoccur. That is why, as stated in the earlier chapters, it is important to have a support team you trust and feel comfortable reaching out to. This may take some time and research.

Social Phobia

Social phobia is also known as social anxiety disorder, or SAD (not to be confused with seasonal affective disorder, which can also be known by the acronym SAD). This disorder is diagnosed when your child has a persistent fear of social situations, performing, and talking in front of others, especially if she will be around unfamiliar people. Your child may be terrified of being criticized, judged harshly, or embarrassed. Social phobia affects one in every twenty-five children, and it seems girls are diagnosed about twice as often as boys. Conversely, clinical samples are either equal on gender or show more males with the diagnosis. Children, especially adolescents, can be preoccupied with how they compare to their friends, so being a little self-conscious is normal. SAD is diagnosed when the symptoms are extreme. Parents can also exacerbate social anxiety disorder if they are fearful, withdrawn, or shy, or if they unintentionally reward their child's fearful behavior.

Symptoms
To be diagnosed with social phobia, a child's symptoms must last at least six months, which distinguishes it from the short-term social discomfort that many children briefly experience in new situations. There is no one sign that indicates that a child has social anxiety. However, if your child experiences several of the following, SAD may be part of the picture:

- Fearing scrutiny by other people in social situations
- Avoiding situations that trigger the fear
- Crying, throwing tantrums, clinging, and freezing in specific social situations
- Complaining of sickness to avoid going to school
- Feeling unwilling or unable to participate in school activities such as sharing with the class, group projects, reading in front of the class, or raising a hand
- Isolation at the playground, feeling outside of the group and not joining in, having no friends or one or two friends

 Fact

Approximately four out of every ten, or 43 percent, of children with social anxiety refuse to attend school because of their anxiety. If your child is refusing to go to school, or goes and then spends most days in the nurse's office, it is time to seek help from a licensed psychologist.

When your child is faced with something she fears, she may have physical symptoms like blushing and sweating, dizziness, heart palpitations, tense muscles, dry mouth, trembling, and nausea. These symptoms magnify the production of anxiety. Interventions such as biofeedback or energy work can teach your child how they have the power to influence their bodily responses. This can be a very rewarding and empowering experience for your child.

Risk Factors

If your child has social phobia, he may have trouble speaking up in class, making or keeping friends, taking tests or keeping up with schoolwork, receive poor grades, not feel able to turn in homework, and feel isolated. You also might notice he is afraid that others will see his anxiety and think he is weak or immature. Your child might fear that he will faint, lose control of bowel or bladder functioning, or not be able to concentrate. Social skills training along with a therapist who understands social anxiety disorders is important.

Generalized Anxiety Disorder

In children, generalized anxiety disorder (GAD) is also called over-anxious disorder. Children and teens with GAD will have excessive concern and worry about the past or future, look for the worst in situations, and often have fears that are out of proportion to what you might have expected. GAD affects approximately 3 to 5 percent of children age six to eleven years old. From early adolescence on, girls outnumber boys with this condition approximately two to one, and 50 percent of adults diagnosed with GAD had it during their childhood or adolescence.

Causes

GAD can be linked to an overactive thyroid gland, and a mal-function of this gland can cause the symptoms associated with anxiety. Children with chronic conditions, such as diabetes or high blood pressure, can be prone to anxiety as well. Frequently this disorder starts out slowly and then sneaks up on your child, so exact causes have been difficult for researchers to confirm.

Symptoms

Your child may be filled with self-doubt that he feels he is unable to control and be highly critical of himself. He may be preoccupied with being on time and adamant about doing things "perfectly." Children with generalized anxiety disorder do not have occa-sional worries or fears; for them this disorder weaves throughout their entire day and all they do—schoolwork, appearance, money, friends, their health, the future, the past, what they said and did, and to whom. Unfortunately, as you can imagine, these symptoms can make living life, having friends, or enjoying a hobby or activity pretty difficult. To be diagnosed with GAD, your child must have difficulty controlling the worry, and the anxiety and worry must be associated with one of the following, for at least six months:

- Restlessness and inability to relax
- Lack of energy
- Trouble falling asleep or staying asleep
- Muscular tension, aches, or soreness
- Trouble concentrating
- Irritability

Also, be on the lookout for "What Ifs," excessive perfectionism, frequent need for approval, trouble shutting off anxious thoughts, stomach problems, grinding of teeth, and dizziness.

Risk Factors

Generalized anxiety disorder, like other types of anxiety, can coexist with depression, phobias, and panic attacks. Substance abuse in teenagers can be a problem if they are trying to self-medicate as a way to alleviate their symptoms. In addition, many people who meet a child, especially a teen, with GAD will see how concerned they are with time, schedules, finances, and health and think they are older than their years. Be careful; you do not want to encourage or reinforce these signs of over-responsibility. Certainly, for the moment it is nice to hear your child described in a positive, mature way, but keep in mind that you know that his "impressive" behavior is based on fear and worry, which is actually hurtful for him.

Certain factors may increase your child's risk of having generalized anxiety disorder. A buildup of stress, a physical illness, and a tendency toward being anxious are among the most common culprits. In addition, as previously mentioned, generalized anxiety disorder occurs more frequently in children who have medical issues like diabetes and high blood pressure. Multiple moves, losses, or transitions can also set the stage for GAD. Children and adolescents with general anxiety disorder, as with all types of anxiety, will need to ensure they receive proper sleep, nutrition, exercise, and incorporate some of the self-soothing strategies in this book.

 Question

My child can't sit still. How do I know if this is generalized anxiety disorder or attention deficit hyperactivity disorder?
If your child has anxiety, she might have difficulty paying attention and be hyperactive or fidgety. A key difference to look for is in the "worry." Children with ADHD do not worry more than children without ADHD, whereas children with GAD are compelled to worry about many things throughout the day.

Obsessive-Compulsive Disorder

For some parents, having a child who is neat, organized, cautious, and careful would be a dream come true. Obsessive-compulsive disorder (OCD) is diagnosed when your child takes the positive qualities of neatness, organizational skills, being careful, or cleanliness to the extreme. With this mindset, she is trapped in a pattern of time-consuming, repetitive thoughts and behaviors and she cannot necessarily accomplish what you might think she should. For instance, she will take an hour-long shower that she is hoping will give her a cleaner body; unfortunately, instead she will get red, raw skin, and might walk out of that shower still thinking she needed to clean herself more. Young children find it difficult to recognize their behavior as useless, but older children are more aware yet still find the pattern impossible to stop. These maladaptive obsessions (thoughts) and compulsions (behaviors) can easily imprison your child, and sometimes, your entire family.

There is no evidence that OCD is learned or caused by childrearing choices. Interestingly, OCD is more common among people of higher education, IQ, and socioeconomic status. When in adolescence or older, men and women are affected equally.

Fact

> Obsessive-compulsive disorder usually starts between the ages of six and fifteen for boys, while for girls it often begins later, between the ages of twenty and thirty. It affects between 1 to 2 percent of children.

The Obsession

An obsession is an unwanted thought or impulse that repeatedly occurs in the mind of the child. Repeatedly, the child experiences a disturbing thought, such as, "My teeth are yellow, I have to brush them"; "I think I left my homework on my desk at home, I am going to fail this class"; or "I am going to mess up this relationship with my friend, I know it." These beliefs are felt to the point of being intrusive, consuming, and unpleasant. The obsessions seem uncontrollable to your child and if she does not manage the thoughts through behaviors, she feels she might lose control of herself. Obsession with germs or body fluids and reoccurring doubts are among the most common.

The Compulsion

Compulsions are repetitive behaviors that are clearly excessive, but temporarily reduce the tension and anxiety caused by the obsession. Compulsions can include hand washing or checking behaviors, such as repeatedly making sure their belongings are where they should be, hoarding objects, counting, repeating words, or praying. Because compulsions become rituals, they can take long periods of time, even hours, to complete (particularly if interrupted), which can feel very frustrating to the parent or others who don't understand the child's behavior.

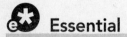 **Essential**

Children who engage in repeated hand washing intended to lessen anxiety about contamination commonly end up with raw skin and dermatitis. Lip-licking and sucking on hands or fingers can have similar results. Be sure to treat these signs early on.

Symptoms

Being able to recognize if your child has obsessive-compulsive disorder can be challenging. Sometimes your child's behaviors will appear obstinate or even lazy. When children obsess, it makes it hard for them to get anything done, especially if there are many items on a list, like chores. All you see as a parent are the hours they spend in the bathroom, or their bedroom, without much being accomplished. At home, children with OCD may have a combination of the following symptoms along with those presented earlier for generalized anxiety:

- Intrusive thoughts and repetitive behaviors
- Extreme distress if their rituals are interrupted
- Difficulty explaining their behaviors
- Seeking repeated reassurance about safety
- Attempts to be secretive about their obsessions or compulsions
- Feelings of shame about the compulsion
- Feeling they can't stop the obsessions or compulsions
- Thinking they might be "crazy" because of their thoughts

At school, the teacher might see:

- Difficulty concentrating
- Isolating or withdrawing from friends
- Low self-esteem socially or academically

Alert

> Environmental stressors such as abuse, changes in living situation, illness, occupational changes or problems, relationship concerns, and school-related problems can worsen OCD symptoms.

Risk Factors

When a child has OCD, peer relationships, school functioning, and family functioning may all suffer. Depression, hair pulling, constantly feeling sick, anorexia or bulimia nervosa, panic disorder, GAD, or social anxiety disorder may develop. For some children, social isolation may increase because of extreme anxiety and a need to limit activities may result. Some children may have thoughts of self-harm. The difficulty is, the obsession temporarily provides relief from anxiety. If you suspect your child is exhibiting the signs, in addition to professional help your child will need to learn and practice other strategies that relief the anxiety such as tapping or EFT (see Chapters 11 and 13). They might also benefit from a cognitive therapy approach where they learn how to experience and change their thoughts.

Because your child may feel ashamed and embarrassed about his OCD, it might be hard for him to talk about. When it all stays in his head, it becomes even more difficult to stop his thinking and your child may even start to wonder if he is crazy. With OCD patience really is a virtue, and that means you will need to take care of yourself as well. To gain the support you need, see Appendix B websites that will connect you with other parents who also have similar situations.

Post-Traumatic Stress Disorder

The diagnosis of post-traumatic stress disorder, or PTSD, was developed to help define the trauma experience of war veterans. What makes this disorder different from many of the other anxiety disorders discussed is that PTSD requires that a specific event occurred before the onset of symptoms. Many upsetting things can happen in your child's life, like a best friend moving or failing a test. While upsetting, these events generally do not develop into PTSD. On the contrary, PTSD is triggered by an event that was terrifying, threatening, and traumatizing for your child either physically or psychologically. Examples include physical, emotional, or sexual abuse, watching someone else being physically assaulted, or being in a disaster such as a flood, fire, or serious accident. Please note that just because your child experienced or witnessed a traumatic event, it does not mean she will develop PTSD. To the contrary, most do not.

 Alert

Energy techniques such as tapping have been used with children and adolescents who have been exposed to school violence. EMDR (Eye Movement Desensitization and Reprocessing therapy) is another technique that has reported positive results. Each of these needs to be applied by a trained professional.

Symptoms

To be diagnosed with post-traumatic stress disorder, your child must have symptoms from these three categories: re-experiencing the trauma; avoidance and emotional numbing; and increased arousal.

Symptoms include:

- Exposure to a traumatic event involving threat or actual injury
- Response involving intense fear, helplessness, or horror
- Re-experiencing the event with distressing memories, dreams, acting, or feeling as if the event is recurring
- Avoidance of reminders of the trauma
- Detachment from, loss of, or limited emotions

- Sleep issues, difficulty concentrating, irritability, guilt, intense panic, and/or angry outbursts

Defining the symptoms of PTSD is a little tricky for doctors and parents because PTSD has different age-specific features. Young children who are not yet verbal might develop stranger anxiety, have trouble sleeping, or regress developmentally. As they get older, some children will act out or engage in play that resembles what they went through. It is also common to see an adolescent express impulsive and aggressive behaviors as a way to deal with intense feelings.

 Question

My twelve-year-old was assaulted on the bus eight months ago and everything has been fine. All of a sudden, he can't sleep and he is angry all the time. Could this still be from the assault?
Sometimes symptoms do not occur until months or even a year after an incident. This can be upsetting for parents because it seems like the symptoms have come out of nowhere. Delayed PTSD is diagnosed if the onset of symptoms occurs six months or more after the trauma. It is often triggered by an anniversary, or something that reminds the child of the original trauma, and it is very real. In this situation, it is best to see a counselor for an assessment.

Risk Factors

The most important factors to consider when identifying how well a child will come through a trauma are the severity of the trauma, how close physically she was to the situation, and how the parents acted in response. Research also suggests that when a child experiences a trauma where someone intentionally hurts another person, she is more likely to develop PTSD.

Depending on age, children with PTSD may have suicidal thoughts, argue with friends, develop stomach troubles, or have poor immune response. They may also engage in substance abuse or disruptive behaviors. The best place to start with your child, if she has experienced a trauma, is to communicate early and often. Allow her time to explore her feelings, and allow her time to recover.

Selective Mutism

If your child talks freely at home but freezes in social or public situations it may be a form of an anxiety disorder called Selective Mutism. This type of anxiety disorder is typically diagnosed early on (before age six) and the symptoms exist for at least one month (not including the first month of school). If you have concerns about your child's inability to speak in front of others it would be a good idea to consult with a speech and language pathologists. They are well versed in development and have ways of assessing whether the difficulty is due to anxiety or a communication disorder. You can also find more information by going to *www.asha.org/public/speech/disorders/SelectiveMutism.htm*.

Night Terrors

If your child wakes from sleep with a sudden episode of intense terror, bolting upright with his eyes wide open, a look of fear and panic, and lets out a scream, he just had a night terror.

Causes

Usually, within fifteen minutes of your child falling asleep, he will begin his deepest sleep of the night, called slow wave sleep, or deep non-REM sleep. Typically this lasts from forty-five to seventy-five minutes. It is during this part of his sleep, just before the transition to lighter sleep, that your child becomes stuck. Caught between stages, your child will have a period of partial arousal. During this time your child will groan, cry, kick, hit, and scream. His eyes may be open or closed; he will look confused, upset, or even "possessed," as many parents have described it. Typically, night terrors last for about ten minutes, although it may be over in one minute, or last as long as thirty minutes.

Night terrors normally affect young children between the ages of three to five years old. Watching a child go through this is very emotional and frightening for most parents, so it is important to know that for the most part, it is a harmless situation. Guidelines to decrease the impact of night terrors include having a strict bedtime and waking time, and dimming the lights one to two hours before sleep; avoiding naps, reading, and watching TV in bed; limiting soda, chocolate, or other stimulants; and eliminating physical exertion and heavy liquids like milkshakes prior to bedtime. Create an environment that is physically safe for individuals that may become disoriented when they wake up at night.

 Essential

In most cases, it is best not to hold or restrain your child while she is experiencing a night terror. Simply sit guard and tune into your child's cues. If your child responds positively to a comforting voice or rubbing his back, do it. If not, do not. Being there to offer comfort to him when he wakes up is critical, however. It is recommended that you not ask about what your child was dreaming about until morning. Keep talking to a minimum. Most important is to protect your child from injury.

Several issues play a part in your child having night terrors. If you or your spouse had night terrors, studies suggest your child will, too. Being overly tired can also play a part. Doctors suggest extra time for sleep and talking to your child to soothe his tendency to worry. If night terrors become frequent and using the guidelines listed previously does not work, then it is time to get professional advice.

CHAPTER 16

Choosing Therapy

If any of the symptoms or types of anxiety seem to fit your child the first appointment you will want to schedule for your child is with your family doctor. Because many physical illnesses are closely related to the symptoms of anxiety, you want a clean bill of physical health. Once that has been established your doctor may suggest a referral to a therapist, and if he does not you can request one. It is important to know that sometimes these referrals are not necessarily based on the doctor's knowledge of the therapist's ability or practice. Instead, the recommendation might be because of a personal friendship, a mutual referral arrangement, word of mouth, or geographic location. This chapter will focus on the information you will need when making such an important decision for your child.

Provider Credentials and Experience

The best referral is usually from a friend or family member who has had experience working with a therapist treating an anxiety. If that is not possible, the next step is to call a professional you trust and get a suggestion of someone they know professionally, and are not involved with socially. Besides your family doctor, sources to ask for a referral from include your minister or rabbi, an employee assistance program at work, your child's school counselor, or your insurance company. Because cognitive behavioral therapy has been the most highly researched, and therefore the treatment most often recommended, you can consult the AABT, the Association for the Advancement of Behavioral and Cognitive Therapies website's directory of providers (*www.abctcentral.org*). Many other therapies have been shown to be effective as well, so do not limit your child to one resource. Other professional websites to check include the American Psychological Association (*www.apa.org*), your state psychological association, or the American Association for Marriage and Family Therapy (*www.aamft.org*). Also, you could look at the Directory of Providers on the Anxiety and Depression Association of America website (*www.adaa.org*).

Credentials

You want to find a therapist who has either a master's or a doctorate degree in a mental health field like psychology, marriage and family therapy, social work, or counseling. A licensed professional who has an advanced degree and has taken an exam given by the state she is practicing in will often be more specialized. This is important when dealing with children.

Experience

Once you have gathered some names from trusted sources, it is important to either spend a few minutes on the phone or have a session with each candidate, so you can decide who might be best for your child. Treating an anxiety can take months or longer, depending on the severity, so this relationship is not one to rush into. Take your time to find someone who meets the high standards you want as you will trust your child's well-being to them.

Questions you might want to ask include: What type of experience, training, and license do you have, and for how long? What training and experience do you have specifically in treating anxiety disorders? What is your basic approach to treatment for a child? Do you have training in alternative therapies or do you work with other professionals that do? Can you prescribe medication or refer me to someone who can, if that proves necessary? Have you ever had a license revoked or suspended, or been disciplined by a state or professional ethics board? (You can call the clinician's state licensing board to check on license, credentials, and any ethical violations.)

 Fact

Taking the time to ask questions and find a therapist who seems to connect with you and your child naturally will increase the chance that your child will want to go to therapy and stay in therapy.

Therapeutic Style and Importance of Rapport

Rapport and comfort are essential elements in the therapeutic relationship, and have a lot to do with the outcome of therapy. Some studies have suggested that rapport is actually more important than the type of therapy provided. Because of that, initially you will want to think about whether a male or female therapist would be best for your child. Take into consideration whether your child's anxiety is related to a trauma, and who the key players were in the experience. After you have decided male or female, you will also want to have an idea about which type of approach and demeanor might be best. Some children feel more comfortable with a therapist who has a "down-to-earth" approach, wears jeans and sneakers, and loves to get on the floor to play games. Other children might feel best talking to someone who is more reserved, wears a suit or dresses up, and sits behind a desk or in a chair in front of them. It might help to think about what teachers your child seems to like best, if she has already started school.

Think about the children she has played with and any comments she might have made about the moms and dads she has met. Or maybe she is on a sports team and feels really comfortable with a certain coach, or a dance teacher. Whoever it is, think about what qualities that person has, seeing how comfortable your child has been around them, and keep that in mind as you look for a therapist. You may be able to read something about their style when listening to their answers in your initial phone conversation. Rapport can start as early as listening to a voicemail or gel as late as the third session. If you or your child are still not feeling a connection with the therapist after three sessions, you may need to reconsider who you are seeing.

 Alert

Do not let anyone, not a doctor, therapist, friend, or family member, tell you there is one single best way to deal with your child or his anxiety. The mind and body are complex structures, not an absolute science, and therefore many different approaches could be helpful.

Do Not Limit Yourself

Trust yourself to know what might work best for your child. If what you come up with is "I'm just not sure," then that is what you know; go with it. What that means is try a few different styles, both male and female, and let your child decide who felt the best and was the easiest to talk to. Finding a good therapist is a process, and there is no "one size fits all." Sometimes it takes a few tries before you and your child will feel comfortable and safe, and you know you have found the right place for your child to do her work. Your approach can be "let's give a few people a try, and then pick who we liked best." Nevertheless, try to limit yourself to two or three to begin; you do not want to overwhelm your child with choices, and you want to start making progress as soon as you can. There might not be an option as to whether or not your child goes to therapy, but that doesn't mean you can't take a collaborative approach to finding the right one.

What Collaboration Looks Like

After each initial appointment, on the way home, you and your child can openly rate how you each felt and make a game out of it. For example, you can make a chart that has certain factors listed on it, with a rating scale already made up and ready to go. Rate on a scale of 1–5:

1 = *awful, no way* 3 = *okay, or maybe* 5 = *great, let's try it*	
How did the office feel when you walked in?	
Did the therapist seem to value your input?	
How caring did this therapist seem?	
Did you feel safe when you talked to him?	
Did she know how to talk with you about your feelings?	
Does he have a good plan to help with your anxiety?	
Does she seem like someone you could talk to again?	

This kind of activity will help your child feel empowered and supported, setting the stage for a more positive therapy relationship to develop. He will feel as if you are all in this together, and that you care about how he feels by allowing him to be a part of the process. For a child with anxiety, that can be invaluable.

Clinic or Private Practice?

Choosing between seeing a therapist at a mental health clinic or a private practice is an individual issue. Each setting has pros and cons, depending on the type of services your child needs. When making your decision, what is most important is how you and your child feel about the person and the services being provided.

Private Practice

In order for a therapist to work privately, and charge your insurance company for the visit, she must be licensed by the state she works in. Some psychologists in private practice do not take insurance at all, or only work with a select few insurance companies. Always ask what the fee is. Sometimes it can be more than in a clinic setting. Often with a private clinic or practitioner, you will pay the full cost of the services, less the amount paid by your insurer. If you need medication, group, or other services, you might be referred out to another provider. Some therapists in private practice run their own support groups, but they are usually specialized. Examples include groups for eating disorders, anger, anxiety, or depression.

Services Offered by a Private Practice

Many private offices have specific times when the office is open and when the therapist will be available to return phone calls. When you see someone in a private practice, he may or may not be more accessible than a provider in a clinic setting. Some private practitioners answer the phone themselves and schedule their own appointments, and others use answering services. Some private offices have an after-hours answering service or offer emergency services. Sometimes you can get an appointment within a week or two of your first phone call, and can be seen regularly right away, but it may take weeks before you can get in for an appointment if the therapist is good. Many offer early morning, day, and evening hours, and sometimes see clients on Saturdays. Some offer a sliding fee based on your income. Often psychologists in private practice have an office and waiting room that is specially designed with the client in mind. They will create a space that feels comforting, warm, and relaxing, very much like a living room.

A Clinic

Unless you are calling for a specific person you might be given to the therapist who is next in line for a referral. However, many clinics use triage systems to determine the best fit between a client's needs and therapist availability. Always ask about the therapist you are scheduled with if someone has not given you a specific name to request. Therapists might be right out of school, be licensed or not, be receiving supervision or not, or be degreed in psychology or not. Often you can wait weeks to get an appointment, similar to private practice, and if the clinic is busy, your child might not be able to be seen again, by the same person, for another month. It can take a while to get on a therapist's schedule with frequency. Often clinics offer a sliding fee scale and many try to become a provider for every insurance company possible, including medical assistance/Medicaid and Medicare. There are some clinics that have a psychiatrist and vocational counselor on staff, or can provide testing and assessment as well, providing you convenient access to multiple services under one roof.

Services Offered at a Clinic

Usually you will find a multitude of options at a mental health clinic because of the number of counselors or mental health workers on staff. Most offer psychological and psychiatric evaluations, medication and medication management, psychological testing, individual, group, and family therapy, play or art therapy, crisis intervention, and twenty-four-hour emergency services. Most clinics have a larger waiting room, similar to a doctor's office, where you will sit with a number of people waiting for your appointment. A clinic will usually have a business office, several people who do your scheduling, and an office manager. A clinic normally offers evening hours for appointments and may also have weekend hours.

Things to Consider

Pay attention to the surroundings and the staff, noticing if they feel comfortable in the space and are respectful and warm to one another. Check to make sure client confidentiality is protected. Use your own instincts; knowing your child best, you can make a good determination of what would be a comfortable setting for him.

Essential

If when you first meet the counselor she does not greet you warmly with eye contact, seems distracted, rushed, or not able to find a sense of ease with your child, you might need to look for another therapist.

When you do choose a therapist or psychiatrist, find out who covers for her when she is not working, or is on vacation. Always ask who does the billing for insurance, and how co-pays or the fee is collected.

 Fact

Anyone in the mental health profession who carries a license is required to maintain a certain amount of professional development to utilize his license. Therefore, it is appropriate for you to ask the therapist about the latest research and techniques available to treat anxiety.

How Long Should You Wait?

There are two questions here. How long should you wait to get in to see a therapist, and how long should you wait before you decide if this therapist is the right one? If your child is having significant difficulty, waiting more than two weeks for your first appointment is not reasonable. When your child is hurting, two weeks can feel like forever. It is important to note that some insurance companies may offer "crisis appointments." However, the next available provider may not be located in an area that is convenient for you. Consider this carefully before agreeing to a stopgap measure that may not be practical in the end. If you decide your child seems to have a problem, but it is not damaging to his daily life yet, waiting two to three weeks for the first appointment is reasonable. After that first session, though, it is important to have your child seen weekly, at least until the flow of therapy is established. Not only has it been shown that weekly therapy helps establish rapport, it is also necessary so your child can get some quick symptom relief.

 Essential

Here are a few questions that are important to ask when looking for a therapist: What is your experience and basic approach to treatment for a child? Can you prescribe medication or refer me to someone who can, if that proves necessary? How long before you have room in your schedule? How frequent are the sessions, and how long do they last? Do you include family members in therapy?

If a therapist tells you she is a month out on her calendar, you need to question whether this is the right person for your child. When a therapist is that heavily booked out of the gate, the time she can fit you in will likely be limited, and as noted earlier, taking children out of school brings with it a host of other issues.

 Alert

If after three months of therapy you have not noticed a difference in your child, and your child has not been given specific things she can do to help her when she is feeling anxious, then it is time to look for another therapist.

Is This Therapist the Right One?

In regard to how long before you know whether you've found the right person to work with your child and family, give the therapist three to four sessions. By then you will know if your child has connected and can form a trusting, open relationship with this person. The therapist will have also had the time to decide on goals and should have discussed a plan with you. By all means, ask any questions and raise any concerns you might have; a therapist's ability and willingness to address these issues can say a lot about her as a professional.

Resources for the Uninsured

Many communities have Community Mental Health Centers. Usually, for a reduced or sliding fee scale determined by your income, you can receive mental health services at your local center, which may in some cases be a county agency. Sometimes these clinics require you to be a recipient of public assistance or have a private insurance plan through the state. Often, to receive a reduced rate, you must live in the city or county in which the clinic is located. Many such centers are nonprofit agencies.

Your church or synagogue is also an excellent place to call. Often they will have a rabbi or certified pastoral counselor available for appointments. Many have professional counseling experience and provide services on a sliding scale, or a no-fee basis. It is important to verify credentials when choosing clergy for counseling.

 Essential

Another option is to have your child join a self-help or support group in school or in the community. They are generally free and can be found in virtually every community in America. Many young people like the group process because it helps them realize they are not alone with their anxiety, and it gives them a sense of belonging.

Public Assistance is another place to look. Examples of such programs are Social Security, Medicare, and Medicaid. Some have specific requirements such as age and income limitations. It will be necessary to call your government office and find out eligibility requirements.

Parent Involvement

Parents are often eager to support their children's learning, but can feel at a loss when dealing with their child's anxiety. Increasing your communication with your child about feelings, goals, and tools can be helpful. In fact, studies confirm parent involvement has positive effects on a child's anxiety when it is seen as encouraging and loving.

Parent Involvement in Cognitive Behavioral Therapy

A well-known study in 1996 by Barrett, et. al., found that children who had parents who were involved in their therapy had success rates that were significantly higher, 84 percent as compared to 57 percent for children who did not. In 2001 Barrett and colleagues found that, five to seven years after their original study, the children were able to maintain their gains. These same children, whose parents were involved in their care, also were significantly less fearful at long-term follow-up. Researchers believe the children were successful in part because of the added component of giving parents the skills needed to improve their own anxious feelings.

 Alert

Another positive aspect of having parents involved in their child's therapy is that support can be given for tasks, or "homework" the child will be requested to do in between sessions. When your child feels understood and supported in therapy, the gains are usually greater.

Other Ways Parents Can Help or Hinder

You can facilitate treatment by providing invaluable information regarding your child's history, extended family history, how functional your child is on a daily basis, issues with school and peers, and what other factors might be causing anxiety. It is just as important to tell the clinician, in front of your child, what you enjoy about her, what other kids seem to like or admire about her, and what assets she brings to school, family, and fun. Sometimes a parent can unwittingly impede his child's treatment by overfunctioning or underfunctioning in the therapy session, or at home. If you try to rescue your child from an anxiety-provoking situation, she might not be able to challenge herself and move past her fears. When you have difficulty setting limits, your child might have difficulty setting her own boundaries. Also, your child might be confused about how to attach to the therapist without hurting your feelings. Last, even though it can feel hard to find the time to take care of yourself or your own anxiety, it is important to remember that your child loves you and will want to model you. All of these issues can, and should, be addressed in therapy.

Individual, Family, and Group Therapy

There may be almost as many types of therapy as there are settings that provide them. It is important to keep in mind that not all therapists are skilled in all types of therapy, and that the approach used will be based on your clinician's training and the setting in which she practices. In general, there are three basic types of therapy: individual, family, and group, and many of the therapies described in the following sections can be used in all three settings with a child with anxiety.

Individual Therapy

Individual, "one-to-one" or "talk therapy," is the most common psychological therapy for children and adults. Individual therapy is based on the premise that when a trusting relationship with a therapist is established, a client can increase self-awareness and change destructive or unhealthy patterns of thought, emotion, and behavior. A real-life example is when you feel relief from and resolution to an issue by talking it through with a supportive friend.

Though theoretical approaches vary, most individual therapy is based on the concepts outlined as follows. However, it is important to keep in mind that some schools of thought, such as behaviorism, focus almost exclusively on behavior change and bypass the importance of the therapeutic relationship and the need for emotional catharsis, or release.

"Name It, Claim It, and Tame It"

In a broad sense, "name it, claim it, and tame it" captures the essence of personal growth, both in therapy and in life. The ability to identify a problem or pattern such as anxiety, take ownership of the problem, and take steps to change it are at the root of personal development. Individual therapy is designed to facilitate this process while offering support, suggestions, affirmation, and a compassionate ear.

Problem Patterns and Positive Psychology

Individual therapy usually begins with an assessment of "what's not working" for a client with respect to thinking, emotions, relationships, and behavior. A skilled therapist will help clients identify maladaptive or unhelpful patterns, and set measurable goals to decrease them while increasing more positive, productive patterns. Because of the inherent negativity in anxiety, a therapist who helps your child own and build on her strengths can be essential.

Catharsis and Release

Many schools of therapy are based on the idea that examining patterns of thought, emotion, and interaction can bring up strong feelings that a client can then release, or let go. Hidden or buried emotion may be discovered and integrated as well, and it is believed that this process leaves room for new, more effective patterns to emerge. A child with anxiety, or his parents, for example, might find that they have underlying grief or sadness about the limitations and losses associated with anxiety. Spending some time with these feelings may allow them to transform and dissolve, making way for empowerment and new hope for the future.

 Fact

> For younger children, the use of play, art, or other child-centered techniques will almost always be incorporated into the session, and for adolescents, who are more verbal and reflective, "talk therapy" is more common. Tweens may do best with a combination of both approaches.

Creating Change

The crux of any successful therapy is the ability to which it is effective in creating lasting change. Usually, therapy continues until the changes are stable; that is, new patterns of thinking, acting, feeling, and interacting/socializing are used more often than not to meet life's challenges. Careful observation and goal setting at the beginning of therapy are crucial to being able to assess the extent to which a child has been successful in changing old, less functional patterns. It is exciting to see how each change your child is able to make creates opportunities for more learning and growth to occur.

Family Therapy

Historically, family therapy grew out of individual therapy as psychologists began to realize that family patterns, interactions, and wounds contribute to both the problem and the solution to emotional and behavioral troubles. There are several schools of thought that drive family therapy, but the overall premise is that families exist as systems, and that "the whole is greater than the sum of its parts." With younger children, parenting and/or family therapy may be preferred, as parents and siblings have the most direct impact on a child's world. Other components, such as individual play therapy or skill building, can be added to your child's plan of care based on his needs.

Family Dynamics

Family dynamics is a term used to describe the general pattern and functioning of your family. Family therapists look at patterns of communication, alliances, problem solving, and the assignment of power and resources, among other things, to determine a family's overall style and then assess what about that style is working and what is not. Family therapists also assess a family's adjustment to various transitions, coping, parenting styles, and marital stability to determine which areas might need to be addressed.

 Essential

In order to fully assess and treat a family, it is generally best for all family members to attend sessions. Children who are very young or older children who may not live full-time with the family may not be included, or included in specific sessions only.

Homeostasis

A primary theory in family therapy is the tendency of families to seek to maintain sameness, even in the face of extreme external changes. This is not unlike an automatic piloting system, which is set to maintain a certain course no matter what the weather or currents. An example of homeostasis is a child with anxiety who is learning to be more independent and spend more time away from home, whose parents may miss her company, or be afraid she will not do well, and subtly discourage her progress.

Enmeshment and Disengagement

Enmeshment and disengagement are classic terms used in certain forms of family therapy to describe how close (enmeshed) or distant (disengaged) family members are from one another. The goal in this aspect of family functioning is to seek a balance between these two polarities, and to enhance a family's ability to move, flexibly and adaptively, between the two extremes.

Families who are extremely disengaged may be more likely where there is depression or schizophrenia. An extremely disengaged family system can produce anxiety in children if they feel there is no one to connect with, or to protect them. This can be especially true for children who live in high-crime neighborhoods.

 Alert

In families in which one or more members have anxiety, the trouble is usually enmeshment, or too little "personal space" between family members. As you saw in Chapter 7, being overprotective can be one form of enmeshment, blocking children from establishing independent, confident selves.

Extended Family

Extended family, such as grandparents, aunts, and uncles may be included in family therapy for a number of reasons. This can be especially important if extended family provides care for your child or if the contact is especially close, so that your child's new skills and the techniques he's learning are supported and reinforced in as many settings as possible. If you have a strong relationship with your family already and feel they can be team players, you will more than likely be able to enlist their support for your child without the assistance of a therapist.

Parent Coaching

Parent coaching can be offered individually or in groups, and is often woven into individual therapy when a therapist provides focused time for parents without the child present. It is typical for therapists who specialize in play therapy to offer parent coaching versus family therapy, as they see the child as the "primary patient," but still want to offer guidance to the parents. Parent coaching can be an essential tool in helping parents to ally with each other, and help their children by reducing anxiety created by mixed messages or approaches.

Group Therapy

Group therapy can be a powerful tool for decreasing isolation, increasing confidence, and practicing emotional expression and social skills. One of the primary benefits of group therapy occurs when a child realizes that he is not alone in his fears and struggles, and that he is not as different from others as he may have come to believe.

 Fact

Although true for most children, teens and tweens can especially benefit from group therapy. This is because of their strong need to connect with, and be accepted by, peers. Groups are also excellent ways to help kids reduce feelings of isolation and alienation. This concept in itself can go a long way to reduce anxiety.

Behavioral Groups

Behavioral therapy in the group setting is designed to help people learn new skills and let go of old, ineffective ones. Training and practice in social skills and assertiveness can be especially helpful for children with social phobia, and teaching relaxation and other coping strategies can be done effectively in a group setting. The group itself allows for trial and error, direct feedback, support, and opportunities for immediate reinforcement of new skills.

Parenting Groups

Parenting groups that provide opportunities for both peer support and skills training are available in many communities. Systematic Training for Effective Parenting (STEP) is one such model. Though many parenting groups are based on childrearing and discipline, there may be specialty groups in your area that are suited to your particular needs. Your care providers, insurance company, or local hospital or clinic may be able to help you pinpoint resources. Early Childhood Family Education (ECFE) and places of worship may offer group-parenting therapy as well.

Supportive Approaches

Supportive therapy is a general term to describe any number of interventions that are intended to reduce discomfort and enhance the effectiveness of therapy for your child. Supportive therapy can be used together with individual, family, or group therapy, and may be recommended by your mental health provider if she feels it will be helpful for you and your child. Several types of supportive therapy are highlighted here.

Coordination with Other Providers

It is sometimes essential for a care provider to coordinate with others who support your child. For example, therapists often consult closely with pediatricians or psychiatrists to help monitor a child's response to medication. If your child shows school avoidance or refusal, contact with his teachers and other school staff can ensure that his transition back to school is the smoothest it can be.

Peer Counseling

The intent behind peer counseling is to help your child build trust, gain support and confidence, and decrease isolation through her connection to a peer counselor. Peer counseling may be available at your child's school, either in groups or one-to-one, and community resources may offer similar opportunities for you or your extended family.

Mentors

A mentor is an older, more experienced person who can take you or your child "under his wing" for support and education. Good mentors for children with anxiety might be older students, siblings, or family members who have tackled anxiety issues, or school personnel who have had similar experiences. Make sure that you know and trust your child's mentor(s) so that your own anxiety will not complicate your child's opportunity to benefit from the relationship.

Calming Animal Companions

Pets can be wonderfully supportive: They ask for little, are great listeners, and generally do not talk back. Companion animals and their therapeutic benefits have become more popular over the past decade, and there have even been specific "animal therapies" developed for special populations.

 Fact

Research shows that sitting with and stroking a cat or dog reduces muscle tension and blood pressure, and slows breathing and heart rate. As such, a child who may feel challenged learning relaxation techniques may benefit just as much by sitting quietly with her pet.

To enhance your child's ability to achieve relaxation while connecting with a pet, you can encourage her to slow down, speak softly (or not at all), and breathe deeply. Finally, the responsibility of caring for a pet is a great way for an anxious or worried child to develop confidence and mastery.

Play Therapy

Play therapy is a projective technique in which your child's conflicts and desires are revealed through her play and her interaction with the therapist. Generally, play therapy is the mode of choice for children under the age of ten to twelve, as they are less verbal and abstract than older children. As children mature, their ability to "think about thinking" and work with their emotions directly increases, and play techniques give way to more traditional talk therapies, which focus directly on emotional expression, problem solving, and behavioral change. It is important to note that play that occurs in a professional setting is different from play that occurs outside of the office. Unless your child's therapist guides you, it is generally unwise to attempt to make free play "therapeutic."

 Essential

> Some therapists are taking therapy outside and using nature as a way to connect and help children and adolescents discuss and develop new ways of thinking that are more productive.

The Symbolic Nature of Play

Play therapists work from the assumption that the symbols your child uses in his creative play are windows into the deeper recesses of his fears, desires, and motivations. When he expresses these through his play, they gradually become a part of his awareness; that is, he can learn about himself when guided by someone who is observant and responsive to his nonverbal messages. When your child feels fully understood, he is more likely to trust that he can manage his emotions and solve his problems.

The Cathartic Nature of Play

When your child expresses her inner nature through her play, a natural emotional release, or catharsis, occurs. This emotional response can also uncover other, related emotions. For example, a girl who re-enacts a fight with her father in play therapy may feel relief, or might move from anger to sadness as her role in the conflict becomes clearer. Your child can then use her insights to change her self-talk and behavior about the situation, and make future adjustments. When an anxious child expresses fears or worries in therapy, they lose some of their power to torment her in her daily life.

 Fact

Self-talk is a term coined from cognitive behavioral therapy. It refers to the things you say to yourself in your head about your experiences, like "She didn't say hello to me, so she must not like me." These powerful thoughts influence your core beliefs and your emotions, which in turn influence your behavior. Learning to change self-talk is essential in managing anxiety.

Learning New Behavior Through Play

Play therapists are trained to gently comment on and intervene in play to help your child learn new behavior. For example, in the situation just described, a therapist might model a father and daughter having a talk together or making up, or suggest that a child come up with a different, more satisfactory scenario. In addition, though much of play therapy itself is unstructured, there are multiple opportunities to teach social skills such as developing confidence, taking turns, following the rules of a game, and negotiating. Play therapists incorporate all of these skills to help a child with anxiety develop confidence, decrease his need for control, and tolerate anxiety.

Tools of the Trade

A therapist who uses play therapy with children will usually have an array of items at hand to meet your child's particular needs and concerns. The experience of play therapy includes not only the play itself, but also the opportunity to build trust and cooperation, which sets the stage for change. The most common props used in play therapy are described in the following paragraphs.

Dollhouse

A dollhouse is a common tool. It is used in therapy to help your child express thoughts, feelings, and experiences about her family and other people in her world such as pets or neighbors.

Games

Games are used by many child therapists to help establish comfort and trust, to provide a window into a child's experiences, and to serve as a tool for skill building. There are many therapeutic games available to help children act spontaneously and express opinions and emotions in nonthreatening ways. Games may also be targeted toward specific objectives, such as making friends or expressing anger. Games provide a backdrop for children to express and work on issues of control and mastery, which are especially important for children with anxiety. In addition, playing games with children in therapy provides a perfect opportunity for therapists to help children improve their social skills.

Puppets, Dolls, and Animals

Puppets can often convey feelings or thoughts a child is afraid to express because they let the child feel "once removed" from his direct experience. This emotional distance can allow a child to feel freer to fully express his needs and emotions. Dolls and animals serve a similar purpose, allowing your child to project his inner self without having to use more complicated means of expression. It is common for a child in therapy to choose a stuffed animal to "speak for him" or to say or do things he may feel he is unable to. Sometimes, therapeutic suggestions from "an older, wiser being" (like a well-worn teddy bear) are received on a deeper level than would be possible in simple "talk therapy."

Sand Play/Sand Tray

Sand play incorporates specially designed trays of sand in which children can form menageries of animals, people, houses, and other symbols that represent their internal world. Sand tray therapists are trained to interpret the scenes your child creates in the sand and to use these to help your child in therapy. The therapist may also use your child's creations to help her tell "stories," to express strong needs and emotions in a nonthreatening way, and to point to recurring themes, which may indicate your child's concerns, strengths, or weaknesses.

 Essential

> The practice of "acting as if" can encourage a child with anxiety to try on new ways of thinking and acting, which may bring relief from fear, worry, or withdrawal and lead to new ways of acting outside the therapy office. Storytelling and role-playing are also techniques that draw on "make believe."

Art and Music Therapy

The creative arts are a perfect medium for the expression of personal experiences, emotions, desires, and aspirations. Therapists skilled in these areas may use a variety of techniques to identify and address problem areas for a child. Opportunities for creative expression also allow children to build on strengths and increase confidence.

Music Therapy

Music therapy is commonly offered in a group setting, such as residential treatment, and is relatively uncommon in general practice. Music can be a great vehicle for eliciting and expressing emotion, such as fear or sadness. In fact, if you were to watch a movie without the music track, you might find the drama of the story far less compelling. A music therapist can play particular music to draw on certain emotions that your child can explore more fully. Conversely, a music therapist may suggest your child use various musical instruments to express a particular feeling or problem.

Art Therapy

Art therapy can use any medium to help your child explore and express his experiences and emotions. Drawing, as you have seen, can be a useful tool in both assessment and therapy. The use of paint, clay, chalk, and collage materials is also common in art therapy.

 Alert

There are many programs available through schools, libraries, community centers, and art centers from which you and your child might choose. If your child has anxiety, try to give her two or three options to choose from, and then help her stick to her commitment.

Do You Need a Specialist?

In many areas of the country, it may be hard to find specialized art and music therapy. However, therapists may incorporate art or music into sessions with your child, depending on their skill and interest. It is worth mentioning that building confidence through art, music, or performance can be extremely helpful for children with anxiety. However, if a child shows high levels of performance anxiety, this type of therapy may be too overwhelming and may not be appropriate.

Cognitive-Behavioral Therapy

Cognitive-behavioral therapy (CBT) is probably the most widely researched of all types of therapy. It was developed in the 1970s as behavioral psychology began to push the field toward more specificity, effectiveness, and measurability. Cognitive therapy focuses primarily on how to change destructive thought patterns, and behavioral therapy helps people identify and change unhelpful behaviors, and replace them with new, more effective skills. Put the two together and you get CBT. CBT is offered in both group and individual therapy, and may be used as a component of family therapy as well. Cognitive therapy is useful for tweens and teens who are developing the ability to monitor and change their thinking, and behavioral therapy can be especially helpful for younger children who need their world to be manipulated more directly.

Thoughts Rule

The term "cognitive" refers to the thought processes, both positive and negative, which in turn drive our emotions and behavior. Cognitive statements include messages you give yourself about events in your life, messages you have internalized from and about your past, and messages about your future success or failure. The goal of cognitive therapy is to minimize negative, self-defeating thoughts, and to maximize positive, supportive, and growth-oriented thoughts. As you can see, cognitive therapy is one of the most crucial components of treatment for anxiety, no matter the age of the client.

Skills Training

Simply titled, skills training is used to help people learn new patterns of behavior and to replace older, less effective patterns. Skills training is crucial for children with anxiety so that they can gradually build small skill sets (like calling friends) to develop larger skill sets (like going on a sleepover). Skills training can be used along with behavioral management to increase the impact of practicing the new behavior. Other uses of skills training for children with anxiety include teaching a shy child to ask for help, or helping a teen learn to be more confident by building social skills.

Assertiveness as Antidote

Assertiveness has been well researched as an antidote to anxiety, and has been popular in both group and individual therapy for decades. Though many people feel anxious when they anticipate having to assert themselves, the act of self-assertion actually decreases anxiety by producing a sense of mastery and control over the environment. Even small children can benefit from assertiveness training at very basic levels, by learning to identify and express their feelings and to ask for help if they are worried or uncomfortable. This is particularly crucial for a child with anxiety, who may feel so overwhelmed by emotion that she can't soothe herself or garner support.

 Question

Have you ever felt a sense of relief or elation after standing up for yourself?
If so, you may have experienced the "biochemistry of assertion." Some researchers believe that there may be specific neurobiological structures that produce pleasure when you assert yourself. Happily, this sense of well-being builds on itself, encouraging future assertion.

Behavioral Management

Though behavioral management is not always viewed as an aspect of CBT, it is a useful tool in helping children with anxiety. A typical use of behavioral management in therapy is for you, your child, and his therapist to develop a systematic plan to reinforce, or reward, his progress. For example, if a child who has been school-avoidant attends school for a full week, you might reward him with a special treat, outing, meal, or quality time together.

CHAPTER 17

Additional Help

Once you find a trusted, knowledgeable therapist who has just the right mix of humor, empathy, and helpful tools, he might also ask you to take your child to see a psychiatrist for an evaluation. A psychiatrist is simply a medical doctor who has special training in the field of psychiatric medicine. She can provide a diagnostic evaluation, consider physical factors that might suggest a physical diagnosis, or prescribe medications. Be sure to ask whether she specializes in treating children. This may seem like a common-sense question, but you would be surprised how many people do not ask it.

How Can a Psychiatrist Help?

Because a psychiatrist is a specialist in how the body and brain work, she can assess the causes and potential treatments for your child's anxiety more fully. She will discuss with you whether medication could be helpful with your child's type and level of anxiety, and which medications might work best. She can also provide additional support, treatment options, and encouragement.

Why Was My Child Asked to See a Psychiatrist?

It could be that your therapist wanted a second opinion about your child's diagnosis, level of functioning, or the treatment plan.

Even though your child might benefit from medication, in most cases a therapist cannot provide that (there is change coming, though; New Mexico was the first state to allow psychologists with specialized training to prescribe medications because of need in more rural areas). In addition, the psychiatrist can give a second opinion on possible medical factors suspected of contributing to the anxiety. Websites such as the American Academy of Family Physicians and the Anxiety Disorder Association of America, that can be helpful as you look for a psychiatrist, are located in Appendix B.

What Happens When You See a Psychiatrist?

Just as with your family doctor and therapist, the psychiatrist will meet with you and your child to look at family history, address physical symptoms, and discuss your child's general development. Often the first time you meet will be a longer session because the psychiatrist will be gathering all the information needed to address the possibility of prescribing medication. Share any issues with sleep, appetite, or energy level. This will help your psychiatrist have a thorough understanding of the difficulty your child is experiencing. It is also essential that the doctor know about any current or past medications your child has been prescribed, as well as who prescribed them. Tell the doctor if your child has begun therapy and with whom as well.

Find the Right Psychiatrist for Your Child

Your HMO or insurance company usually has a list of pediatric psychiatrists who are in your network. Sometimes you need a referral, so when you contact your insurance company for the list, ask about the proper procedure. You can also talk with your therapist, family doctor, other mental health professionals, your child's school, family members, or friends. As with the referral to a therapist, you want to ask for a few names and call each one with a list of general questions.

Questions to Ask a Psychiatrist

When looking for a psychiatrist, you might find the following list helpful. These questions are similar to the ones you want to ask when you look for a therapist:

- What experience does she have with children and anxiety disorders?
- Are there other forms of alternative treatment she would recommend?
- What insurance does she take, and who files the insurance?
- Can she offer your child before- or after-school appointments?
- What are the possible side effects of the medication she is prescribing?
- How long will it take the medication to work?

Also, ask if your child should avoid other medications or certain foods while she takes the medication, what to do if the medication does not work, and how to stop the medication when it is time.

 Question

What is a psychiatric nurse, and how can she help?
In many clinic and hospital settings, a psychiatric nurse acts as "the right hand" of the psychiatrist. Psychiatric nurses often gather history and background information at your visits with the psychiatrist. They will often be your first point of contact, and will interface with the doctor about your concerns. Some psychiatric nurses can even recommend an increase or decrease in your child's dosage as well.

Involving a Primary Care Physician

Primary care physicians are clinicians that are trained in general medicine, pediatrics, gynecology, or family practice. A PCP, as they are also known, establishes the first point of entry for a patient who is not feeling well and is not exactly sure why. The primary care provider can treat a wide range of health concerns and typically is well educated in a broad number of areas. Some will even be comfortable managing a child's psychiatric medications, particularly if your child has taken them before and shown stability over time. You can think about the primary care provider as the doctor who has to know enough about every area of medicine to make the proper referrals to the appropriate specialists.

 Alert

Because of recent concerns with suicidal thinking and behavior in children taking antidepressant/antianxiety medication, it is recommended that your child receive regular follow-up, especially when starting or stopping a medication. Your PCP, NP, or GP may offer this option, though you may have to ask for it.

PCPs are considered the primary gatekeeper in health plans, authorizing referrals to specialists for more complex and time-intensive diagnostic procedures. After taking on a patient, they often will manage the long-term care of that person if the patient has a basic medical condition that is nonsurgical in nature.

Can My Regular Doctor Prescribe Antianxiety Medication?

If your child's anxiety is severe, and it has been decided that medication is the best route along with therapy, you might be wondering if your family doctor can write the prescription.

Many general practitioners are comfortable and competent prescribing medications for basic or uncomplicated anxiety and depression. Some are not, as they may feel that it is out of the scope of their practice. If your child has overlapping conditions such as ADHD and anxiety, or a more complex condition such as OCD, it is invaluable to have the input of a psychiatrist. Because your child's pediatrician typically can see your child immediately, start with her. The wait to see a psychiatrist, particularly one who sees children, can be anywhere from four to twelve weeks. If your child's pediatrician is comfortable prescribing for anxiety, she can get you help as soon as possible. In the meantime, schedule an appointment with the psychiatrist, and by the time you have your first appointment, you will have weeks of data to share about your child's mood and behavior, and how the medication is working. The psychiatrist is in the best position at that point to evaluate what to do next.

Help from a Nurse Practitioner

A nurse practitioner (NP) is a registered nurse (RN) who provides high-quality medical care similar to a doctor. They have a minimum of a master's degree and are trained to diagnose and manage common medical conditions, focus on health education, and counsel you about your child's illness. Like a PCP, they will educate you and your child on how actions and lifestyle can affect your well-being. A nurse practitioner can be a patient's regular health care provider, and in most states, many nurse practitioners have a DEA registration number so they can write prescriptions for "controlled" medications.

Why Choose a Nurse Practitioner?

An NP is an excellent point of entry into the medical system because she may provide services for an entire family, is easily accessible, treats the mind and body, can fill prescriptions, and bills insurance for services performed. With an NP you get the full package, from diagnosing, treating, evaluating, and managing non–life-threatening acute and chronic illness and diseases, to providing primary and specialty care services, performing minor surgeries and procedures, and collaborating with physicians and other health professionals as needed. She can order, perform, and interpret basic diagnostic studies as well.

 Essential

Because anxiety can be due to a poor or inadequate diet, a health professional might recommend a visit to a dietitian or nutritionist who will create a food and meal plan specifically with your child's physical and mental health needs in mind.

Treatment Plan for Anxiety

It is helpful that everyone who is involved in your child's care is a specialist in anxiety if possible. You want to be assured they understand the complex and pervasive impact anxiety can have, or has had, on him. When making the treatment plan, discuss a combination of therapy, skill building (personal and social), assertiveness training, relaxation skills, and self-esteem building. Also, include in your plan an educational component so you and your child can understand how anxiety affects the mind and body. It is also helpful to include your ideas about whether medication will be considered, at what point, and how. Part of the plan also needs to include how and with whom information will be shared, and who will be included in the support system. For example, many families choose to share the treatment plan with the counselor, nurse, and teachers at school, and family members who live at home, too.

 Alert

It is always best if everyone is moving in the same direction, so as your child takes baby steps to facilitate change, others throughout his day can provide support and understanding. Having a clear, written plan will assist you in this.

Building on Your Child's Strengths

When you are discussing treatment choices and selection with the therapist or psychiatrist, it is essential to consider how to positively reinforce your child's strengths. It is best to create a treatment plan that includes strategies to manage the negative symptoms accompanying anxiety, but also includes opportunities to build on what's right, enhance your child's self-concept, level of confidence, autonomy, resilience, and a sense of self-efficacy.

An important reminder for every parent: More often than not, it is the strengths your children acquire, sometimes through adversity, that bring with them a vision of what their lives can be and what their true potential is. It is there that they find hope and the inspiration to proceed through difficulty. With that in mind, building a well-balanced, strength-based treatment can be the foundation for long-term health.

CHAPTER 18

To Medicate or Not

The use of psychiatric medication, especially in children, has been under close scrutiny for over two decades. Reports of antidepressants causing suicidal behavior in children, and outcry against the overmedication of children for ADHD have raised both public and professional concern. A concern about the "quick fix" mentality of the pharmaceutical industry has made many potential consumers skeptical about the rationale and safety behind the use of psychiatric medications. This chapter will help you to consider all the facts and make a decision about medication that you will be comfortable with. If you are uncomfortable with the idea of medication, use the other resources offered throughout this book.

Is My Child's Condition Simple or Complex?

Determining whether your child's situation is straightforward or more complicated is important in helping you to decide whether (and what type of) professional help will be most beneficial to your child. If your child's condition is relatively simple, such as trouble going to bed at night or playing at other children's houses, you may opt to address the issues at home. If, however, your child's anxiety interferes with many areas of her functioning and prevents her from living her life fully, or if her anxiety overlaps with other conditions, this increases the need to seek professional help, including considering medication.

 Essential

The decision about whether to use medications in treating children with anxiety is one that is highly personal, and often complex. It is best to make the decision with solid education and support from professionals whom you trust, and who know your child well.

Nature Versus Nurture

A classic debate in psychology is the degree to which innate biological characteristics (nature) or environmental influences (nurture) cause disturbances in thinking, emotions, and behavior. Research has certainly demonstrated a strong biological component in conditions such as schizophrenia, bipolar disorder, major depression, and, to a certain extent, anxiety. For milder conditions, however, like panic attacks and adjustment problems, the waters are a bit murkier.

If you feel that your child has both nature and nurture in her way—that is, if there is a family history of anxiety, and your child experiences one or more of the issues discussed in this chapter—your best course of action may be to consult with a psychiatrist.

Dual Diagnosis

Dual diagnosis is a psychiatric and medical term used to describe a situation in which a person has two, often overlapping, conditions. Medically, this might include someone who has diabetes and obesity, or asthma and allergies. As you have learned, it is common for psychological conditions like depression and anxiety to overlap, and for chemical dependency to overlap with anxiety and other conditions. In children, it is common for anxiety and ADHD to produce mild depression. Children with persistent medical conditions like asthma or diabetes may experience both depression and anxiety, and as you've seen, anxiety and depression can result from loss and trauma. For example, consider a child who has separation anxiety. If she has trouble being away from home, she may feel sad about not having many friends and feel even more isolated. As you can see, the anxiety and depression spiral in on themselves, making the situation more and more difficult to unravel.

 Essential

In teens, anxiety and depression can overlap with, and even cause, substance abuse. This often occurs as a teen self-medicates social anxiety or internal feelings of hopelessness or chaos by using drugs or alcohol.

Family History

If you or anyone in your extended family has suffered from anxiety or related conditions, it can be especially important to seek evaluation for medication. Studies show that children of parents with anxiety disorders are more likely to have difficulty with anxiety, and it is clear that early intervention improves your child's ability to recover fully from anxiety. If you are not sure about whether your family members have had troublesome anxiety, consider gently asking, for the benefit of your child. The good news is that if you are alert to patterns that already exist in your family, you are in prime position to intervene early and ensure the best care for your child, regardless of whether you choose medication as an option.

Medical Complications

Children with medical conditions such as diabetes, asthma, or cerebral palsy, among others, may be at risk for increased anxiety or depression due to the chronic nature of these ailments. Other complicating factors might include serious illness such as leukemia, growth or hormonal deficiencies, or serious injuries or accidents. The anxiety may be a side effect of a treatment, an aspect of the illness itself, or simply a psychological reaction to coping with such an illness.

Types of Medication

Though there is good evidence to support the benefits of medication in treating adult anxiety, the long-term research needed to validate safety, effectiveness, and developmental effects in children is ongoing. Due to the tightening FDA regulations, those who prescribe medication for children may only have a few options to work with, especially if they practice in a managed-care setting. Following is a list of typical types of medication that your child's doctor may prescribe. Some newer medications are formulated so they need only be taken once a day. They may have the designations CR (controlled release), SR (sustained release), ER or XR (extended release), or LA (long-acting).

 Fact

Remember, if you've responded well to a medication yourself, your child's physician may want to consider the same medication as a first course for your child. Be sure to let your child's doctor know if you've responded well to a medication for anxiety or depression.

Antidepressants

Antidepressant medications have been used for decades to reduce anxiety, whether or not depression is present. There are three basic types of medications, and they are grouped based upon the neurotransmitters they act upon. In general, antidepressants work by helping the brain to restore the optimal chemical functioning that it needs to improve mood, thinking, and physical troubles such as sleep, appetite, and energy. In addition, the overall support of brain chemistry by antidepressants can help stop negative, unproductive thinking and behavior.

Some FDA approved brand medications for anxiety include: Luvox, Zoloft, Anafranil, Prozac, Tofranil, and Effexor. As always, it will be important for you to follow up with your doctor within a month of starting treatment.

Is Medication Safe?

When taken as prescribed by a doctor skilled in treating children and adolescents, medication can be helpful in reducing or eliminating symptoms that interfere with your child's daily functioning. Unfortunately, the long-term effects of such medications on a child's development and health are little understood due to the lack of research. Be sure to ask your child's doctor about any FDA warnings associated with your child's medication, and if you research medication online, be careful to make sure your sources are valid and reputable. Your pharmacist can often provide education and support as you investigate your child's medication.

Special Considerations with Children

Because children's brains and bodies are still developing, most practitioners use caution in prescribing psychiatric medication, especially for children under twelve. In addition, longitudinal studies on the way medication may affect children's development are only recently coming available, and are nonexistent for newer medications. Because there is an indication that antidepressant medication may increase suicidal thinking and behavior in adolescents, it is especially important to monitor your teen carefully, particularly during the initiation, change, or cessation of a medication. For example, do not be fooled if your teen seems to have more energy after beginning a medication. This might actually be a risk factor for suicide if he continues to have suicidal thoughts along with increased energy, for example.

Allergic and Toxic Reactions

Rarely, a child may have an allergic or toxic reaction to medication. This is different than a side effect and may require IMMEDIATE MEDICAL ATTENTION. Typical signs of an allergic reaction might include disorientation, extreme lethargy or agitation, bizarre physical sensations (tingling, numbness, buzzing), debilitating headache, vomiting, skin rash/mottling or hives, difficulty breathing, or trouble with coordination.

 Alert

If your child experiences any allergic reaction symptoms while on a medication, it is important to speak with your care provider without delay. If your child becomes unresponsive, unconscious, or if she can't breathe, call 911 immediately!

Monitor Responses to Medication

All of the warnings and precautions in this chapter may cause many of you to feel skittish about considering medication as a part of your child's treatment plan. For some children this is an essential component in their care, and the benefits far outweigh any risks. Remember that if you choose to have your child evaluated by a psychiatrist, you are not obligated to accept or fill a prescription. In some cases, a psychiatrist will determine that your child may in fact not need medication, but would be better served by another therapy.

Starting a Medication

Medication is often started at a low dose. After the body becomes reregulated with the medication, it is then increased.

If your child has bothersome side effects, a dose can often be reduced until his body adjusts. Make sure to have all your questions answered, and see that your child takes his medication at about the same time every day. Be sure to ask the doctor or pharmacist about any interactions that might occur with other medications your child is taking.

 Fact

> Some children may have no side effects at all, but others may be troubled either by side effects or by how a medication makes them feel. In general, antidepressants reach full effect about four to six weeks after the full dose is reached. Some patients may respond after a week or two, and for some it may take longer. Your pharmacist and doctor will provide you with a list of possible side effects.

Changing Medications

Cautions are in order when changing a medication, which may produce new side effects. There may be an additive effect if the new medication is to be used along with one your child is already taking. There may be effects from decreasing or discontinuing a medication, as the new one is added. Normally, your doctor will have a standard protocol for changing medications, and if your child is changing medications within the same class, side effects can be minimal or nonexistent.

Going Off Medication

There has been recent press about the problems associated with discontinuing medication, particularly SSRIs. The adverse effects, though rare, are referred to as SSRI discontinuation (or) cessation syndrome. This syndrome is caused by what is referred to as the "half-life" of a medication, which refers to the extent to which it remains in the body after being discontinued. Symptoms can include dizziness, vertigo, lightheadedness, a whooshing or shocking sensation in the head, flashes of pain or discomfort, sweating, headaches, irritability, lethargy, nausea, diarrhea or vomiting, disrupted sleep, and general malaise. The best defense against these effects is to decrease a medication slowly, taking breaks until symptoms abate. Sometimes another medication is prescribed at a low dose to alleviate withdrawal symptoms, and many of the complementary and alternative therapies included in this book may be able to help. It is never advisable to stop a medication "cold turkey" unless there is a toxic or allergic reaction to it. Make sure you receive clear instructions and precautions from your doctor if your child will be stopping a medication.

Team Approach

It is true that "it takes a village to raise a child." The more resources you are able to use, the more powerful the intervention will be for your child. The sections that follow highlight areas you may wish to consider as your child begins taking medication for anxiety.

 Question

What if you are uncomfortable with the recommendations?
If you are uncomfortable with any recommendations you receive from a care provider, discuss them first with your provider and then seek a second opinion if you feel it is warranted. Often people are concerned they will offend a doctor if they seek a second opinion; if your doctor is offended, get a different one. You do not need your doctor's ego getting in the way of your child's well-being.

Coordination of Providers

As previously mentioned, it is ideal if your child's care providers consult and coordinate with each other regarding your child's care. You will need to sign consent forms for this to occur, and you may have to advocate for coordination if your child's care providers do not normally work in this way. These days, providers can use phone, fax, e-mail, and regular mail to contact each other. In more complex cases, scheduling a team meeting involving all of the players may be essential to ensure everyone is working toward the same goal.

Combining Therapy and Medication

Combining therapy and medication has often been shown to be more effective than either therapy or medication alone. In fact, it is recommended by the AACAP and other professional organizations that if a child takes medication, she is seen by a therapist as well. For example, your child may find that medication decreases her anxiety even a little, which helps her tolerate distress as she is learning or retrieving skills under the supervision of a therapist. The new skills, once cemented by practice in and out of therapy, should remain once the medication is discontinued.

 Fact

You will likely need to sign a consent form for your child to take medication at school, and may need to develop a protocol together with the doctor and school nurse for when and how (as needed) medication should be taken.

School

Your child should not need to take anxiety medications at school, as they are administered once or twice daily and can be taken at home. However, some shorter-acting medications for acute anxiety may be given at school. Your child's doctor will need to contact the school (often by fax) with the pertinent information.

Decide together with your child and care professionals how and who to inform about your child's medications. For example, some families may be comfortable informing a school nurse and social worker, but not the primary teacher.

Dealing with Friends

It is not uncommon for children who are anxious to worry about what their friends and other important people in their lives will think about their treatment. Unfortunately, there is still a great deal of stigma associated with mental health care, and even your extended family may question your choice to seek treatment for your child. You yourself may be confused about what to share about your child's troubles, and with whom. In fact, these issues are great topics for discussion in therapy, and can help your child "own" his condition and take some pride in the fact that he is taking control of his problems. The best rule of thumb is for you and your child to decide, with the help of a therapist if you wish, "the story" you'd like to present publicly. Developing a list of "pat" responses such as "I am getting help because I worry too much," or "I need to see a doctor to help my brain from working overtime" can afford you and your child some confidence in managing the curiosity of others.

 Essential

At times, you may find yourself wanting to act as an advocate and educator for other parents and children with anxiety. Remember, though, that some children are more private than others, and unless you feel it is detrimental, try to respect your child's wishes regarding privacy.

All in the Family

There are many reasons and ways to involve family in your child's care, which are discussed in other chapters of this book. The focus of this section will be on how to help your family understand and support you and your child's choice to include medication in your child's care plan.

Getting Everyone on the Same Page

Getting everyone on the same page is especially important in families with joint custody arrangements. It is equally as important in blended families, where there may be two sets of parents to consider and siblings as well. Honesty, education, and opportunities to ask questions and communicate about medications will help in your child's recovery. Make sure those closest to your child, especially if they will be caring for him, know the name, dosage, and reason for any medications your child is taking. This is especially important during any start, change, decrease, or discontinuation of medication so that others can help you watch for any signs of trouble. Do not hesitate to use resources like NIMH (*www.nimh.nih.gov*), NAMI (*www.nami.org*), or ADAA (*www.adaa.org*) to help those in your child's life to learn more about anxiety and its treatment.

Involving Siblings

Often siblings are either a great source of comfort or a great source of distress. With regard to medication, it is probably most important for your child's siblings to be supportive of your choice, and encouraging to your child with anxiety. Remember to keep in mind the age of your child when educating her about her sibling's care, and do not let an older child be responsible for ensuring her sibling takes her medication.

When to Seek Help for Yourself

It sometimes happens that a child's diagnosis with anxiety, depression, or ADHD causes a parent to feel an eerie sense of familiarity and recognize that he may have a condition similar to that of his child, and to consider medications for himself. If this is true for you, you too can discuss this with your child's doctor, your doctor, or the therapist.

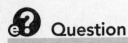 **Question**

Should I tell my child's doctor about my own anxiety?
It is important to discuss your own anxiety with your child's doctor or therapist. Your child may have a sense of "not being so alone in the world" if she sees that you have struggled, too. As previously mentioned, a family history of anxiety may increase the likelihood your child could need medication. Also, there are many benefits to learning and practicing anxiety management with your child.

Working with Extended Family

Your child's grandparents, aunts and uncles, and cousins may need to be informed about your child's medications for several reasons. Letting the family at large know that your child's condition is serious enough to warrant medication will help them to understand that your child is not just "going through a phase," or "being difficult." Sharing information about your child's condition and care may also help your extended family reflect on potential problems they might have with anxiety, and this could make big changes for the better for everyone.

CHAPTER 19

Creating a Promising Future

Many parents who have anxiety themselves or who are raising a child with anxiety are often worried about the future. Questions such as, *Will my child grow out of this*, *Will she be able to live a healthy, happy life*, and *Will it ever be easier for her* may frequently visit their minds. This is particularly true if it concerns your firstborn or only child. In your heart you may want to be hopeful for a promising future, but your mind tells you to be uncertain and afraid. This chapter offers you a glimpse of how children who may have experienced anxiety at one point in their lives look in the future. In addition, for children and adolescents in therapy, this chapter covers how and when to end these types of supports.

What Is the Goal?

The long-term goal for assisting children with anxiety is twofold: First, for your child to feel confident that she is capable of handling just about anything that is presented in her life; and second, for her to recognize her own internal and external discomfort as an opportunity for growth. This means rather than being overwhelmed or pulled along by her feelings, she will embrace them as part of her wholeness. Your child's feelings and physiological responses are not the problem. It is how she chooses to perceive them and thus react that determines whether she will learn and thrive from anxiety.

Letting Go

Looking ahead to a promising future requires a bit of letting go on your part. As much as you may dread the future or your child growing up too fast, the reality is that he too will be an adult someday, and adulthood comes with everyday stressors, challenges, and in some cases hardship. If you have an attachment to how you would like the outcome to be, or put pressure on yourself to do things right, you may actually contribute to a future of struggle.

The path of letting go requires you to experience your fearful thoughts. Parents who choose to ignore, disregard, or distract themselves from their own fearful thoughts may inadvertently project them onto their child. Projection comes in many forms, and even if you are not verbally expressing your fearful thoughts your child can sense them. They may notice that you make yourself so crazy busy that you develop a frightening look in your eyes. On the outside, you are juggling many things. On the inside, however, what gets sacrificed is the experience of allowing yourself to feel your emotions. Part of letting go means making time for yourself, and tuning into your senses through practices that connect you to feeling rather than doing. Take a moment and imagine a tightly wound ball of yarn. Now imagine gently loosening the yarn with your fingers while breathing in and out of your nose slowly. Letting go is similar only, instead of yarn, emotions such as fear have been tightly wound up. Consider the symptoms of anxiety (often experienced in the chest and head) to be a road map of where in your body you may be holding tension. It is as if your body is saying here it is, now relax and breathe and you will soon see how you have the ability to convert this tension into letting go.

Surrender Expectations

Anxiety and expectations go hand in hand; therefore, if you or your child are experiencing symptoms it is likely that expectations are in the mix—expectations of yourself, your child, school, siblings, parenting partners, work, etc. Learning how to recognize and surrender expectations allows you to understand, grow, and be empowered by your symptoms. The following steps will show you how:

1. Identify what expectations feel like. Some people can identify them by an urge or impulse to make things different. For example, you expect your child to clean up and then immediately do it for him because it makes you feel too anxious to wait.
2. Ask yourself, "What am I expecting right now of myself and others?" For example, are you expecting things to be done quickly or without discomfort?
3. Once you identify your expectations begin to disarm them. To do this bring the expectation in your mind and then imagine yourself pushing the disarm button. For example, imagine pushing the disarm button on your keychain for your car. Take a couple of minutes and one by one begin to disarm the two or three of the expectations you may be carrying.

The road to a promising future means keeping realistic expectations, which for some parents and children means accepting the fact that emotions are not designed to go away, but rather are a part of the way human beings connect, learn, and evolve.

See the Blessing

Whether you have modeled these strategies to your child or implemented them with him, there are mostly certainly blessings that you have experienced from your experiences. To help your child move toward a more promising future it is important to periodically review the progress the two of you have made. Think of all the times you choose to take a breath and watch your words rather than react impulsively. Encourage your child to think of the things he has learned about himself, what worked and did not work, and yet how each and every step (immediately successful or not) helped prepare him for where he is today. Reflect on what a gift it has been to walk alongside your child through this process. As your child moves toward adulthood, you will continue to walk with him, but instead of side by side he will gain confidence and begin to lead the way.

New Wealth

Remember that one of the goals of transitioning your child into adulthood is to help her recognize that she can handle anything that comes her way. In order to do this well, it is important for you and your child to value your health as your wealth, physically, mentally, and emotionally. If you feel good inside, this will be reflected on the outside. Explain to your child that she'll know when she is feeling good when she is able to make responsible decisions, see mistakes as opportunities for growth, and see problems as feedback and opportunities rather than obstacles. In order to keep healthy in mind and body, you and your child will need to consistently create healthy boundaries between work, rest, exercise, and play. This will allow you to more easily recognize when you are overextended (this often shows itself through forgetfulness, or making careless errors). The self-love strategies in this book or ones that you create on your own are a part of how you live your life, rather than something you hope to try one day.

Trust Yourself

As you embark on the pathway to a promising future you will find trusting yourself comes more easily. As a parent, you know your child better than anyone else in the world. If you are able to see yourself clearly as well, you are in a great position to use your intuition and a bit of courage to know when to step back and hand your child the reins. This means that sometimes you may have to stand by as your child moves through discomfort, let him experience his own consequences, and manage your own anxiety all the while. You may also have to encourage other family members to do the same. Trust your instincts also if you truly feel that your child is overwhelmed by the strategies and other goals you've set together, or if the pace is moving too rapidly or too slowly. Remember that there will be times when your child takes the lead, as well as times when you will choose to take a step forward and get more involved.

Launching

Just as the job of a good therapist is to prepare a client to end therapy, your job as a parent is to make sure your children have the skills they need to fledge, and use their new wings to continue growing and learning from all the experiences in their life. For many parents, a child's increasing independence can be scary, lonely, confusing, and sad. Sometimes it helps simply to reassure yourself that it's nature's plan for your child to leave the nest, and continue to do your best to allow your child to soar.

As you learn to let go of your child, it is important to stay flexibly connected, securely but not too tightly. It is important for parents to be prepared to handle strong emotions as children become less dependent upon them. This can be especially true when separation anxiety is an issue. As you've learned, it is always best to try not to let your own fears interfere with your child's desire and need to push forward. Draw on your inner and outer resources, and know that you and a million other parents have learned to let their children go on to be competent, productive, resilient, responsible adults.

Practice Makes Permanent

Scientists have known for years that learning involves physical changes in the brain. Eric R. Kandel, a neuropsychiatrist who received the 2000 Nobel Prize in Medicine for his groundbreaking work, proved that the release of neurotransmitters increases as learning occurs, creating new neural structures and connections, which multiply and further enhance learning. It has also been established that learning interpersonal skills and social interaction is more complex, and therefore requires more repetition to acquire. This, of course, has applications to managing social anxiety, assertiveness, and learning when and how to seek support from others. Practices that relieve stress and anxiety are a lifetime commitment, and with that comes the reward of being able to access your higher potential at each state in your entire life span.

 Essential

Conventional wisdom has it that it takes twenty-one attempts at a new behavior before it becomes a habit. However, the rule of twenty-one actually has no basis in fact. There are simply too many intervening factors to make a sound prediction regarding anyone's learning curve. So keep the faith and encourage your child to be patient, and to stay open to learning more and more about the magnificence of his brain and body.

Also, keep in mind that your child is unlearning old, unhelpful behavior at the same time that he's learning new skills. Following Kandel's observations, though it does not take long for the brain to store a new image or idea, new cell growth and connection does require quite a bit of repetition and reinforcement to truly take root. For these reasons, it is important for your child to continue practicing new skills such as better self-talk and self-calming skills.

Taking Stock of Your Toolbox

After a couple of months of implementing strategies and other possible interventions, it will be important to reflect on the progress you and your child have made in your work to overcome his anxiety. The questions that follow can help guide you. These same questions may be used as a way to determine whether to discontinue other supports.

- Have you and your child learned what anxiety is, and how it is triggered?
- Have you addressed any medical, nutritional, or environmental concerns that contribute to your child's symptoms?
- Has your child improved in his ability to identify and express his needs and feelings effectively?
- Are you and other family members more able to share your needs and concerns without undue upset or conflict?
- Have you, as a parent, addressed your own expectations and fears?
- Does your child use skills such as breathing, relaxation, and imagery with minimal or no prompting from you?
- Can your child self-soothe in other ways, such as yawning, bathing, music, exercise, and breathing?
- Are self-love strategies a part of your daily lives?
- Does your child know what an emotion is, and how to experience it without fighting or being overwhelmed by it?
- Does your child set healthy boundaries for technology and media?
- Does your child have a plan for how to handle times he feels stressed?
- Has your child experienced relief from the strategies you have implemented?

Weaning Gradually

When your child hears about his growth and gains from people such as his teachers, family members, or therapist this can be a great source of pride and accomplishment. However, as your child becomes more confident in her abilities and more self-assured, you may begin to decrease support. For example, if your child is receiving extra help from a tutor, or support from a school counselor or nutritionist, you may start scheduling more space between appointments.

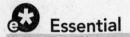 **Essential**

When ending support services, keep in mind that your child (and you) may have developed a strong attachment to the individual. Honor the effort and the relationship, and avoid ending abruptly, unless you have reason to believe it is harmful or inappropriate for your child to continue. To help with closure and acknowledge your child's accomplishments, consider planning something special for the final session, or ask about exchanging touchstones.

Knowing When to End Medication

Research shows that many people are able to manage their anxiety effectively after stopping medication, typically if they have received therapy to learn ways to work through their symptoms. Specific data on exactly how this applies to children with anxiety is less conclusive, due to the fact that children's development is dynamic and ongoing, along with the current lack of longitudinal research.

Basic Guidelines

In general, it is common practice for a child to stay on a medication for at least six to twelve months in order to obtain maximum benefit. However, timeframes vary depending on the class of medication. For example, it is typical to see benefits from antidepressants in around four to six weeks. In addition, if it takes time to reach the therapeutic dose of the medicine, or if another medication is added, it may take longer to see optimal effects. Your child's age, the length and severity of her symptoms, and the co-occurrence of other mental health issues will also determine when it is reasonable to discontinue a medication.

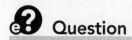

Question

Are there any times when my child should *not* go off medication?

Yes, in fact. It may be beneficial for your child to stay on medication through times of transition or particular stress, during anniversaries of loss or trauma, or during the fall and winter months if seasonal affective disorder is a concern. It may be unwise to risk further unbalancing your child when times are already difficult.

Though most medical professionals would agree that a child shouldn't take medication she no longer needs, there are just as many reasons to continue until full benefit can occur. Unfortunately, it can sometimes be difficult to determine just when to discontinue a medication, especially if it has been used for an extended period of time.

Three Steps to Smother-Free Support

Throughout this book you've received many pointers on how not to let your own fears and needs interfere with the well-being of you and your child. This section offers a three-step plan to help keep yourself in check as your child grows and becomes more independent.

1. **Encourage Independence.** In order for your child to have the confidence that he can manage on his own, he needs to feel that you believe that he can do it. Always let your child make an attempt, no matter what his age, before you step in. This applies all the way from learning to walk to applying for college. If your child seems to have trouble managing on his own, offer support while respecting his growing independence by considering the tip that follows.

2. **Ask Before Offering.** This strategy can be applied to young children, and is especially important to cultivate as your child ages. If you see your child struggling, simply ask her if she needs feedback, assistance, or direction. If she does, help her make a plan by using the "baby steps" concept presented earlier. As your child becomes stronger and more independent, she may begin to decline your assistance; take this as a sign of growth and accomplishment, not as rejection. As mentioned previously, the best strategy is always to allow your child the time and space to figure it out on her own before you step in. This is especially important for young adult children who have moved out or gone away to college. Always be sure to lend a sympathetic ear, but use your reflective listening skills (see Chapter 6) to guide and encourage, rather than dictate. Be careful in offering advice that is unsolicited.

3. **Have a Plan.** As your child grows, it will be important for her to learn how to be aware of when normal stress develops into anxiety. Occasional anxiety is normal (e.g. finals week at school); however, teach your child to pay attention to the frequency, intensity, or duration of symptoms. Symptoms such as worry, perfectionism, panicking, or insomnia are signs that your child may need support or to make some changes. Comfort your child that symptoms are the body's way of communicating that it is out of balance. Sometimes a simple shift in schedule (e.g. decrease in work hours or class schedule) can ease the pressure, allowing your child to resume a balanced lifestyle. Other times, it may be a sign that your child needs a tune-up. Therefore, it is important that you maintain connections with your support system or develop new ones. Professional and nonprofessional people that your child can go to during times of stress such as transition times, unemployment, holidays, break up of a relationship, or dip in

grades are some examples. It may be something as simple as checking in with a nutritionist.

 Essential

When looking at colleges and other places to live, be sure to look into what is available on and off campus to support healthy living. Many colleges now offer yoga classes for college credit, free meditation groups, stress management courses, massage, healthy foods, counseling, gyms, healthy eating options, and housing that is less noisy than a dorm room.

Moving Out

Whether it is a new apartment, shared housing with friends, or the transition to college, your child may experience his first real sense of independence when he moves out of your home. For some, this can be exhilarating; for some, frightening; and for most, a combination of the two. To help your child manage separation and general anxiety, make a plan for how you'll stay connected, and acknowledge that this is a big change for both of you. Clarify guidelines for how often you will talk on the phone, and set limits if you feel either you or your child is too dependent on the contact. If your child will be living nearby, you might consider starting a Sunday dinner ritual, a monthly night at the movies, or a Saturday coffee break. Children are often comforted by care packages, impromptu grocery deliveries, or occasional offers to help with housework. Remember, though, to ask before you offer, and respect your young adult's need for privacy and the right to establish a life of his own.

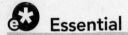 **Essential**

Many colleges have functions and activities that give parents opportunities to visit their child on campus, experience a meal, and perhaps meet professors. You can stay connected with your child by attending performances and sporting events, and perhaps by volunteering in some way.

As you conclude the final chapter of this book, ask yourself and your child if anxiety could speak words what would it say? Perhaps it would say, *Thank you for taking the time to notice the symptoms and for having the courage to speak up and attend to it, rather than ignore or shove it away.* It might say, *I never wanted to be fixed, but rather loved and treated with kindness and respect.* It may whisper *Good job, you have everything you need to be the best you can be.* It may reveal that this was all part of your personal story of how you learned to receive the moment, be yourself, trust your higher guidance, and love yourself well.

Anxiety Questionnaire

If you think your child may have an anxiety disorder, please answer the following questions, and show the results to your child's health care professional:

Yes ○ No ○	Does the child have a distinct and ongoing fear of social situations involving unfamiliar people?
Yes ○ No ○	Does the child worry excessively about a number of events or activities?
Yes ○ No ○	Does the child experience shortness of breath or a racing heart for no apparent reason?
Yes ○ No ○	Does the child experience age-appropriate social relationships with family members and other familiar people?
Yes ○ No ○	Does the child often appear anxious when interacting with her peers and avoid them?
Yes ○ No ○	Does the child have a persistent and unreasonable fear of an object or situation, such as flying, heights, or animals?
Yes ○ No ○	When the child encounters the feared object or situation, does she react by freezing, clinging, or having a tantrum?
Yes ○ No ○	Does the child worry excessively about her competence and quality of performance?
Yes ○ No ○	Does the child cry, have tantrums, or refuse to leave a family member or other familiar person when she must?
Yes ○ No ○	Has the child experienced a decline in classroom performance, refused to go to school, or avoided age-appropriate social activities?
Yes ○ No ○	Does the child spend too much time each day doing things over and over again (for example, handwashing, checking things, or counting)?
Yes ○ No ○	Does the child have exaggerated fears of people or events (for example, burglars, kidnappers, car accidents) that might be difficult, such as in a crowd or on an elevator?
Yes ○ No ○	Does the child experience a high number of nightmares, headaches, or stomachaches?
Yes ○ No ○	Does the child repetitively re-enact with toys scenes from a disturbing event?
Yes ○ No ○	Does the child redo tasks because of excessive dissatisfaction with less-than-perfect performance?

Diagnostic and Statistical Manual of Mental Disorders, Fourth Edition. Washington, DC, American Psychiatric Association, 1994.

Additional Resources

Wagner, Aureen Pinto PhD. *Worried No More: Help and Hope for Anxious Children.* (Rochester, NY: Lighthouse Press, Inc., 2002).

Ellsas Chansky, Tamar. *Freeing Your Child from Anxiety.* (New York, NY: Broadway Books, 2004).

Manassee Buell, Linda. *Panic and Anxiety Disorder: 121 Tips, Real-Life Advice, Resources and More.* (Poway, CA: Simply Life, 2001).

Nardo, Don. *Anxiety and Phobias.* (New York, NY: Chelsea House Publishers, 1992).

Burns, David D. *When Panic Attacks: The New Drug-Free Anxiety Therapy That Can Change Your Life.* (New York, NY: Morgan Road Books, Random House, 2006).

Dispenza, Joe. *Evolve Your Brain: The Science of Changing Your Mind and Breaking the Habit of Being Yourself.* The Aware Show interview. November 2013. *www.theawareshow.com.*

Foxman, Paul PhD. Director of Center for Anxiety Disorders. Affiliate of The Life Skills Progam. *www.chaange.com. The Worried Child: Recognizing Anxiety in Children and Helping Them.* (Alameda, CA: Hunter House Publishers, 2004).

Foa, Edna B. PhD, and Wasmer Andrews, Linda. *If Your Adolescent Has an Anxiety Disorder.* (New York, NY: Oxford University Press, 2006).

Fox, Bronwyn. *Power over Panic: Freedom from Panic/Anxiety Related Disorders, 2nd Edition.* (NSW, Australia: Pearson Education Australia, 2001).

Lee, Jordan. *Coping with Anxiety and Panic Attacks.* (New York, NY: The Rosen Publishing Group, Inc., 1997, 2000).

Gardner, James MD, and Bell, Arthur H. PhD. *Overcoming Anxiety, Panic and Depression.* (Franklin Lakes, NJ: Career Press, 2000).

Bourne, Edmund J., PhD. *The Anxiety and Phobia Workbook, Third Edition.* (Oakland, CA: New Harbinger Publications, 2000).

Websites

About Our Kids, New York University Child Study Center
Articles, research, programs, and education about children.
www.aboutourkids.org

American Academy of Child and Adolescent Psychiatry
Information about diagnosis and treatment of developmental, behavioral, and emotional disorders that affect children and adolescents.
www.aacap.org

American Academy of Family Physicians
www.aafp.org

American Medical Association
www.ama-assn.org

American Psychological Association
Helps you find a psychologist in your area.
www.apa.org

Anxieties.com
Self-help site with tests, publications, and information.
www.anxieties.com

Anxiety and Depression Association of America (ADAA)
Comprehensive website about anxiety.
www.adaa.org

Common Sense Media
Use this website for advice on all types of media and technology.
www.commonsensemedia.org

Healthy Place
Offers information, live discussion, and chat groups.
www.healthyplace.com/index.html

Healthychildren.org
Includes guidance on family media, TV, and cell phones.
www.healthychildren.org

Mental Help Net
Resource for consumers and professionals.
www.mentalhelp.net

National Alliance on Mental Illness (NAMI)
General mental health resource includes opportunities for support and networking.
www.nami.org

National Institutes of Mental Health (NIMH)
Up-to-date news, research, and treatment information about anxiety.
www.nimh.nih.gov/health/topics/anxiety-disorders/index.shtml

Psych Central
A mental health website that has created a social network run by mental health professionals.
www.psychcentral.com

Specialty Resources

Communication
Advocates for Youth website provides a good resource for multiple issues with children.
www.advocatesforyouth.org

This web page gives a list of feeling words to help you and your child learn ways to express emotions.
www.psychpage.com/learning/library/assess/feelings.html

Massage
Massage Magazine has articles of every kind about massage and studies about the health aspects of massage for children.
www.massagemag.com

Biofeedback
Association for Applied Psychophysiology and Biofeedback, with information about providers, research, and treatment.
www.aapb.org

Conscious Living Foundation has books, stress-management tools, CDs, and movies to guide children in relaxation techniques and understanding how the body works.
www.cliving.org/children.htm

Aromatherapy
Aromatherapy and Children article by Kathi Keville, Mindy Green (excerpted from *Aromatherapy: A Complete Guide to the Healing Art* found at the Health World website).
www.healthy.net/scr/Article.asp?Id=1714

Chiropractic
The International Chiropractic Pediatric Association is a resource that provides an accumulation of research and a membership directory for the layperson interested in chiropractic care for his or her family.
www.icpa4kids.org

Resource to find studies and articles on chiropractic care for children
www.chiro.org/pediatrics/ABSTRACTS/Chiropractic_For_Children.shtml

Homeopathic Medicine
National Center for Homeopathy
The National Center for Homeopathy has created a website to provide access to studies, resources, and practitioners.
www.homeopathic.org

National Center for Complementary and Alternative Medicine
National Center for Complementary and Alternative Medicine is an excellent resource for alternative options.
http://nccam.nih.gov

Other Sites

The Self-Love Movement
This movement encourages people to sign up to commit to take care of themselves daily. Inspirational videos and quotes are shared on this site along with a free guidebook.
www.facebook.com/TheSelfLoveMovement

StressFreeKids
Books, CDs, curriculums, and other products designed to empower children, teens, and adults.
www.stressfreekids.com

The LifeSkills Program
An audio taped learning process designed for the anxious person ages six through fifteen. Lifeskills can be used by a professional therapist, classroom teacher, or monitored by a parent.
www.chaange.com/about-lifeskills

Young Living
A resource for purchasing essential organic oils.
www.youngliving.com

Youthbeat
An empowering website for youths ages six through eighteen.
www.youthbeat.com

InspireMeToday.com
Recommended for short inspirational daily readings.
www.InspireMeToday.com

APPENDIX C

References

Amen, Daniel G. *Healing ADD*. New York: Putnam's, 2001. Print.

American Academy of Pediatrics. "Managing Media: We Need A Plan." October 28, 2013. *www.aap.org/en-us/about-the-aap/aap-press-room/pages/managing-media-we-need-a-plan.aspx*

American Psychological Association. "Violence in the Media—Psychologists Study TV and Video Games for Potential Harmful Effects." November 2013. *www.apa.org/research/action/protect.aspx*

American Psychological Assocation. Forty to fifty percent of marriages in the U.S. will end in divorce. *www.apa.org/topics/divorce/*

Anderson, Craig A. "Violent video game effects on aggression, empathy, and prosocial behavior in eastern and western countries: a meta-analytic review." *Psychological Bulletin* 136, no. 2, 151–173 (2010).

Anxiety and Depression Association of America (ADAA). "Anxiety affects one in eight children." *www.adaa.org/about-adaa/press-room/facts-statistics*

Blakeslee, Sandra. "Complex and Hidden Brain in Gut Makes Stomachaches and Butterflies." *New York Times.* January 23, 1996.

Boyle, Sherianna. *Powered by Me for Educators Pre-K–12*. Balboa Press. 2012.

Breuning, Loretta, PhD. "Five Ways to Trigger Your Natural Happy Chemicals." Wisdom New England Edition. January/February 2013, p. 24.

Brown, Brené. *The Gifts of Imperfection*. (Center City, MN: Hazelden, 2010).

Challem, Jack. *The Food-Mood Solution*. John Wiley & Sons. Hoboken, New Jersey, 2007.

Chaplin, T.M., and Aldao, A. "Gender differences in emotion expression in children: A meta-analytic review." *Psychological Bulletin*. Advance online publication. December 26, 2012.

Church, Dawson. *The Genie in Your Genes*. (Santa Rosa, CA: Energy Psychology Press, 2009).

Cohen, Lawrence. *The Opposite of Worry*. Ballantine Books, New York, 2013, p. 177.

Cope, Stephen. "Depression manifests as our inability to be present for the experience of life." Excerpt taken from the foreword in *Yoga for Depression* by Amy Weintraub (New York, NY: Broadway Books, 2004).

Danzig, Marsha Therese. *Children's Book of Mudras*.

Dispenza, Joe. "Thoughts are the language of the brain and feelings are the language of the body." *Breaking the Habit of Being Yourself.* Ted Talk. Hayhouse Summit. Published Oct. 23, 2013.

Eden, Donna. *The Little Book of Energy Medicine.*

Emmons, Robert and Michael McCullough. "Counting Blessings Versus Burdens: An Experimental Investigation of Gratitude and Subjective Well-Being in Daily Life." *Journal of Personality and Social Psychology* 84, no. 2 (2003): 377–389.

Foxman, Paul. "Anxiety Disorders in Children and Adolescence." PESI, Inc. Cape Cod, MA. November 14, 2013. "5000 children rated number one fear as school performance." "90 percent of children will learn and remember if it were experienced, as opposed to 20 percent if they only hear it."

Foxman, Paul. *Anxiety Disorders in Children & Adolescents: Recognizing & Treating the Emerging Epidemic.* (Eau Claire, WI: PESI Publishing & Media, 2013).

Foxman, Paul. *Dancing with Fear.* (Alameda, CA: Hunter House, 2007).

Foxman, Paul. *The Worried Child.* (Alameda, CA: Hunter House, 2004).

HealthyChildren.org. "Anxiety in Teens" audio essay. Teen Health Issue, 2013. *www.healthychildren.org/English/health-issues/conditions/emotional-problems/Pages/Anxiety-and-Teens.aspx*

Hutchinson, Courtney. "Evening T.V. and Violent Cartoons Disrupt Preschoolers' Sleep." *ABC News* via *Good Morning America.* June 27, 2011.

Kornblum, Nestor. *The Healing Power of Sound and Overtone Chant. www.globalsoundhealing.net/en/content/healing-power-sound-and-overtone-chant*

Kwik, Jim. "Practice makes permanent." Jimmy Kwik is the CEO of Kwik Learning and founder of SuperheroYou. *www.youtube.com/watch?v=JzQ-ISbuzmA*

McTaggart, Lynne. *The Intention Experiment: Using Your Thoughts to Change the World.* (New York, NY: Free Press, 2007).

National Institute of Mental Health. "Anxiety Disorders in Children and Adolescents (Fact Sheet)." *www.ftp.nimh.nih.gov/health/publications/anxiety-disorders-in-children-and-adolescents/index.shtml*

Nelson, Jane. *Positive Discipline for Blended Families.* Prima Publishing. Rocklin, CA. 1997, p. 82.

Newberg, Andrew, and Mark Robert Waldman. *Words Can Change Your Brain.* (New York, NY: Hudson Street Press, 2012).

NurrieStearns, Mary and Rick. *Yoga for Anxiety.* (Oakland, CA: New Harbinger Publications, 2010).

O'Neill, Catherine. *Relax.* Child's Play (International) Ltd. New York, Swindon, Toronto, Sydney.

Ortner, Nick. *The Tapping Solution.* Hay House, Inc. 2013.

Parry, Marc. "Young People Let Digital Apps Dictate Their Identities, Say 2 Scholars." October 28, 2013. *http://chronicle.com/article/ Growing-Up-Theres-No-App-for/142655/*

Paul, Annie Murphy. "The Uses and Abuses of Optimism and Pessimism." *Psychology Today*, published November 1, 2001 (reviewed July 16, 2013). *www .psychologytoday.com/articles/201110/the-uses-and-abuses-optimism-and-pessimism*

Penn, Audrey. *The Kissing Hand*. Child Welfare League of America, 1993.

Perry, Susan. "Mirror Neurons." Neuroanatomy, BrainFacts.org. November 16, 2008 (reviewed Feb. 20, 2013). *www.brainfacts.org/brain-basics/neuroanatomy/ articles/2008/mirror-neurons/*

Rossman, Martin, MD. *How Your Brain Can Turn Anxiety Into Calmness*. Uploaded March 12, 2010 (YouTube).

Simmons, Rachel. *Odd Girl Out: The Hidden Culture of Aggression in Girls*. (New York, NY: Houghton Mifflin Harcourt, 2002.)

Small, Gary, and Gigi Vorgan. *iBrain: Surviving the Technological Alteration of the Modern Mind*. New York, NY: HarperCollins, 2008.

Taylor, Jill Bolte. *My Stroke of Insight*. (New York, NY: Penguin Books, 2009).

Wangen, Stephen. *Healthier Without Wheat*. (Seattle, WA: Innate Health Publishing, 2009).

Weintraub, Amy. *Yoga Skills for Therapists*. (New York, NY: W.W. Norton and Company, 2012).

World Health Organization. Parent Skill Training for Management of Emotional and Behavioral Disorders in Children. *www.who.int/mental_health/mhgap/ evidence/child/q5/en/*

Zeidan Fadel, Katherine T. Martucci, Robert A. Kraft, Nakia S. Gordon, John G. McHaffie, and Robert C. Coghill. "Brain Mechanisms Supporting the Modulation of Pain by Mindfulness Meditation." *Journal of Neuroscience* 31, no. 14 (April 6, 2011): 5540-5548.

Index

HILLSBORO PUBLIC LIBRARIES
Hillsboro, OR
Member of Washington County
COOPERATIVE LIBRARY SERVICES